5/24

THE
DEATH
OF AN
HEIR

PHILIP JETT

THE
DEATH
OF AN
HEIR

ADOLPH COORS III
and the MURDER THAT ROCKED
an AMERICAN BREWING DYNASTY

ST. MARTIN'S PRESS
NEW YORK

www.stmartins.com

The Library of Congress Cataloging-in-Publication Data is available upon request.

ISBN 978-1-250-11180-7 (hardcover)
ISBN 978-1-250-11182-1 (ebook)

Our books may be purchased in bulk for promotional, educational, or business use. Please contact your local bookseller or the Macmillan Corporate and Premium Sales Department at 1-800-221-7945, extension 5442, or by email at MacmillanSpecialMarkets@macmillan.com.

First Edition: September 2017

10 9 8 7 6 5 4 3 2 1

For Austin and Brandon

PROLOGUE

At barely half a rod wide and three hands deep, Turkey Creek was not unlike hundreds of tributaries snaking their way through Colorado canyons. That would soon change. The creek flowed only a few miles, spanned here and there by rough-hewn lumber bridges like the one in Turkey Creek Canyon, with its crude railings and two wooden tracks burrowed in gravel, wide enough for a single car to cross. Fewer than half a dozen vehicles crossed Turkey Creek Bridge each morning. That included the local school bus and a milk delivery truck—and for the last month, the white-over-turquoise International Harvester Travelall driven by Adolph Herman Joseph Coors III.

The name fit for a crown prince belonged to the forty-four-year-old chairman of the board and CEO of the multimillion-dollar Adolph Coors Company in Golden, Colorado, and first-born grandson of the brewery's founder. Known simply as "Ad" to most who knew him, he was well-liked by associates and employees for his friendliness and reserve. And despite being the eldest successor to the giant Colorado beer empire and an accomplished man, Ad preferred the simple life on his horse ranch southwest of Denver, where he lived contently with his wife, Mary, and their four young children.

On the crisp, windy morning of Tuesday, February 9, 1960, Ad rose before sunrise and began his daily exercise regime. After showering, he dressed for work and joined Mary at the kitchen table for coffee. They talked as they did every morning.

Before leaving for the brewery, Ad headed outside to check his horses, pitching hay and breaking ice in their troughs. He soon returned to kiss Mary and his children goodbye, but his children had boarded a school bus minutes earlier. Grabbing a tan baseball cap and slipping on his favorite navy-blue nylon jacket, he stepped out onto the carport, started his Travelall, and headed down the driveway. He waved to his ranch manager as he passed. It was 7:55 a.m.

Ad's normal route to the brewery, twelve miles away, would have carried him less than a mile to paved US Highway 285, but a section of the highway had been closed for construction since January. The closure forced him to detour along a winding, lonely stretch of gravel road for four miles to Turkey Creek Canyon, where it connected to a state road that led back to Highway 285.

As Ad drove along the secluded road that morning, his Travelall rambled around the last bend before reaching Turkey Creek Bridge, just out of view. Waiting on the bridge was thirty-one-year-old Joseph Corbett Jr., who had stalked Ad for many months awaiting the chance to carry out his scheme. The road closure and detour across Turkey Creek Bridge gave him that chance.

Corbett backed his canary-yellow Mercury sedan onto the one-lane bridge just minutes before Ad's arrival. Handcuffs and leg irons lay on the back seat. A ransom note in an envelope ready for mailing later that day lay in the glove box. Concealing a pistol in his coat pocket, he exited the four-door car, leaving the driver's door open. He opened a rear door and raised the hood, signaling engine trouble, and stood by the car, waiting for his victim. All he had to do was lure Ad away from his Travelall. Then the Coors CEO and heir wouldn't be so rich and powerful. Instead, he'd be a hostage worth many times his weight in gold and, if all went according to plan, would make Corbett a very rich man by week's end.

As Ad drove around that last bend, he spotted the yellow Mercury stranded on the narrow bridge. It was 8:00 a.m. Just as Corbett had planned, Ad pulled onto the bridge behind the Mercury. He shouted through a rolled-down window, asking if he could help. Corbett shouted back his rehearsed reply. Eager to get going, Ad stepped out of the Travelall and shut the door, leaving the engine running and radio playing. He didn't expect to be long. He figured he'd help push the stranded car out of the way and give its driver a ride to the nearest filling station.

But as Ad approached, Corbett stepped forward and drew his pistol, taking the beer magnate by surprise. Ad was an intelligent but stubborn man, not the kind to don shackles and meekly slide into an assailant's car. As Corbett drew nearer, the six-foot-one, 185-pound Ad Coors seized his abductor's hand that gripped the gun. The two, almost identical in height and weight, struggled. Ad shoved his younger assailant backward, and they slammed against the crude bridge railing. Ad's baseball cap along with Corbett's fedora flew into the creek. Ad's eyeglasses fell, too, cracking the left lens on impact. Ad pushed his antagonist away and made a break for the Travelall. But Corbett, seeing his ransom trying to escape, extended the pistol and fired. The sound of shots echoed up the canyon.

> "It was about eight o'clock," Rosemary Stitt would later testify in the First District Court of Colorado. "Right after I sent my kids off to school, about twenty minutes after. First, it sounded like somebody hollered down at the bridge. I was sittin' in front of my sewing machine by the window. It sounded like one or two words is all. It was two different people, I think. Then I heard a crackling noise like lightnin' striking a tree. I looked out the kitchen window to see if a tree fell down out back but didn't see nothing. So it was then I got to thinking it might be a gunshot. Just one shot. Or, it coulda been two really close together."

Those two shots set off the largest US manhunt since the Lindbergh kidnapping. State and local authorities, along with the FBI, burst into action, attempting to locate Ad Coors and arrest his kidnapper. Ad's influential father demanded that the perpetrator be caught and his son returned, and FBI director J. Edgar Hoover gave assurances that he would make it his top priority domestically. Once the evidence pointed to Corbett, Hoover backed up his promises by placing Corbett on the FBI's Ten Most Wanted list, describing him as the most hunted suspect since John Dillinger. The manhunt would span the continent and involve hundreds of law enforcement officers. Yet as months passed with little success, Ad's tormented wife and children clutched tenuously to their hopes. Like them, everyone wondered where Colorado's favorite son and his abductor could be.

I

THE
PLAN

CHAPTER 1

Windshield wipers squeaked back and forth to reveal the white stripes flashing along the Colorado highway that cold February Sunday afternoon in 1960. Despite a heavy cloudburst, Joe Corbett Jr. spotted the sun reflecting on the mountain peaks in the direction he was traveling. On the back seat lay two polished high-powered rifles in cases along with a fully-loaded .22-caliber target pistol stuffed in the glove compartment. He'd left .45-caliber and .38-caliber revolvers and a 9 mm Llama automatic pistol with a stockpile of ammunition on the closet shelf in his Denver apartment. All of his weapons were capable of blowing a sizeable hole through anything or anyone. And he knew how to use them.

"They're for target shooting," he'd tell anyone who glanced in his car or ventured into his apartment. "I enjoy target shooting."

Target shooting was one of Corbett's hobbies, all right, as it was for many Coloradans. He frequently searched for a place to shoot that wasn't posted, much like searching for a good fishing hole, some out-of-the-way place where he could take aim and fire at bottles, cans, or rats—anything would do to keep his aim sharp.

Most days, Corbett satisfied himself with excursions to mines, caves, and ghost towns abandoned decades earlier. He reconnoitered farther out sometimes, like Central City, Sedalia, and Morrison and as far south as Colorado Springs near the US Air Force Academy. Sometimes to shoot, sometimes to scout for places to shoot, and sometimes to just sit and watch.

This Sunday, he sat and watched. An hour passed. Still, he wasn't satisfied. It might take longer today to observe what he was looking for. He was used to waiting. While he waited, he opened a book. Corbett was an avid reader and a thinker. Once, he'd been a Fulbright Scholar enrolled at the University of California–Berkeley, but he had dropped out of college after his mother died. Soon afterward, in December 1950, he stole a car and shot a hitchhiker twice in the back of the head during a botched robbery, leaving behind a horrific scene of blood and brain tissue. The young Corbett was tracked down and spent a year in San Quentin and three years in Soledad and Terminal Island on a second-degree-murder plea deal. He gained his warden's trust and received a transfer to a minimum-security prison, the California Institution for Men in Chino, where he escaped three months later and hid in Los Angeles before fleeing to Colorado in November 1955.

Though no longer behind bars, Corbett found himself in another sort of prison, where he was forced to work dead-end jobs surrounded by men whom he believed read nothing more challenging than the sports page or girlie magazines. Unlike them, he possessed a library card from the Denver Public Library and regularly checked out books on multifarious scholarly subjects, such as chemistry, physics, math, philosophy, psychology, vocabulary, and foreign languages, like Russian and German.

And so he waited with a book in his hand until the rain stopped.

Though his love for shooting explained his guns, his hobby couldn't explain the mail orders he'd received during the past few months— four pairs of leg irons and four pairs of handcuffs. He'd also purchased a Smith & Wesson K-32 Masterpiece revolver, for which he signed a statement: "I am over 21 years of age, have never been convicted of a felony, and am not now under indictment or a fugitive." It gave him a big laugh.

Nor could simple curiosity explain the most recent titles checked out on his library card—books about traveling to foreign countries, learning the Spanish and Portuguese languages, and understanding criminology and methods of detection. Even the book he was reading on this Sunday, *The FBI Story*, detailed several federal crimes, including insurance fraud, embezzlement, and kidnapping.

No, there was no simple explanation, at least not one that would make sense to any law-abiding citizen, because Corbett's reading and thinking had mutated into scheming, and his target shooting into stalking. He'd been planning a crime that would yield him loads of money since the first day he'd stepped his fugitive foot on Denver soil. But who would notice? No one knew where he was. No one could find him.

Even though he'd robbed a supermarket of $700 in Los Angeles after his escape from Chino, his illicit gains had not been so forthcoming since fleeing to Colorado. He'd planned to rob a liquor store and then considered robbing a coworker's family business in Denver, but didn't go through with either plan. In the summer of 1957, he and coworker Dave Reigel tried to rob a Texaco Bulk Station, but were unable to crack the safe.

Corbett's natural proclivities soon demanded more audacious plans to quench his greed. He plotted a bank heist, yet decided against it.

"That would only net me about $5,000 to $10,000," Corbett told coworker, Arthur Brynaert. "Enough of that small-time stuff. I'm planning something big. A big score. I'm talking a few hundred thousand to a million. With that kind of cash, I can go to Mexico or Australia, or maybe a country without an extradition treaty with the United States and never be heard from again."

Maybe Corbett was shooting his mouth off. Perhaps that's why he generally kept to himself, so his mouth wouldn't get him into trouble. But those who knew him, like Brynaert, a coworker with a shadowy past himself, believed something might be in the works.

"Said he'd been planning something for two and a half years, something very big," Brynaert told lawmen later. "Said he attempted to go into this venture, whatever it was, the previous summer, that would be the summer of '58, during his two-week vacation. That something backfired and he wasn't able to accomplish it, and had to postpone his plans. . . . Didn't say why or what exactly he planned to do. I took it at first as just general bragging—you know. I've been in trouble with the law myself, nothing big, you understand, just little stuff like vagrancy, laying hot paper, you know," Brynaert said.

On this rainy Sunday, Corbett's subterfuge had taken him from the streets of Denver to rural Jefferson County. That's why Corbett picked an out-of-the-way spot, parking on a seldom-traveled gravel road, alone. After all, if anyone asked him, what was he doing wrong? Only reading—and watching.

"Be sure and tighten that front cinch," Ad Coors said to his sixteen-year-old daughter, Cecily, on that rainy Sunday after Ad's return from the US Brewers Foundation convention in Miami the day before. "Need some help?"

"No. I can do it."

The rain had stopped, so the two mounted their horses and rode along the trail away from the corral.

"Come on, Daddy," Cecily said, riding ahead.

They headed southwest in the direction of the Dakota Hogback, a ridge rising up from the prairie that formed a beautiful boundary around the south end of the ranch. The sun was peeking through leaden clouds, spraying its rays of sunshine down on the colorless winter countryside, save for a sprinkling of emerald pine trees. Snowfall from two days earlier had all but melted in the lowlands, leaving muck for the horses' hooves when they strayed off the sand-and-feldspar paths.

Ad looked out over his ranch from the saddle. He'd missed the crisp air and the mountains while in Miami. This was the beginning of his second full year as a part-time rancher, and his enthusiasm hadn't waned one bit. Since they'd married in 1940, he and Mary had always lived in Denver in a very nice section of the city. But over the last few years, Ad's dreams of leaving Denver and living on a ranch had grown stronger. That's all he talked about—a ranch with cattle and prize-winning bulls and quarter horses. Anything to counter the long days spent inside his office behind a desk. In 1956, his dream had come true at last. Mary acceded to relinquish her urban conveniences and build a new house on 480 acres above the Bergen Ditch in the Willow Springs area, south of the small town of Morrison, about fifteen miles south of Denver. After all, it wasn't that far away, especially from the fashionable Cherry Creek area Mary enjoyed, maybe a twenty-minute drive. And Ad could make the twelve-mile drive to Golden without having to battle Denver traffic and lights.

The deal Ad struck with Mary seemed a natural one. He would design their home and its exterior and make the ranch whatever he wanted while the décor of the interior, the family's living space, would rest solely within Mary's province. Construction was completed in the summer of 1958, and the family moved into their ranch-style house. It was a beautiful residence with beautiful surroundings—hundreds of acres of Dakota red sandstone and prairie grass lying at the foothills of the Rocky Mountains with a magnificent view of Pikes Peak to the southwest. Though it was hardly luxurious by the standards of the rich, Ad was happier than he'd been in years. At long last, he was going to be a rancher in his spare time, and he hoped it would be full-time very soon.

Ad had always loved the rugged outdoors, and he'd remained active despite sitting in an office. His physique was that of a younger, vigorous man. Every morning, Ad did push-ups and sit-ups, and he hiked the Colorado terrain and worked his ranch when he could. He also was a superb snow skier and an avid hunter. And his four children—Brooke (Brookie), eighteen; Cecily (Ces), sixteen; Adolph IV (Spike), fourteen; and James (Jim), ten—kept him busy joining them in their activities as he was doing with Cecily on that Sunday afternoon.

"Look, Daddy, there's that car again." Cecily pointed at a car with a single occupant, a man wearing a brown hat and dark-rimmed glasses. "I saw it earlier out the living room window. It's been there for like an hour. Brookie saw it, too."

Mary had told Ad the same thing. Her maid, Thelma Coffman, said she'd seen the automobile several times while Ad and Mary were in Miami the week before. Sometimes with one person, other times with two men inside, she thought, if it was the same car.

A parked car along a quiet country road, not known as belonging to a neighbor, generally raised suspicion that the occupants might be up to no good, like hunting on posted land, looking for something to steal, or worse.

"Let's go see what we can do for him. Might be a poacher," Ad said as he kicked his horse a bit to trot over.

No sooner had Ad and Cecily prodded their horses than the car spun away down the wet gravel road.

"Guess he wasn't in the mood for conversation," Ad said, believing that by the man's actions, he must have been a poacher.

When Ad and Cecily arrived at the barn, Cecily told Bill Hosler about the car while unbuckling the girth from her saddle. The ranch manager shook his head and turned to Ad, saying, "I seen that same yellow car parked on the road one day last week. Seen others, too. Hunting for game off the preserve, I bet."

"Can't they read? Our land's posted everywhere you look. I may have to place a call to the sheriff if they keep coming out here."

Ad was referring to the metal placards tacked up on fence posts, gates, and utility poles surrounding his property that read:

NO HUNTING
Trespassers Will Be Prosecuted

Ad was more observant on the ranch than he'd been while he and his family lived on 840 Steele Street in Denver. The same man had parked near Ad's house then, too, only in a 1957 two-tone white-and-gray Ford Fairlane Club Sedan. No one had really noticed the car parked down the city street among other cars lining the curb.

When the mysterious man in the brown hat and eyeglasses had to change his plans because of Ad's move to the ranch south of Morrison, he continued to watch just as before, but now folks were beginning to notice the stranger on the remote country road.

> "Yes, sir, I saw an older-model car parked at the mouth of a cave fifty feet from Turkey Creek Bridge. I was on my way home from my waitressing job. It was Saturday, Saturday the sixth of February," answered Mrs. Virginia Massey to a question posed by assistant district attorney Richard Hite in a stuffy Jefferson County courtroom in March of the following year. She explained the type of car and its color the best she could recall, and then she looked at the defendant and declared, "Yes, sir. That's the man."

Viola Merys hurried along the third floor of the Perlmor Apartments in Denver, anxious to return to her room and relax after a long day. Though only fifty, she appeared older, wearing a hairstyle and floral dress similar to those of her mother, with a pair of eyeglasses that rested crookedly on her nose.

"Oh!" Ms. Merys squealed when the door to room 305 swung open. "Why, hello," she said to a tenant. "You scared me. How are you tonight?"

"I'm fine," said the tall, lanky tenant, stooping slightly as he ambled along the hallway.

"I'm doing fine, too," Mrs. Merys offered. "Oh, and before I forget, are you sure about that parking space? I don't want to give it to somebody else and then you change your mind." (The apartment had only eight parking spaces for thirty rooms.)

"I'm sure. I've leased a spot in a garage. Good night," he called back.

The lease extension stated the tenant's name as Walter Osborne. California prison records identified him as the fugitive Joseph Corbett Jr. The fastidious tenant kept a spotless apartment. He even folded his dirty laundry. His car was no different. He'd recently sold his 1957 gray-and-white Ford Fairlane to a used car dealer named Nathan Yanish. "It was immaculate, unusually spotless, and purred like a kitten. One of the very few cars I have purchased that I didn't have to do anything to before I sold it," said Yanish. The man known to his neighbors and former coworkers as Walter Osborne bought a 1951 yellow Mercury sedan two weeks later and kept it out of sight inside a garage, protected from the harsh Colorado winter and anyone who might be seeking to bother it—or him.

The studious-looking young Corbett reached the end of the hallway and started down the stairwell, flanked on the street side by large window panels that split the front of the apartment building in two.

"Good night," Mrs. Merys said as she stopped to empty an ashtray into a metal trash can before also heading down the stairs. *Such a quiet, courteous man*, the landlady thought. *I wish all my tenants were like him.*

The night of Sunday, February 7, 1960, was bitterly cold. Denver had collected another layer of snow the day before, and its icy surface crunched beneath Corbett's shoes as he made his way to King Soopers grocery around the corner. He struggled back home against a bone-chilling wind, clasping his coat's collar tightly around his neck. Once inside, the cool stairs and hallway did little to relieve his chill. At last, he stepped inside his warm apartment.

The thin-walled studio apartment had welcomed him as its only tenant since it opened in April 1956 when Corbett moved from an older apartment on South Santa Fe Drive. The room was small, like most of the Perlmor Apartments, providing a mere four hundred square feet of living space for seventy-five dollars a month, though it seemed larger because of the bare white walls and scarcity of furnishings. A golden-brown sleeper couch along with a small black-and-white TV took up the far end of the apartment. The studio also had a miniature refrigerator and kitchen table, with a hot plate and toaster oven on a counter by the sink. A tiny bathroom lay off the kitchen area. The typical personal adornments were noticeably absent—no photographs of friends or family, no sports memorabilia, no souvenirs of trips taken, and no knickknacks. Only a portable transistor radio sat atop the TV. He didn't even have a telephone.

Corbett rarely watched television and listened to the radio sparingly. Like many folks during that era, he preferred to read. "The most distinguished thing about him was there was nothing you would remember him by," said Charles Spencer, who lived down the hall.

Corbett was a frugal man, having resigned from his job two months earlier. Forced to scrimp with money running low, he had decided the time had come to find a better job. To Corbett, this was something he really wanted. He began to think of his future. No more job hunts. No more wasting his life. He hoped this would be his last job, one that would provide him with a comfortable life full of good food, luxurious accommodations, and travel to exotic places. On his chrome-bordered kitchen table rested a new Royalite portable typewriter that would help him obtain that job. Once a proficient typist who could type fifty to sixty words a minute, Corbett was rusty, and so was his old Underwood typewriter. Casting the Underwood aside, he was anxious to give his new typewriter a trial run.

Typically dressed in creased khakis, starched white shirt, and black oxfords, Corbett poured himself a cup of coffee and cranked a sheet of paper into the typewriter. He wanted this letter to be perfect, wholly free of errors. He knew the correct margins and punctuation to use. While in college, he'd worked for a typing service. He typed business documents, papers for other students, and correspondence.

His run-in with California authorities over shooting and killing a man a decade earlier had taken him away from college after his junior year. Though he assured his family and acquaintances he would be going back after his release from prison, perhaps returning to the University of California–Berkeley to study courses in engineering or premedicine one day, he instead escaped and his family hadn't heard from him since.

After absconding to Denver four months later, he told his landlord he was enrolling at the University of Colorado–Boulder. Instead, he took a job as a laborer at Colorado Cold Storage for a few weeks, and then at Chemical Sales Company for three months, before finding a better job as an alkyd resin cooker at the three-story Benjamin Moore & Co. paint factory north of downtown Denver. It paid $2.70 an hour, earning him about $110 for the week. He worked the night shift, 3:15–11:30 p.m., with a single coworker. No one else was in the building after 5:30, which suited Corbett's desire for solitude. Though Benjamin Moore wasn't the job he desired, he was a loner, not liking to be around people since high school, never going to parties or participating in other social functions.

Corbett's former production manager at Benjamin Moore, Don Herring, described "Walter Osborne" to a *Rocky Mountain News* reporter: "Everyone liked him. When we needed a cooker, we put an ad in the paper and 117 people applied. Walt was head and shoulders above the others. He never missed a day's work in the three years he was with us. The only thing you might call unusual about him was that he always kept to himself. No one ever knew anything about his personal life. But that seemed natural enough to us, since he worked the night shift, with only one helper. When Walt left, he resigned. We were very sorry to see him go."

Sitting with his back erect, Corbett pushed his horn-rimmed glasses to the bridge of his nose and commenced typing scales he'd learned to increase dexterity before attempting the letter. Minutes later, he selected more substantial text from the February 1960 issue of *Popular Science* magazine he'd just purchased at King Soopers—an article about a nuclear-bomb shelter that could accommodate a family of up to six comfortably.

The typewriter keys clacked as they struck the paper loudly, and the ding of the bell sang out, signaling to the practicing typist to swipe the return lever, whisking the carriage to its starting position with a zing. Flipping to page 103 of another magazine, *Popular Mechanics*, he continued on with a story about flying saucer sightings.

If he made a mistake, he'd rip out the paper, crumple it, and toss it into the trash can. Other times, he'd shove his chair back and stand up to pace about the room. Corbett's mercurial temperament could make him his harshest critic. He was a perfectionist about many things, yet he could be perfunctory about important matters, like failing to finish college and quitting his most recent job.

Across the hall from Corbett lived Vivian Cherveny in apartment 306. When asked, Miss Cherveny agreed with her neighbor Herman Rask when he said: "He was a good neighbor. Never gave anyone any trouble."

But that night, they heard their typically quiet neighbor typing very late into the evening. For more than an hour, Corbett flipped through magazines and typed advertisements and news stories as the keys clacked loudly and the bell rang repeatedly. He eventually moved on to the letter and kept working at it until the letter was perfect—precise alignment, no misstrikes of the keys, and two spaces after a period, like he'd learned in school. And the words were carefully chosen to convey to its recipient his qualifications and commitment to success.

"Understand this: Adolph's life is in your hands. We have no desire to commit murder. All we want is that money."

CHAPTER 2

When Ad arrived at the Coors brewery around 9:30 on Monday morning, February 8, he was greeted by his secretary, Jo Ann Pfalzfraf. Rather than arriving at his usual time of 8:15 a.m., Ad had taken a different route to work, one that didn't take him across Turkey Creek Bridge, going to Denver for an errand before arriving at the brewery.

"Ad always had time to speak and give you a smile," Jo Ann said. "He had a large volume of daily personal work, but he was never overbearing. I'd turn on his dictation recorder, and Ad's voice frequently started out with instructions something like this: 'Now, you don't have to rush with this.'"

His brother Joe quickly pointed out the weeklong backlog of paperwork on Ad's desk. Joe spoke in a low voice, and he was the tallest and quietest of the Coors brothers. He always talked about the "Red Menace," most often the Soviet Union, with its *Sputnik 3* satellite passing over his head every 105 minutes.

Despite the fact the multilevel Adolph Coors Company spanned nearly 1,600 acres, Ad and his younger brothers, Bill and Joe, shared a single office on the third floor, each sitting behind a gray metal desk butted against a gray-tiled wall one foot apart from his closest brother's desk. No wood-paneled walls; no ornate mahogany desks; no paintings and sculptures, only tradesmen's calendars and framed black-and-white photographs of the Coors plant from days gone by. If someone came in to speak with one brother, he'd have to do so in the presence of the other two.

Like the Earp brothers of old Tombstone, the Coors brothers of Golden stuck together at work and play. Everything Ad did, just like his father and brothers, was exemplary, from administration and sales to designing his home, to skiing, piloting the company Piper Comanche plane, and even playing the piano and the drums. There were three areas in which the Coors family demanded excellence from their children: education, athletic ability (for the sons), and physical appearance. Education was extremely important. No one married before graduating college. (Ad did have a sister, May Louise. She was the youngest. While at Vassar College, she'd met Joseph Tooker Jr. from a wealthy New York family, and after their marriage in 1948, she left Colorado to live in Greenwich, Connecticut. Mr. Coors didn't mind. After all, she was a daughter; she'd never run the brewery.)

At six foot one, Ad was the shortest of the three brothers. All of them were slender, but Ad's countenance was fuller and softer, with blue eyes and light brown hair, having taken after his mother, whereas Joe and Bill had bony features like their father, Adolph Coors Jr., known to all as "Mr. Coors," the firstborn son of the founder of the Adolph Coors Company.

Mr. Coors was six feet tall but dreadfully thin, always dressed in a dark blue or gray suit and vest from a bygone era, high-button goatskin shoes, a starched white shirt with bow tie, topped with a gray derby he wore when coming and going from the brewery. He was a shrewd businessman, and the only thing on Mr. Coors's mind was the brewery. So much so that he worked twelve to fourteen hours a day and often forgot to eat, becoming so thin at times, nearing 110 pounds for a man over six feet, that his wife insisted he check into a Santa Barbara sanitarium to gain weight.

By contrast, he insisted his sons dress casually, because he did not want the Coors family to be viewed by the locals as too haughty. They wore khaki pants, button-down shirts, and high leather shoes, almost identical in appearance, except Bill sometimes wore a bow tie and Ad often wore a long-billed tan cap.

"Ad dresses casual because he feels he is on the same level as the laboring man and can do any job in the plant," observed Kenneth Malo, a longtime friend.

One employee explained Ad's ways to an out of town reporter differently: "Ad's most outstanding trait is that he is not outstanding. Often he is mistaken by new employees and suppliers as a run-of-the-mill employee. None of them would ever dream he's Adolph III, chairman of the company."

Despite the appearance of a middle-class existence in public, the Coors brothers belonged to several social clubs in the Denver area, like the Rolling Hills Country Club, Lakewood Country Club, Denver Country Club, University Club, Cherry Creek Country Club, Garden of the Gods Club, and the Denver Club. These were private clubs, local playgrounds for affluent white Protestant men and their families. Places where the Coors brothers could mingle with others of similar station without rousing their father's unease about upsetting the lower class. Places where husbands smoked cigars, traded golf stories, and transacted business, and wives drank martinis and talked about kids, the latest fashions, and tennis.

At work and at home, though, their casual business wear and easy-going personalities were indicative of their modest lifestyles. The brothers and their wives and children lived much like everyone else, without limousines, private schools, or bodyguards. The kids played on public school playgrounds, swam in the city pool, and slept over with friends, never standing out from the rest. The wives frequented the local beauty parlors, dress shops, and the neighborhood King Soopers or Safeway. They lived in middle-class homes and drove ordinary cars. Mr. Coors saw to it. After all, he owned the company stock and controlled the purse strings.

Mr. Coors believed he had reason for his family to maintain a low profile. He'd always feared that Prohibition, the law against the brewing, sale, and transport of alcoholic beverages passed in 1916 in Colorado and not repealed until 1933, might someday be voted back into law. Prohibition had almost ruined the Coors brewery when he was younger and, some believed, helped shove his eighty-two-year-old father and company founder off a sixth-floor Cavalier Hotel balcony in Virginia Beach in 1929. Mr. Coors reasoned that if he prohibited advertisements of beer that contained images of people drinking, and forbade his family from parading their riches, people would not begrudge their wealth from alcohol and support a return of Prohibition.

But his foremost concern was the possibility of kidnapping. Thirty years earlier, just months after the infamous Lindbergh baby kidnapping, in February 1933, Mr. Coors's good friend Charles Boettcher II, the son of the wealthiest man in Colorado, had been kidnapped and held for two weeks until released in exchange for ransom. The crime made the kidnapper the country's first "Public Enemy No. 1," hunted by the fledgling FBI and state and local law enforcement. One item found in the kidnapper's possession was a crumpled list of five potential victims. Mr. Coors's name was on that list.

Though he'd dodged the first public-enemy kidnapping, Mr. Coors didn't have long to savor it. Seven months later, he was informed of a separate plot by two former Prohibition agents to kidnap and hold him in a secluded cabin for ransom; however, the out-of-work revenuers were apprehended before they could put their plan into action.

Yet those incidents had occurred decades ago, and the Depression-era gangsters were now just old movies on the late, late show. Kidnappings of wealthy or famous individuals were almost unheard of in the United States since then, thanks to the Federal Bureau of Investigation and the advent of sophisticated criminal-detection techniques. And so the Coors brothers gave their father's stories little consideration and simply grew accustomed to living a lifestyle leaner than most sons of multimillionaires, believing Mr. Coors would not have been such a curmudgeon had he not lived through those difficult times.

But sometimes with age comes wisdom.

Six weeks earlier, cash registers at the Sears, Roebuck & Co. department store in Cherry Creek rang up sales during Christmas 1959. It was a good sales season for the mail order catalog and retail company even though it competed with the May-D&F and Denver Dry Goods Company stores frequented by Denver families, like the Coorses, since the Colorado silver rush. Among those who returned to the department store after the holiday season searching for bargains on overstocked or unpopular items was Joe Corbett, on Monday, December 28, the first shopping day following Christmas.

"Can you tell me where the camping gear is?"

"Yes, sir. Third floor. On the left near the back."

Corbett stepped on the escalator and patiently rode upward behind other shoppers as the sound of Christmas songs still filled the air. Once on the third floor, he spotted a red-and-white Coleman display. The display's shelves were lined with the items he sought: tent, kerosene lantern, sleeping bag, blankets, cooking set, canteen, twelve-piece aluminum picnic set, and a small propane stove.

A store clerk helped Corbett carry the camping gear to the checkout counter.

"Will that be cash or charge, sir?" asked Harry Ilgen, a clerk in the sporting goods department, readying a pencil to fill out a charge slip.

"Cash."

As the clerk rang up Corbett's purchases, the electric cash register flashed its white numbered cards indicating each item's sales price in the register window. Buying his camping supplies amid throngs of rabid shoppers gave him a headache. Motionless, like in one of his hunting stances, Corbett strained a gaze over the heads of shoppers milling about the store, avoiding direct looks and conversation with those around him.

"I lived with him for two and a half years and never got acquainted with him," said J. H. Hannah, manager of the Perlmor Apartments till August 1958, speaking of the man he knew as Walter Osborne. "Spoke with a middle-west accent; was refined, polite, and courteous. . . . He went in for athletic stuff. I remember he got some barbells through the mail, and a camera, and he liked to fish and shoot."

"My only real conversation with him was about hunting," Mrs. Merys added, who assumed management of the Perlmor from Mr. Hannah.

As the clerk continued to ring up the items, he looked at the tall, thin customer with a high forehead and eyeglasses and asked, "Whatcha doin' buying all this stuff in the middle of winter?"

Corbett glared and said nothing. When the clerk appeared uneasy, Corbett replied, "I like to camp in winter. I'm going to camp this winter in the mountains."

The clerk shuddered as if cold and handed Corbett his sales receipt. "Thank you for shopping at Sears." Corbett crumpled the receipt into a ball and dropped it in the sand-filled ashtray lid of a trash can beside the checkout counter as he walked away. But the cash register had kept its own receipt that would go to the store manager at the end of the day—a paper record listing the date, sale number, amount, type of transaction, and clerk.

Once back home, Corbett opened the trunk of his automobile and, with three trips, carried his purchases upstairs to his third-floor studio apartment. He didn't unpack those in boxes. There'd be time for that later. He stacked everything inside a tiny closet that stored his firearms, fishing gear, and other equipment. Corbett had grown up in Seattle, near mountains, rivers, and lakes, and he enjoyed the outdoors, whether it was camping, hunting, or fishing for trout. One of his favorite fishing spots was on the Blue River near Dillon, Colorado. But for now, his mind was on more serious matters, and he needed some rest. He stretched out his lanky body on the sleeper couch. The day was dark and gray, shining very little light between the cracks of the pulled blinds. He fell asleep. His preparations were almost complete.

Golden, Colorado, is home to the Adolph Coors Company. For many, the Adolph Coors Company is home to Golden, Colorado. The small town was incorporated in the Colorado Territory in 1871, a mere two years before Adolph Coors arrived from Germany and started his brewery. Until the 1950s, Coors employed more workers than the town had people. As the population of Golden grew during the '50s, however, so did the "difficulty" between management and workers.

"I don't know of anybody who didn't like Ad Coors. He was never a part of the difficulty at the brewery, as far as I know," Golden's city manager and former classmate of Ad Coors, Walter G. Brown, later said to a reporter for *The Denver Post*.

Workers at the world's largest single brewery were unionized as members of Local 366, part of the International Union of United Brewery, Flour, Cereal, Soft Drink, and Distillery Workers of America, which in turn was part of the AFL-CIO. The Coors family had gotten along fine with workers, but merely tolerated the union. Coors paid less than some, but Mr. Coors paid a large Christmas bonus if the company had a good year. Also, open beer taps stationed around the plant enabled employees to have a little libation during the workday.

Unions were at their pinnacle of power in the United States by the 1950s, and national union leaders were strong-arming companies all around the country, demanding better wages and benefits for their members. Tensions strained to the point that the moment had come to show who was boss in Golden.

"The electricians are still talking about a strike," said Bill Coors to his brothers after hanging up the telephone in their common office. "That was Russ Hargis [Coors' personnel director]. He heard it on the floor."

"You know, if the electricians go, the whole brewery might go like last time," Ad said on that first business day back from Miami.

The last strike had been in 1957, and it was the worst strike the brewery had witnessed. Picket lines formed in front of the brewery, the porcelain factory in Golden, and the Coors warehouse in Denver. Incendiary speeches berating the company and maligning the Coors family followed. Tires were slashed, punches thrown, windows broken, and threatening calls made to Coors management and anyone who crossed the picket line. When more than eight hundred workers and their families took to the streets, the Jefferson County sheriff asked the governor to call in the National Guard to disperse the crowd. Security was added at the plant, and members of the Coors family were careful not to place themselves in harm's way. Fortunately, that strike was settled without incident. But the possibility of a company-wide strike was always of concern.

The brothers had been discussing the issue of a strike just days earlier before Ad and Mary left for the brewers' convention in Miami. Ad's secretary walked in and heard them talking. It was a discussion she was becoming more and more accustomed to hearing from them. "Excuse me. Ad? Your father wants to see you. He's in his office."

"You in trouble, Ad?" asked Bill with a grin.

"Not that I know." He smiled.

Ad ambled down the hallway, stopping outside his father's office door. He stood a little straighter and cleared his throat before going in.

Despite his age and thinness, Mr. Coors was not decrepit. On the contrary, he was tough and intimidating. Mr. Coors walked about the plant floor six days a week and sometimes half a day on Sunday, oftentimes registering an impressive three miles a day, checking not only how the brewing was progressing but also uncovering employee infractions. Any transgression, no matter how big or how small, drew a stern warning from the company's chief. He never gave a second. "[Mr. Coors] would eye our desks, and if everything wasn't in place," remembered one female employee, "he'd tell us to straighten it up. . . . When you left at night, there literally couldn't be anything on top of your desk—even your phone. You had to put it in your desk drawer. And you didn't dare leave a sweater on the back of your chair!"

Yet many employees liked and admired their austere employer. "On Saturday afternoon, he'd come down to the lunchroom and have a beer with us," one employee recalled. "He'd have this small cup with him, and after a first beer, I'd ask him if he wanted another. 'Just half,' he'd say, and he meant it. He always stressed economy."

Adolph Coors, the company's founder, had granted control to Mr. Coors while he was young, yet at seventy-four, Mr. Coors wasn't ready to relinquish ownership. His adult sons, now in their forties, held various positions in the company but owned none of the stock and thus had none of the control. They lived off a salary that was more like a child's allowance, an allowance that might seem outrageous to a worker filling beer bottles on the plant floor for $2.23 an hour, yet meager compared with that received by sons of other multimillionaires they knew.

Ad was a man of few words and rarely stood up to his father, despite holding the positions of chairman of the board, chief executive officer, and director of sales and marketing. Much of Ad's silence could be attributed to Western stoicism, but he also possessed a natural reserve, even shyness, attributed to an upbringing where children spoke only when they had something important to say. "[My father] believed if he showed affection, it would spoil me and my brothers," recalled Bill. "There was no levity in the house, no idle chatter at the dinner table. If you didn't have something worth saying, my father felt you shouldn't say it." Some of Ad's quietness was caused by an affliction he'd suffered since childhood. As Coors employee Clyde Ellis told a newsman for *The Denver Post*: "I've been here thirty years and I never seen [Ad] blow his stack at anybody. If he was upset, he wouldn't let you know it—the only way I knew was 'cause he'd start stuttering—then you knew somethin' was up."

When Ad stepped inside the office, his father was sitting behind the rolltop desk that had belonged to Ad's grandfather. A painting of Adolph Coors hung above it, his ever-watchful eyes gazing down on his brewery and its caretakers.

"Yes, sir? Jo Ann said you asked to see me."

"Hargis stopped in to tell me about the electricians. You boys handling that?"

"Yes, sir. We're discussing it now."

"What's to talk about? Fire the whole bunch with my blessing." Mr. Coors's antipathy toward the union was no surprise to Ad. Mr. Coors would pull an electrician off a job to make him sweep or perform some other menial task not in his union contract's "job description." Interestingly, his concerns about harm coming to his family physically or financially through kidnapping, or any other way, did not interfere with his toughness as an employer where disgruntled or terminated workers might harbor grudges.

Ad responded, "Yes, sir. We will if we have to. Bill's already hunting for replacements."

"See that he does. That's all, son."

"Yes, sir."

"Oh, son?"

"Sir?" Ad said, turning as he stopped near the office door.

"You boys don't let this get out of hand while your mother and I are in Hawaii. I don't want reporters hounding us. You go ahead to the convention in Miami, but if a problem comes up, you hightail it back here. Understand?"

"Yes, sir."

Stepping back into the hallway, Ad was relieved that he'd commanded his urge to stutter, which angered his father. He was the oldest son, and following Coors tradition, his father had named him chairman of the board and chief executive officer overseeing all company operations. But his stutter prevented him from being placed in charge of the day-to-day operations of the brewery like his father and grandfather before him. The person who runs the brewery must also run the workers, which means holding employee meetings and speaking to the press, sometimes during very tense times. Because of Ad's shyness and stutter, his father did not want the embarrassment. Another imperfection that prevented Ad from being a brewer was even more embarrassing to his father—he was allergic to beer.

Ad returned to the brothers' office. The last thing they needed was a plant-wide strike. They had warehouses full of orders to fill. (At that time, Coors only distributed to an eleven-state area, not yet commencing distribution east of the Mississippi.)

There was no question who would handle the negotiations. Joe handled the porcelain workers; Bill the brewery workers. Joe was the youngest son, and though he wasn't allergic to beer, he hated its taste, so he was placed in charge of Coors Porcelain, which fashioned fine china, chemical crucibles and dishes, and other porcelain products, located a stone's throw across Clear Creek from the brewery, where he kept his main office. (Profit from the Coors Porcelain factory, along with the production of near beer and malted milk, had kept the brewery from going under like most breweries during Prohibition.) Joe had taken the confrontational lead on behalf of Coors Porcelain when the strike was settled in 1957.

Bill, the second born, was president of Adolph Coors Company, in charge of the brewery's daily operations. No one ever questioned Bill's engineering and problem-solving skills. He was a fixer, no matter if it was an intricate corporate matter or a malfunctioning boiler valve. A year earlier, he had gained international notoriety for perfecting the aluminum can, whereby soon all soda and beer cans would be aluminum. Coors started a separate aluminum can company, Coors Container, which would become the largest aluminum can–producing plant in the world. He also was the first to pay a penny deposit in order to recycle aluminum cans. And almost as famously, he substituted cold filtering for hot pasteurization, preserving the fresh taste of beer.

Bill was often criticized, however, for being mule-headed and intolerant. He had been the brewery's outspoken vanguard during the last union strike. Bill and the Coors family firmly believed in the classes of America, the haves and the have-nots. To him, the haves ran the company; the have-nots worked in the company. And there was no way the have-nots were going to tell the Coors family how to run its brewery. The company paid employees well and provided safe working conditions. The Coors family believed there was no need for unions to "protect" Coors employees. Union leaders believed otherwise, hence the acrimony between the two sides, though the bitterness had not yet risen to the dangerous heights of 1957 when the union last struck.

The Coors family's views were well-known throughout the plant, including the family's conservative beliefs, whether those beliefs concerned unions, activists, homosexuals, or government mandates. Because of Ad's stutter and quiet disposition, he was not as visible or vocal as Bill and Joe about union matters or family ideologies, usually voting in agreement with his brothers behind the scenes without receiving the bad press his brothers received.

So on that Monday afternoon on February 8, 1960, when word of an electricians' strike that might spread to the brewery was again in the air, the brothers stood in a small circle in their office, symbolic of circling wagons before an attack, discussing how best to deal with the possibility. They agreed to take it up at their weekly executive committee meeting at 10:30 the following morning.

"I don't think Ad had an enemy in the world," Bill said to a reporter two days later, who had asked if Ad may have been harmed by a union member. "Revenge isn't a part of this. If it had been Joe or myself, then maybe I could understand it."

Corbett drove south of Denver to scout for camping sites. He took a route he'd taken before, turning off Highway 105 near Sedalia, in western Douglas County. He drove up Jackson Creek Road as the asphalt turned to gravel and then to dirt and mud. At seven thousand feet, he pulled over on the side of the narrow, rutted road at a garbage dump tucked away in the pines. A sign with a six-pointed star at its apex flanked on each side by the symbols for Venus proclaimed the garbage belonged to "Shamballah Ashrama—The Brotherhood of the White Temple." Corbett laughed. The first time he'd seen the sign with the odd name a few weeks earlier, he thought it was some kind of men's club, like the Shriners or the Elks, only for foreigners.

"Nope," replied W. C. Benson, operator of the Sprucewood Lodge located three miles northwest of the dump. "It's not one of them fraternal orders. About fifteen year ago, this fella named Claude Doggins from Oklahoma bought property up yonder and started callin' himself Dr. Doreal, sayin' he was some kinda prophet or somethin'. Built a church settlement and called it 'Shamballah Ashrama.' He told his followers a nuclear apocalypse was comin'. Gobs of folks believed 'im and settled in the commune. Said they'd be safe up there in the mountains 'cause lead in the rock would protect 'em from the fallout."

Corbett chuckled again before exiting his car at the crest of a hill. He opened a gate beside the road and entered a fenced property. It was the tiny community's garbage dump, covering an area about seventy by forty feet, small compared to a municipal dump. It was not an ideal place for camping, but it was a great spot for hunting. A dump attracts wild animals, including some dangerous ones, like wolves, bears, mountain lions, and bobcats.

Carrying a rifle he'd withdrawn from the back seat, Corbett came across a warm, flat boulder to sit on while he waited for an animal to scavenge through the garbage. He'd seen tracks of a three-pawed bear that were fresh, the tracks of the same bear he'd seen before and told a coworker of weeks earlier, but as one o'clock turned to two without a sign of anything other than prairie dogs, Corbett decided to shoot at cans and bottles.

Corbett fired several shots. He was surprised he'd missed a few times. He didn't miss often. He lifted the barrel of the rifle and inspected the gun sights.

The wind soon picked up and grew cold against Corbett's face. He decided to head down the mountain. Tossing his rifle on a blanket in the back seat, Corbett navigated his car down the rough road, now deeply rutted from the snow thaw during the sunny afternoon.

About halfway down the mountain, with Devil's Head still in full view to the south, he remembered he'd forgotten to do something at the dump. He stopped his car and removed an object from the trunk. It wasn't in a box, bag, or blanket. He carried the heavy object in both hands about fifty feet into the thick pine trees and brush. He dropped it in the dense forest. A bell dinged. He was glad to be rid of it. He wouldn't need it anymore.

Mr. Benson at the Sprucewood Lodge would later recount to the FBI how a man matching Corbett's description had frequented the lodge. "Came three times as I remember. Carried a paperback book and read while he ate. Ordered a cheeseburger and beer every time. First time was in January. Asked where he could go camping. Last time I seen 'im was first week in February. Haven't seen 'im since."

Incredibly, just weeks earlier, Corbett encountered another man while on one of his expeditions who also would later tell his story to the FBI. Apparently unconcerned about being remembered or just simply overconfident, Corbett stopped near the entrance to an old mine shaft, which lay only 150 yards from Turkey Creek Bridge. "Hey, mister. I'm searching for a place to do some shooting practice. I saw the mine over there and wondered if I could take a look around."

Hilton Pace, a roofer and part-time miner, answered the stranger's questions in an unfriendly voice, all the while doing a little surveying of his own, curious about this stranger who looked more like a college professor than a sportsman—starched white shirt, brown hat, eyeglasses.

"Yes, sir. It was in December. He was drivin' a gray-and-off-color-white Ford," Pace told an FBI agent later. "Asked me if I was workin' the mine, and I said I was part-time, mostly weekends and nights. He asked me how deep the mine was. . . . Yeah, and he asked where Four Corners Mine was and whether it connected with this mine up near Turkey Creek Bridge. I got the first two letters off his plate if that helps any—*AT*."

Corbett didn't tell Pace his name, but when Pace was shown Corbett's photograph, he recognized him right away. "I remember 'cause his two front teeth slanted backward a bit, kinda like a gopher's. . . . Said he wanted to go shootin'. Seemed to me to be just skulkin' about, up to no good. I told 'im I was rentin' and it'd be better if he did it somewheres else, 'specially since most of the land 'round the mine is game preserve. Anyways, who target shoots in mine shafts less you wannabe buried under a mountain of earth? I do a little shooting myself, but never in a mine. . . . [W]e talked maybe fifteen, twenty minutes, and the whole time I thought it were strange—"

"What? What was strange?" asked the FBI agent who interviewed Pace.

"That he weren't wearin' a coat. My wife, Clara Jean, felt the same way. She come out after he pulled up. It was cold as blue blazes, and I thought to myself a man wouldn't go shootin' without a coat in this kinda weather. . . . Clara Jean said he looked crooked as a Virginia fence, but I never dreamed . . ."

Mr. Pace never dreamed, but Corbett did. Not only of target shooting but pulling a job that would make him a fortune. And his planning was almost done. It soon would be time.

CHAPTER 3

Snow swirled past the windows outside Ad's barn at eight o'clock on the night of Monday, February 8. Ad wanted to confer with his ranch manager about when they would auction the cattle. They decided to wait a bit, when the market was up. He also asked his manager if he would accompany him Saturday to size up some horses in La Junta, and he agreed.

Mary called Ad to dinner. Afterward, Ad sat at the kitchen table near sweat-streaked windows, reviewing some of the ranch accounts. He was bushed and hoped to turn in soon. He'd been back from Miami for forty-eight hours, and his first day at the brewery had been a busy one, with more meetings and telephone conferences scheduled for Tuesday. At least his father was on vacation in Hawaii with his mother and wouldn't return for another two weeks. Things wouldn't be as tense with Mr. Coors away.

Cecily was seated across the kitchen table from her father with Spike seated beside her, both doing homework. The youngest of the Coors children, Jim, lay on the den floor in front of the fireplace with a toy truck and horse trailer he'd gotten for Christmas. Mary sat watching television with the volume low so not to disturb those at the table. She'd finished putting the dishes away earlier with the help of Brooke, who now stretched out in the hallway floor with the telephone.

Mary couldn't help thinking how nice it was to be home with the kids and Ad and her fireplace and her favorite chair and everything feeling like it should. She wished she could freeze the moment and keep things just the way they were forever. She knew things at home were changing and the kids were growing up. What Mary didn't realize was that night would be the best it would be, forever more.

"Three dollars—regular," Corbett told gas attendant Lynn Westerbuhr at the Conoco Service Station on East Fourteenth Avenue, around the corner from Corbett's apartment.

It was a cold night, and the young attendant inserted the hose nozzle into the automobile and turned the pump lever. He stomped his feet on the icy concrete and cupped his gloved hands, blowing on them to provide a little warmth.

"He stopped by regularly, usually once a week. He asked for three dollars' worth of gas every time," said Westerbuhr. "Never told me his name. Always paid cash."

The attendant removed the hose and hooked it on the side of the pump. "That's three dollars," said Westerbuhr, waiting for Corbett to slip three bills through the sliver of open window. "Whatcha got back there? Moving?"

"A sleeping bag and tent."

"You going camping in this weather?" asked the attendant, just like the clerk had at the Sears department store.

"Here's your money," said Corbett. He detested snoops.

"He was driving a dark maroon Dodge, 'tween a '46 to '49 year model, I think," Westerbuhr soon would tell authorities. "Around Christmas, I seen him in a bright-yellow Mercury and again in January, 'bout through the second week of January, I'd say. I seen him in several cars over the last year, though—a light blue Ford wagon, gray-and-white Ford sedan. He liked cars. Most times, he was by himself. Sometimes with another man. A big fella, about thirty-five, usually in dirty work clothes, might 'ave been an Indian or an Italian, I don't know."

After leaving the station that Monday night, Corbett returned to his Perlmor apartment. Soon, metallic sounds filled the air. Gun chambers snapped, shackles clanked, and handcuffs clattered eerily in the sparse room. Corbett was making ready for the following day. He brushed his coat and spit-shined his shoes, like preparing for a job interview, a compulsion he'd picked up in prison. He'd gotten a haircut earlier in the day. A freshly dry-cleaned suit hung on a doorknob.

Later that evening, Corbett hurried down the back stairs to the first-floor hallway and out the back door. A pistol, a rifle, cuffs, and leg irons draped in a blanket filled his arms. A sedan waited for him across the alley behind his apartment with its trunk raised and front- and rear-passenger doors open on the passenger side. He'd already loaded blankets, canned food, water in glass jugs, and his Coleman stove, lantern, and other camping equipment in the trunk. He checked for anyone who might be watching him before stretching out the blanket and removing the pistol and placing it in the glove compartment.

"He seemed like he was in a hurry," said Terrence Smith, a tenant in room 106. "I saw blankets on the back seat, two rifle cases, a telescopic case, and a pistol case, all zipped up along the side."

Corbett slammed the trunk closed, removed his hat, and wiped his forehead, running his fingers through his hair that was soaked with sweat despite the cold night's sleet pelting down. Scaling flights of stairs half a dozen times made him perspire, but he was also full of nervous anxiety from fear of detection. He was afraid, all right, even though he'd spent months, almost thirty of them, planning this job. Despite being proud of his intellect (he'd been tested as having an IQ of 148) and his methodical, almost obsessive analytical approach to things, he knew he wasn't infallible. After all, he had been captured for shooting a man and imprisoned in California a decade earlier.

To calm himself, he sat in his apartment and turned on the television to *Peter Gunn*. Soon, he pulled open a drawer and stuffed the letter he'd perfected into the pocket of his coat hanging in the closet. He planned to mail it the next day.

Corbett hadn't seen his family for ages, and if the letter procured him what he expected, he doubted he'd have a chance to see them for a long time to come. He didn't have a family of his own, not yet, only a father, stepmother, and stepbrother.

"It says here that he's got a wife—name's Marion," said one of Corbett's former bosses reviewing his employment records with an FBI agent later. "Some of the boys said Walt told 'em he was married. But later he said he was married to 'Anne' and listed her as his wife on his company health insurance policy. Seems to me a man should know the name of his wife, and polygamy is frowned on in Colorado."

His female neighbors, however, never saw a wife or a girlfriend or any woman visiting, for that matter. If any woman said hello, she was lucky to receive eye contact from Corbett, much less a response. Many of his female neighbors who'd been rebuffed by Corbett's shyness and abrupt exits referred to him as "Mystery Boy."

"When we'd go to the city café to eat, which we did a lot, he'd never talk to the waitresses," said one of Corbett's coworkers. "Some were interested, but he'd never say as much as a how-do-you-do. He'd just order his food."

"Women aren't to be trusted," Corbett would say. "They're dirty, disagreeable, expensive, and worst of all, can't keep confidential information to themselves."

Corbett clicked off the television set. He had things to do tomorrow—confidential things. He stretched out on his sleeper sofa. It was dark, but trails of light passing through the metal venetian blinds laid stripes across a portion of the ceiling and one wall. He stared at the faint luminescent strands above him. It was late. His preparations had taken longer than he'd planned. But he wasn't sleepy. Adrenaline pumped through his veins. Soon, his mind raced through the details of his plan. It was a good plan.

CHAPTER 4

Darkness filled the hallway as Ad ambled to the kitchen. It was 5:30 in the morning. Sunrise wasn't due for another hour and a half. He flipped on the kitchen light and started the percolator as he did every morning. The smell of brewing coffee soon filled the kitchen.

After a cup, Ad stepped into the basement, removed his flesh-colored rimmed glasses, and began his daily exercise routine. Push-ups, sit-ups, jumping jacks, and other calisthenics kept him a slender 185 pounds.

Mary was awake by the time Ad stepped into a steaming shower. She could hear him whistling as she slipped on her robe. Ad was a morning person. Mary envied her husband's predawn sprightliness. She poured a cup of coffee and was sitting at the kitchen table looking out a frosty window toward the Dakota Hogback when Ad, dressed for work, joined her.

They discussed the routine matters that a husband and wife share: how they slept, what time he'd be coming home, what he'd like for supper. At last, Mary stood and walked down the hallway toward the kids' bedrooms to awaken them for school.

Ad took another sip from his mug and slipped rubber boots over his dress shoes. He stepped outside to check the horses and to piddle away a few minutes, breaking ice in troughs, pitching a little hay, and pouring a little feed. He stopped for a second to look across the bluff toward the rolling hills past the road. The morning felt warmer than last. The warm weather would make the day's chores a bit more comfortable for his ranch hands, who'd be arriving soon.

The Coors household came very much alive when Mary awakened the kids at 6:30. Spike and Jim dressed in a flash and were at the table, ready for breakfast, whereas Brooke and Cecily required more time.

Outside the large kitchen window, the kids could see their father stirring about, though they really didn't think much about it. He was always outside doing something when he wasn't in his basement office.

At 7:40, the sound of the school bus's diesel engine moaned up the hill to a stop at the bottom of the Coorses' driveway. The kids scattered from the table and raced for the door, picking up books and satchels along the way. They didn't see their father as they trotted down the driveway.

The bus driver spotted the kids hurrying downhill and waited. Soon, the doors folded shut, and the Coors children seated themselves about the school bus. They were off to another school day filled with the usual. Simply another school day in their young lives filled with school days. But this one they'd never forget.

Mary cleared away the dishes and left them in the sink. She heard Ad step inside the back door. He removed his rubber boots, and she could hear him going down the basement stairs. Mary left to pick up Marie Miller, a woman hired to do the household ironing every Tuesday, who lived just minutes away. When back, Mary clicked on the television and sat in her housecoat and slippers, relaxing in the warmth of her den to the welcome quietness while Mrs. Miller worked downstairs.

"I was doing the ironing in the basement," said Mrs. Miller. "Mr. Coors was in his office. He didn't say anything. He was busy. I remember he wrote out two checks and then went upstairs to leave for work."

Mary was drinking her coffee watching the early news when Ad ascended from the basement. "Gotta go, honey." He bent down and pecked her on the lips. "Have a nice day."

"You, too, sweetheart," said Mary, who stayed seated. Like most weekday mornings, they'd had little chance to talk. There'd be time to talk that evening.

Ad grabbed his tan baseball cap and slipped on his favorite navy-blue nylon jacket, which he wore almost every day during the cold months. The hoodless parka doubled as a suit coat. If he had a meeting, Ad would slip on a tie and zip up the parka so that only his buttoned-down collar and tie would show.

He stepped into the cold garage and started his 1959 white-over-turquoise International Harvester Travelall, a perfect vehicle for the rutted gravel roads sprinkled with potholes and fist-sized stones in the Colorado countryside. Most folks called it an oversized station wagon or a carryall (an early version of a four-wheel-drive SUV).

Ad backed his Travelall out of the garage and eased down the winding drive to a gravel road that would lead him to the brewery in Golden, twelve miles away. He spotted Bill Hosler outside the barn with fellow ranch hand Peter Puck, who'd just arrived. Ad gave a wave. Hosler waved back. It was 7:55 a.m.

Ad's deerskin gloves gripped the cold, hard steering wheel, waiting for the Travelall's heater to warm as he rambled north toward Morrison and on to the brewery. His normal route would have carried him less than a mile along a straight gravel road to paved US Highway 285, which would lead him to Golden. Yet that route had been closed for the last month while state workers repaired a two-mile stretch of highway. The detour took him along a winding, lonely stretch of road for four miles, barely wide enough for two cars, requiring that one pull over and let the other pass.

The night had been stormy, but it was now a warm forty-two degrees with only a slight sprinkling of rain. He had a few telephone calls to make and then his 10:30 meeting with his brothers. After lunch, he had one or two more meetings. Not too stressful a day, but lots more paperwork to catch up on.

Fewer than five minutes from his home, Ad's Travelall rambled around the last bend before reaching a rough-hewn lumber bridge, twenty-three feet long and fourteen feet wide, with crude wooden railings on each side and two wooden tracks burrowed in gravel, wide enough for only a single car to cross, shadowed by a pair of scraggly leaf-bare trees and a telephone pole laden with sagging wires. Turkey Creek Bridge, locals called it. On the other side of the narrow, shallow creek lay State Road 70, also gravel, lined with hackberry and cottonwood trees. A right on Route 70 and then a left on Soda Lakes Road would take Ad to the town of Morrison and the busily traveled Highway 285.

The gravel road mixed with snow and mud revealed that only the school bus had traveled the road that morning. Its driver was S. C. Nielson, who'd crossed the bridge at 7:35 a.m. and back again ten minutes later with the Coors children aboard.

"I can't recall seeing any cars at all," Mr. Nielson later told a Colorado state patrolman.

As Ad approached Turkey Creek Bridge, he came upon an automobile at the far end of the narrow bridge blocking his way to the crossroad. Its hood was raised and driver's-side doors, front and back, were open. Beside it stood a tall, thin man in a dark suit, tie, and brown felt hat, wearing dark-rimmed glasses. He was standing near the open hood, along the driver's side, just standing there watching Ad as he pulled his Travelall on the bridge.

Ad stopped not far behind the stranded automobile and rolled his window down as the man approached.

"What's the trouble?" Ad shouted, stepping out of his Travelall.

II

THE

DISAPPEARANCE

CHAPTER 5

Sounds of shallow water rippling beneath Turkey Creek Bridge were seldom interrupted during the day. But on the morning of Tuesday, February 9, 1960, the timber planks and log supports of the bridge would bear silent witness to a horrifying crime. Yet the seclusion wasn't absolute. There were those who could tell their stories, and they would when asked the next day by law enforcement— for the grandson of the most famous man in Colorado had gone missing.

> "I was driving along State Road 70 that morning," said Dr. John Pallaoro, a Golden veterinarian who knew Ad Coors. "It was muddy and the sun had just come out when I passed by Turkey Creek Bridge. I spotted a large blue-and-white station wagon parked on the bridge. It appeared deserted. . . . No, I didn't cross the bridge because I didn't come that way. I was headed toward Morrison and State Road 70 passes by the bridge. . . . Yes, I remember the time exactly. It was 8:04."

Not until 10:20, almost two and a half hours after Ad stopped his Travelall, did another traveler come that way: Dan Crocker, a twenty-five-year-old milkman for United Dairies in south Jefferson County. He gave his statement to a Colorado state patrolman:

I was making my morning deliveries in the Soda Lakes area when I come up on a blue-green–and-white Travelall on the bridge. It was parked in my way so I couldn't pass. I got out and walked up to the car. The motor was running and the driver's-side window was down and I could hear the radio playin'. I honked the car's horn and waited another minute or two, and when nobody come, I went back to my own truck and rearranged the load, thinking somebody's got to come move it. When they didn't, I honked the horn on my truck and waited again. I probably sat there fifteen minutes honking and waiting till I decided nobody was coming. I got in the Travelall and backed it off the bridge, kinda catty-cornered on the side of this no-name dirt road. I turned the switch off and left the keys in the car and went on my way.

I made a delivery to Mrs. Stitt that took me 'bout a mile down the road. I told her what I seen but she didn't know whose car it was. She didn't have a telephone neither so I couldn't call the highway patrol. So I drove back the way I come. The car was still sitting where I left it. I made another delivery at the Lowdermilk Construction Company, then I went to the old CC camp outside of Morrison and made another delivery. Nobody was there. From there I drove to the Standard gas station on the east side of Morrison and called the Colorado State Patrol and told 'em what I seen.

Offices inside the Coors brewery were coming alive by eight o'clock. Ad's secretary, Jo Ann, arrived and sat at her station, putting away her purse and tidying up for the morning's work to begin. Other secretaries filed into the stenographers' pool, rustling about, removing their coats, scarves, and gloves and slipping off their galoshes. Greetings and nods passed about the room and soon the chatter of "hello" and "good morning" gave way to the sounds of typing and ringing telephones.

By 8:15, Bill and Joe were seated in their office. Joe flipped through a financial newspaper as a radio on his desk announced the morning's news. Bill busied himself reviewing sketches of an additional conveyor system to be installed at Coors Container. The brothers were casual and relaxed. Mr. Coors was in Hawaii and wouldn't return for two weeks. There'd be no stern father making unexpected stops in their office.

The hands of the office's wall clock clicked to ten as Joe and Bill worked. Jo Ann had little to do except answer Ad's telephone line. "He's busy at the moment. Can I take a message and ask him to return your call?"

Jo Ann wasn't alarmed. Ad had been late before, especially when his father was away, though he'd usually telephoned. She continued with her morning's tasks, expecting her smiling boss to walk in any moment.

Sunlight was breaking through dark clouds, and the sprinkles of rain stopped. The office was warming as Bill and Joe sat at their desks, holding calls so they'd be ready for their 10:30 a.m. meeting to discuss, among other things, a possible union strike—but no Ad.

Although their father had handed over most of the decisions, he retained ultimate veto power. As for the sons' votes, they had to agree on all major company matters. Adolph Coors Company didn't run by majority vote. If one son refused his consent, that was the end of the matter, subject only to Mr. Coors's intervention.

"The three of us worked with our father as a team during the 1940s, 1950s, and 1960s," recalled Bill. "Not that there was always agreement—four strong-willed people in one room guarantees conflict. Our father, however, would not tolerate dissension. If there was a difference of opinion, he insisted we sit there and argue things out until we reached unanimity. We were then bound by the decision. . . . It was up to me and my brothers to preserve and improve what he had given to us. We were ready."

The brothers were more than ready to divvy up management duties. They had years of experience working under the tutelage of their demanding father. "I never got a word of approval, nor did my brothers," recalled Bill. "A prefect job was expected of you; anything else was underperformance." They also had first-rate educations. Ad graduated from Phillips Exeter Academy and received an engineering degree from Cornell like his father, where Ad was the president of Quill and Dagger, a prestigious senior honor society. Bill also graduated from Phillips Exeter, but became the only Coors to earn his chemical engineering degree from Princeton. Joe earned his degree in chemical engineering from Cornell. "Ad was the only one of us not to have a chemical engineering degree, and I believe that hampered him," recalled Bill. "Sometimes he had to bite his tongue and go along with the will of the mass."

Military service had not interfered with their educations or tutelage at the brewery. Their father had not served in the military, and none of the Coors brothers had served during World War II or Korea. Ad had a legitimate excuse. He was 4-F for acute nearsightedness. He couldn't see his hands without his glasses. Bill had been in charge at Coors Porcelain, building porcelain insulators for atomic missile research at Oak Ridge, Tennessee, during World War II, which was viewed by the War Department as more important than him trudging across his family's Prussian homeland. Joe's exemption was the weakest. He had been put in charge of the American Dairy Association.

After fifteen minutes had passed and Ad had still not shown up, Bill didn't want to wait any longer. "Jo Ann?" he called. "Ring Ad at home and see what's holding him up. Tell him we're starting without 'im."

"Yes, sir."

The telephone rang at the ranch house.

"Hello," answered Mary, expecting the call to be from a friend anxious to hear about her stay at the luxurious Americana Hotel in Miami where the likes of Frank Sinatra and his Rat Pack frequented.

"Hello, Mrs. Coors. This is Jo Ann at the brewery. How are you?"

"I'm fine, thanks. And you?"

"Fine, thank you. The reason I'm calling is Ad hasn't got here yet, and Bill asked me to call to see if he's still at home."

"No . . . he's not here," replied Mary.

"Do you know where he's at? He was supposed to be here right now for the executive committee meeting."

"Well, I don't know. He left about eight. I thought he was headed straight for the brewery. He should be there," Mary said, not too concerned, because Ad had taken excursions for ranch or beer business. Only the day before, he'd gone to Denver first and arrived at the brewery around nine thirty. "Maybe he had some stops to make," continued Mary.

"Okay. I'll check at the warehouse and Porcelain to see if he's there," Jo Ann said. "Maybe he got stuck on something before he could come into the office. Anyplace else I should call you can think of?"

"Let me see," Mary said. "I'm not sure. Tell you what, I'll call the Jefferson County Grange and see if they've seen him this morning. Sometimes he gets to talking and loses track of time. If he's not at the feedstore, I don't know—"

Jo Ann could detect anxiety creeping into Mary's voice. "I'm sure he's hunky-dory," she interrupted. "You know Ad. He'll pop in any minute."

Jo Ann knew Ad, too, and it wasn't like him to forget to call and let his brothers know he wasn't coming in.

"Call me when he does, okay?" asked Mary.

"I will," said Jo Ann. "And if you hear from him, please tell him to call Bill."

Mary lowered the receiver and wondered where Ad could be. Perhaps he went up in the company plane and that's why no one could reach him. Or he was out inspecting cattle, but Ad usually took Bill Hosler with him, and Hosler was at the ranch. A startling thought suddenly crossed Mary's mind. Perhaps he had a rendezvous . . . but no sooner had the thought crossed her mind than it evaporated. No, Ad wasn't like that. She dialed the feedstore.

Jo Ann called the Coors warehouse in Denver and the Porcelain offices. She checked with all the departments within the brewery. No one had seen Ad. She was starting to become worried.

Though Bill was frustrated, he, Joe, and office manager, Ray Frost, went ahead with the executive committee meeting.

Another hour passed. Jo Ann had had enough. She pulled out the telephone directory and began calling hospitals and doctor offices. She was still making calls when Jack Scanlan from Coors Traffic Department buzzed her.

"Is Ad in?" Scanlan asked.

Jo Ann started to reply that Ad was in a meeting, but didn't. She sensed nervousness in Scanlan's voice. "No. Can I take a message?"

"I just got a call from the Colorado State Patrol. They said . . . tell you what, transfer me to Bill Coors instead."

"Is something wrong? Is Ad hurt?"

"On second thought, tell Bill I'm on my way up to his office."

"Okay." Jo Ann was about to explode. The state patrol meant one thing. Ad was in a car accident. But she knew better than to pry.

"Bill, I just got a call from Jack Scanlan over at Traffic," phoned Jo Ann. "Says someone from the Colorado State Patrol just called him. Jack's on his way to your office."

"What's it about?"

"I asked, but he wouldn't say. I think it's about Ad."

Bill groaned. "Here he is now," Bill said, hanging up the phone as Scanlan entered.

"Sorry to barge in, but—"

"That's okay, Jack. What's wrong? Ad in a wreck?"

"The patrol wouldn't say. Just said they'd found a company car and said for me to get someone from management to call back. That's all they'd tell me. I looked it up, and it belongs to your brother Ad, so I thought I should tell you personally. Here's the phone number," said Scanlan, handing Bill a piece of paper.

Bill dialed the number. "Hello, this is Bill Coors. I received a message—"

"Yes, sir. The lieutenant is expecting your call. Let me transfer you."

"Hello. Mr. Coors?"

"Yes, this is Bill Coors. What's this all about?"

The officer introduced himself and then began. "Our dispatcher received a call from one of our patrolmen, who located a car registered to the Adolph Coors Company." The officer spoke clearly and without emotion. "It's a 1959 International Harvester Travelall, four door, light blue and white, bearing Colorado license plate number RT-2423."

"Is it wrecked? Broken down?" Bill asked.

"No, sir. It appears abandoned, though it's in perfect running order. It was spotted by a motorist, parked on a bridge with the engine running. No driver. Our patrolman radioed it in at 11:35 a.m. as still there. You know who the driver is? Was the car stolen, and if it's not, what's the trouble?"

"It's my brother Ad's car."

"Ad?"

"Adolph Coors III."

"Have you been in contact with him today? Do you know his whereabouts? We'd like him to pick up his car."

"No. He was supposed to be here at the company. He usually gets here around 8:15, but we haven't heard from him."

"I see." The officer paused, hesitating to say more. An abandoned vehicle may have just turned into a missing-person report of a Coors.

"Hello?" said Bill.

"Is your brother married?"

"Yes, he is, but Ad's secretary just spoke with her. She doesn't know where he is either. You say the car's not wrecked? No flat? Plenty of gas?"

"No, it's fine."

"Can I speak to the patrolman at the scene?" asked Bill.

"Yes, we can patch him through to your number via dispatch, but—"

"I'll tell you what. Why don't I come there and talk to the patrolman and see the car in person? Maybe we can straighten this out. What's his name, and where can I meet him?"

"Sure, that might help wrap this up," said the patrol officer. "The patrolman's name is . . ."

Bill listened.

"Patrolman George Hedricks. Okay, hold on a minute."

Bill turned to Joe and asked, "Know where Turkey Creek Bridge is?"

"Over at Turkey Creek Canyon near Ad's house is all I know," Joe said with Ray Frost looking on.

"How about we meet him on the north end of Morrison at the Sinclair station just as you come into town?" Bill told the patrolman. "We can follow him to the bridge from there."

"All right," said the officer. "I'll radio Patrolman Hedricks to meet you. How long will it take?"

"We'll be there as soon as we can, maybe twenty, twenty-five minutes."

Bill hung up the telephone and remained silent. Ray Frost and Joe stared at Bill.

"Well?" asked Joe.

"We've got to meet a Colorado state patrolman in Morrison—now. Drop everything. We've got to go," said Bill.

"What's wrong? Ad hurt?"

"His car was found on Turkey Creek Bridge, but the highway patrol can't find Ad."

Joe lifted his brows. "What do you mean, can't find Ad? Is it parked or on the road or—"

"I'll fill you in on the way. We need to get going."

The brothers were silent for a moment, suspended in disbelief, until Frost broke in. "If it's all right, I'd like to come along."

Bill nodded and then buzzed his secretary. "Phyllis, Joe and I've got to go out for a while. Hold all calls and meetings. We'll be back in, uh, as soon as we can. Maybe three o'clock. Tell Joe's and Ad's secretaries. Ray Frost is coming along, too. Thanks."

Jo Ann got the relay call and stepped into the hallway in time to see the company president, vice president, and office manager marching down the hallway toward the side parking lot. She could see them talking and Joe shaking his head before the three silhouettes passed from view.

Snow in Colorado can be beautiful. A white, powdery blanket stretched over otherwise dirty streets and unkempt yards can be a wonder. Evergreen branches laden with natural flock can be picturesque. Too much snow, however, can be treacherous. Blizzards reduce visibility, and plummeting temperatures freeze everything like stone. Those who camp to see the winter beauty amid peaceful solitude sometimes learn a hard lesson—heavy snow, gusting winds, and near-zero temperatures lead to collapsed tents, frozen drinking water, wet clothing, extinguished fires, and obscured or impassable hiking trails. The result is often frostbite, hypothermia, dehydration, snow blindness, or death.

Winds were gusting on the morning of February 9, and the air was chilly despite a warming temperature. Only patches of snow remained on the grass and in the shade, but weather forecasters were predicting heavy snows moving into the area by Thursday.

Corbett's plans changed that Tuesday morning. Rather than camp in an isolated spot outside Denver, he ran errands around the city. Close to midday, he walked to the Safeway at Colfax Avenue and Pearl Street and grabbed some sandwich meat to make lunch at his apartment. Seated on his davenport, he switched on the television and then the radio to listen to the noonday newscasts. He discovered the news was slow so far. And the weather forecast? It hadn't changed. Lots of snow on the way.

He turned down the radio as he heard footsteps approaching. Several people were walking down the hallway. The footsteps grew closer and heavier. Corbett began to stand, but stopped in a crouched position and listened. The steps came within inches of his studio door, but as quickly they passed. *Get ahold of yourself*, he told himself. *It's not the law. They couldn't know by now.*

Corbett sat back on his couch and, after a sigh of relief, recalled his brush with the law two weeks earlier when he also had to remind himself to remain calm. It was a minor incident, really, but for a fugitive carrying weapons, nothing involving the law is minor. He'd been driving around aimlessly on January 25, again on one of his forays about four miles north of Morrison on Highway 285, when a red revolving light flashed in his rearview mirror. He hadn't had an encounter with the police since he'd scaled the fence at Chino. No, that's not true. Incredibly, he'd been stopped once before and given only a warning for driving with an expired California driver's license. He thought he was lucky to avoid detection that time. Perhaps his luck had run out. He knew his old car couldn't outrun the state patrol's Ford Interceptor, so he pulled over. Corbett was indignant. He should have been courteous to avoid suspicion, but he couldn't help it. He hated law enforcement. The Colorado state patrolman, John B. Kelly, walked to the rear of the yellow Mercury and withdrew a pad, wrote down the license plate number, AT-6203, and after receiving Corbett's license and registration, scribbled the driver's license number D13217 along with the driver's name—Walter Osborne. The officer radioed in the information. It all checked out. He wrote out an eight-dollar ticket for improper passing and handed it to Corbett. The officer could not have known.

"He was always so quiet," Corbett's landlady Viola Merys later told an FBI agent. "Always took his lunch to work, cooked most his meals in, and was hardly ever gone from his apartment for very long. Since I been here, he never took a vacation or went on trips and he never had any visitors. I thought it peculiar that he never received any Christmas packages."

Corbett left his apartment again that Tuesday after finishing off his sandwich. He locked his apartment and walked out the back door. It was around 1:30 p.m. He was away only a short period, as his landlady would describe later.

"Do you have an account with us?" asked Athalee Brehm, a clerk at Gigantic Cleaners & Laundry on East Seventeenth Avenue, sifting through the laundry bag.

"No, ma'am. I'm a new customer," Corbett said, standing at the counter in heavily starched khaki work pants and checkered sport shirt underneath a brown zippered jacket.

"I need to fill out a card on you, then. I need your name and address here." The woman cocked her head to see what her customer was writing. "Okay. 'Osborne, W., 1435 Pearl, 2-9-60.' Should be ready by Friday. Will that be okay?"

"Sure."

Corbett stepped out and saw a ruffled sky with more low clouds rolling in, but no snow yet. He got in his car and searched for news on the radio dial as he pulled on the street. His next stop would be a post office in Denver. He typically dropped his mail inside his box in the apartment entrance, but this was the letter he'd typed so carefully, the one that hopefully promised him a better life. Soon, Corbett stood in front of the intake chute outside the post office. He looked left and then right, seeing cars and pedestrians moving busily about their day. He dropped the letter into the chute and then returned to his Mercury and wiped a smudge from the dashboard. He pulled onto the street. It was nearing three o'clock.

"I suppose you could call him odd, though we all are a little, I guess," Merys explained to an FBI agent. "He locked his apartment door every time he went out, even if he was gone for a minute, like when he'd take out the garbage. And he always used the building's back door, never the front. But the oddest thing was he always put his rent money in an envelope and slipped it under my door. When I first started managing the apartment, he signed the envelope *Walter Osborn*. So I made out his receipt that way, *Walter Osborn*. But after two or three months, he started signing the envelopes with an *e* on the end—*Walter Osborne*. I thought it mighty peculiar, but I don't pry into my tenants' business."

The brothers hardly spoke during the twenty-minute drive south on Highway 285 to Morrison in Bill's company car. When they arrived, Patrolman Hedricks identified himself, and then Ad's brothers followed along behind the patrol car to Turkey Creek Bridge. Frost followed in his automobile. As they drove along the bumpy gravel road, the Travelall appeared, parked off the road near the bridge, its front wheels pointing hard to the left. It was 12:40.

Bill and Joe got out. "A milkman backed it over there out of his way," Hedricks said. The four men walked over to the Travelall. They opened the doors and examined the interior. They didn't notice anything unusual. The men split up and searched for footprints and clues.

The brothers saw nothing out of the ordinary. But Hedricks approached holding a cap and a hat he'd spotted earlier. "I found these washed up on the creek bank by the bridge. They're not soaked through. Still mostly dry. Recognize them?"

Bill took the tan cap in his hands. Joe took the brown fedora.

"This one's Ad's, my brother's," said Bill.

"You sure about that?" Hedricks asked.

"Yeah. That's Ad's cap, all right," said Joe. "Calls it his 'luck hat.'"

"What about the fedora?" asked Hedricks.

"Never seen it before. You, Joe?" Bill asked.

"No. I don't think it's Ad's," said Joe. "Says on the inside here, 'Cruiser' from the May Company, size 7⅜."

Bill examined the inside band, and then looked inside Ad's cap. The worn label displayed size 7⅛. "Different sizes," said Bill. Hedricks had already noticed.

Hedricks returned to his patrol car to place the hats on the front seat.

"I'm going to walk along the creek and see if I can find anything," Joe said. "Ray, why don't you come along with me? You go upstream. I'll search down."

Each hiked slowly, struggling a hundred yards along the stream, and saw nothing. Bill and Hedricks combed the roadway on the bridge's ends. Bill saw what appeared to be tire marks, scratching out gravel, headed east on State Road 70. The four men gathered around the tire tracks.

"Looks like someone left in a hurry," said Bill.

"Maybe some souped-up job," said Joe softly.

"Based on the tire size, it's probably stock," said Hedricks.

Uneasy silence fell over the men. They could hear the shallow creek rippling over the rocky creek bed and the wind whistling as a crow cawed in the distance, all producing an eerie cacophony.

Bill finally offered, "It looks to me like there's only one explanation."

"What's that?" asked Joe.

"Ad's been kidnapped."

"Kidnapped!" barked Ray.

"Looks that way to me, too," said Hedricks. "Hijacked."

"There's another possibility," said Ray. "Ad could've taken somebody to the hospital and went in their car to save time, or maybe Ad was the one hurt."

"And not call the brewery or pick up his car? It's been more than four hours," said Bill. "By the same token, if Ad had been taken to the hospital, they would've called by now. They'd have his billfold with his driver's license, and there's his car with the registration on the steering column. No, I'm afraid kidnapping's the only scenario that makes sense."

Joe dropped his head. There was silence again as the men considered Bill's conjecture. They knew he was right.

"Ray, why don't you fetch Mary? I think she needs to know what's going on. Maybe she can help the patrolman," said Bill, who knew a worried Mary had telephoned the office that morning to find out if Ad had arrived. "We'll look around some more."

"Sure, Bill," answered Ray, who immediately walked to his car, wishing Bill hadn't selected him to be the messenger.

Joe heard Ray's car tires crunching the gravel as it pulled away. He turned with his hands in his coat's pockets and shook his head. "Bill, I think one of us should tell Mary, not Ray."

"All right. Take my car, then," said Bill.

Joe hurried to the car and sped away, hoping to arrive in time to tell Ray to let him do the talking. What Joe didn't know until later was that Ray, unfamiliar with the area, had taken a wrong turn, and would eventually give up and return to the bridge instead.

Mary heard a car and raced to the front door. She saw Joe step out of Bill's car. Joe showing up couldn't be anything but bad, she thought, like when a policeman or clergy arrives with tragic news. Mary fought a sudden weakness coursing through her body. She nearly sank to her knees, but she grabbed a table's edge before stepping outside and meeting her hesitant brother-in-law.

"Where's Ad? Have you found him?" The only thing that prevented Mary from bursting into tears was hope that Joe was going to say Ad was okay.

"We don't know yet, Mary," said Joe in a solemn voice, leading her back inside the house.

"What? You mean you still don't know? Then why are you here?"

"The state patrol discovered Ad's car not far from here, abandoned. Bill is there now with the patrolman. They're searching for clues to where Ad might be. We thought you should come and talk to the patrolman. You might be able to tell him something that can help."

"Has he had a wreck? Is he hurt? Maybe he's at the hospital or out wandering dazed somewhere."

"No, it doesn't look like a wreck. I don't know. Come on and you can ask the state patrolman. I think it'd be better to hear from him and see the situation firsthand." Joe was trying to ease the news and put as much off on the patrol officer as he could.

"Situation?" Mary paused and glared at Joe, who remained stone-faced. "Okay. Let me grab a coat."

Joe waited as Mary hurried down the hallway into her bedroom. She wasn't hysterical or crying, but he could tell Mary was desperately holding back and it could burst out any moment. The possibility made him uncomfortable. Mary reemerged and the two stepped outside and started across the carport. Mary dropped her keys. She knelt and picked them up and motioned for Joe to wait a moment while she hurried back inside. She opened the door and rushed out again, fiddling with her coat and gloves. Joe held the front-passenger door for Mary as she scooted into the car, clutching a framed photograph of Ad she'd brought along to give to the patrolman.

"We'll be there in less than five minutes," Joe said as he pulled down the long driveway.

"That close?"

"His car's at Turkey Creek Bridge."

Joe could see Mary about to break down. Perhaps because the disappearance occurred so close to home. "It'll be all right. Try to be calm. We really don't know anything yet. It may be nothing. Maybe something stupid. I don't know."

"Was he kidnapped?"

Joe was surprised by Mary's question. "Could be. I don't know. It could have been some kind of fender bender and there was a fight or someone got hurt and was taken to the hospital. I don't know. The state patrol is checking with doctors and hospitals now. We'll know something soon."

"A fight?"

"I don't know. I'm just thinking out loud. Like I said, we'll know something soon. Try not to worry." Joe knew the strongest possibility was kidnapping. He simply didn't want to be the one to tell Mary.

Mary sank into the front seat and raked a trembling hand across her forehead to move her bangs blown down on her eyes. She looked at Ad's photo on her lap. *I bought him that shirt and tie*, she remembered. *We were in Phoenix.*

Before the two reached the bridge, Joe slowed the car and turned toward Mary. "There's something else. The patrolman found Ad's cap in the creek with another man's hat. That's why I said there might have been a fight. He'll want you to identify the cap. But there's no question to me and Bill it's Ad's."

Mary let out a sigh and said nothing.

Joe and Mary arrived at Turkey Creek Bridge about 1:15. Mary stepped out of the car and was met by a burst of cold wind. She saw Ad's Travelall parked on the other side of the creek. Funny, she'd seen it many times, pulling into the drive and out, parked in the driveway, always connecting it with a good feeling of Ad. But today, it seemed unfamiliar to her, as if it belonged to a stranger. She didn't want to go near it.

"Wait in the car. I'll get the patrolman," Joe said.

Detectives from the Jefferson County Sheriff's Office had arrived and joined Bill, Hedricks, and Frost. Lieutenant Ray Kechter had already ordered the ends of the bridge roped off as Joe approached. Bill introduced Joe to the county lab technician, Dale Ryder, who was snapping photographs of the bridge, car, roadway, and creek. Two deputy sheriffs, Bob Stockton and Ed Pinson, were combing the bridge and creek sides for additional clues, along with Ed Queen, Al Pedrett, Stanley Smith, and Bill Brandes of the Jefferson County Sheriff's Office. Soon, state patrolmen would be setting up barricades on the roadway.

"I asked Mary to wait in the car," Joe said to Bill as Hedricks approached with the cap and hat in his hands.

"Let's go with him," said Bill.

The three walked toward Mary, who stepped out of Bill's car.

After making introductions, Hedricks said, "I'm sorry, but I have to ask if you recognize these."

Mary reached for Ad's cap. She softly rubbed her fingers along its brim. "Yes. This is my husband's. Ad Coors." She kept examining it, ignoring the patrolman's outstretched hand to retrieve the cap. "Oh, you need it back?"

"Yes, ma'am," said the officer, taking the cap back gently. "And this one?" Hedricks asked, holding it out toward Mary.

Mary shook her head repeatedly, refusing to touch the hat. "No. I don't know who it belongs to. Ad hasn't worn a fedora in years."

The patrolman glanced up at Bill and Joe. His sorrowful eyes broadcast to them he was only doing his duty.

"What time did your husband leave home this morning?"

"Around eight o'clock."

"Was he going to work?"

"Yes."

"Have you heard anything from anyone this morning or seen anything out of the ordinary? Any threats?"

Mary hesitated. "No."

"Thank you, Mrs. Coors. That's all for now. You may be questioned again later by county detectives."

"Where is my husband?"

"I'm sorry, ma'am. We don't know anything yet. We're making calls, and we've alerted all state and local agencies to be on the lookout for him. I see you brought a photograph. Good. That will help. As soon as we learn anything, the state patrol or sheriff's office will contact you."

"Don't worry, Mary, they'll find Ad," said Ray Frost, who'd just returned.

"Over here!" shouted one of the investigators. His yell startled Mary.

Everyone hurried toward the county investigator standing on the bridge. Joe stopped Mary.

"Why don't you wait in the car where it's warm?" said Joe. "I'll be back directly and take you home."

Mary wrapped her arms about her chest and returned to the car with her head down, not noticing the mud and ice she trudged across. She wanted to join the others, but then again, she didn't. She sat in the car and shut the door, not wanting to watch them do whatever they were doing. Instead, she fiddled with her gloves, removing one and then another, and carefully unsnapped her purse and placed them inside. She couldn't do it. She couldn't ignore what was happening only a few yards away. She raised her head and gazed through the windshield.

"Look," said a kneeling Lieutenant Kechter. "Blood. Here, here, and here. And over there," he said, pointing.

"Don't get too close. We have to take samples and photographs," said Ryder.

Bill and Joe knelt beside what appeared to be blood on the dirt edge of the bridge. It was more of a viscous stain, the blood having soaked deeply into the loose dirt. Ruts on the bridge laid bare wooden planks, and gravel and dirt rose like edges of a furrow, having been pushed by traffic to the sides of the bridge, providing a barrier between the middle of the road and the blood.

"I walked by here twice and didn't notice," said Bill.

"Me, too," added Joe.

"It kinda blends in with the dirt over here and then with the shade from the railing and the dark sky today. That's understandable. We know what to look for," said Ryder.

To the Coors brothers, the spot of blood appeared a few inches in diameter, and more like droplets than a solid mass of blood— "Definitely made of drops, individual drops," Bill would tell an officer. They also were directed to a fleck of blood on the railing above the bloodstained soil.

Mary, sitting in Bill's car, saw Joe stand up, looking agitated.

"Bill, I think I'll take Mary home," Joe said, after seeing Mary gazing in his direction from inside the car.

"Good idea. Why don't you stay with her? I'm gonna stay here."

"Okay, but call Ad's house or send Ray to get me if you find something important." Joe hesitated, not wanting to leave, even though it was his idea. He walked to the car, trying to keep his head up so not to alarm Mary. He opened the car door and sat behind the wheel.

"What was it, Joe? What'd they find?"

Joe started the engine and began backing out. "Some blood drops on the ground."

"Blood? Oh, Joe." Mary couldn't contain it any longer. She lowered her face into her hands and started crying. The sounds of her weeping filled the car, making Joe uneasy and awkward.

He stopped the car. "It wasn't that much, really. It looked like a man had been on his hands and knees, maybe bleeding from a hit on his head."

Mary continued crying.

Joe handed Mary a handkerchief. "I'll take you home and call the doctor to come give you something for nerves. I'll stay there with you.

And I'll call Holly. She'll come over, too." Joe's wife, Edith Holland "Holly" Coors, could soothe Mary much better than he.

"I know it sounds bad," Joe continued. "Look, it may not've even been Ad's blood. He may've whapped somebody in a fight. And even if it was Ad's, it doesn't mean he's hurt bad."

Joe was trying his best to calm Mary and did believe what he said. Only, he wasn't a forensic expert. He could be wrong—dead wrong.

CHAPTER 6

The Jefferson County sheriff directed his deputies in the search for Ad Coors from his office at Golden. The wooden placard on his government-issue metal desk made it clear who was in charge: ART WERMUTH SHERIFF. Calls were made to his deputies' homes. Days off were canceled, ranches were left unattended, moonlighters dropped what they were doing. Adolph Herman Joseph Coors III was missing.

All seventy-three Jefferson County sheriff deputies were called in, except for a handful that still had to patrol the county. Colorado state patrolmen and volunteers also joined in the search. The sheriff had an unenviable task. He not only had meager clues, but worse, he had to handle the powerful Coors family, all in front of newsmen and their cameras.

The onetime gas station owner, then part-time evergreen farmer, then part-time insurance salesman and bailiff, was appointed sheriff of Jefferson County by the Board of County Commissioners in January 1957 (elected in his own right a year later) when seventeen-year sheriff Carl Enlow, accused of taking payoffs for ignoring illegal gambling in the county, was sentenced to three years in a federal prison for tax evasion. The board believed they had in Wermuth, a man famous for his courage and toughness, the person best suited to clean up Jefferson County and restore dignity to the office of sheriff.

Eighteen years earlier, the exploits of the stocky, imposing Sheriff

Wermuth were written about in *Life* and *Time* magazines, comic books, and even in packages of War Gum, not as a sheriff but as the "One-Man Army of Bataan." One article stated that the "flamboyant" Wermuth "brags a heap but always makes good." The son of a World War I colonel and a graduate of Northwestern Military and Naval Academy, the athletic young Wermuth entered World War II in the Philippines, where by 1942 he was credited with more than 116 kills single-handedly. Photos of Wermuth in the Philippines and of his mother and sister back home were splashed in newspapers all across the country.

After Bataan was captured by the Japanese, Wermuth spent the next three and a half years as a prisoner of war, moved from prison camp to prison camp, and was attacked by his own country when an aircraft from the USS *Hornet* fired on and sank an unmarked Japanese prison ship that he was aboard. After his liberation by Soviet troops in August 1945, he weighed only 105 pounds. Wermuth, who'd been listed as killed in action, received the Distinguished Service Cross, the Silver Star, the Bronze Star, five Purple Heart decorations, and a promotion to the rank of major.

But on February 9, 1960, Wermuth was engaged in a different type of battle in his quiet Colorado community. Around one o'clock that afternoon, he'd sent his best investigators to identify and process evidence at Turkey Creek Bridge—Captain Harold Bray, Lieutenant Ray Kechter, Corporal Bob Stockton, and lab technician Dale Ryder. Later that afternoon, Captain Bray and state patrol chief Gilbert Carrel set up search headquarters at the bridge site. Recently arrived heads of the Jeep Patrol, Mounted Posse, and Alpine Rescue Team also helped make assignments from the site.

"Tell your men to fan out from the bridge," Wermuth instructed his chief investigator, Captain Bray, on a two-way radio. "Go downstream and up north past Soda Lakes toward Morrison and south toward the Coors house. Let's go for a mile and a half radius. . . . I know that's a lot of territory . . . The jeeps can cover wherever they can go. The posse takes everything else. Tell 'em to look in every hole and behind every rock no matter how tough. It's gonna be dark by 5:30. . . . Hold on, Harold."

"What is it, Lew?" Wermuth said on another bandwidth to Undersheriff Lew Hawley. "Right, right. Okay, tell 'em to remove the whole damn plank from post to post. . . . That's right. We can cut out the piece with the blood here later. . . . Good."

"Harold? You there?" asked Wermuth. "Get some men to scope the area around the bridge on foot. I want 'em close to the ground. Tell 'em to eyeball everything, footprints, wrappers, bottles, anything that appears fresh. . . . I don't care. Do it again. . . . I'd say a five hundred–foot radius from the creek bed to start with."

Deputies in coats and new military-like uniforms (dark green shirts, brown bolo ties and belts, gray trousers, white peaked caps, and brown boots) got busy scouring the area on foot. Several handled a group of bloodhounds, though none located a scent except on the bridge. Ninety-six other men in denim jeans, coats, boots, and cowboy hats, part of the Evergreen Troop of the Mounted Posse, rode out on horseback from the area, similar to the posses of the Old West, slowly combing for clues over rugged terrain, in the cold temperatures and strong winds, leaning from their saddles, looking for anything that might help find Ad Coors. Some wore holsters, others bandoliers, and most carried rifles or shotguns. Another thirty-two were searching as part of the Jefferson County Jeep Patrol. Another nine in the Alpine Rescue Team climbed nearby rocks and mountains. All were experienced and tested, and knew the terrain well.

Altogether, more than 150 men surveyed the snow-patched fields, woods, gullies, and riverbanks, climbed over boulders, cut through thick vines and brush, and crossed over ditches and ravines. They entered old mines and caves, carrying flashlights and torches, careful not to become lost or injured themselves. Others shone lights or were lowered into old wells. And still others entered vacant cabins and vacation homes and stopped at grocery stores to find out if anyone had purchased camping supplies. A sense of urgency pervaded the seasoned men as they searched. The sheriff's office had not been contacted by the Colorado State Patrol until 12:45, when almost five hours had already passed.

"Hey, Harold!" Dale Ryder called from the bridge. "Come look at these scratches. See this here." He pointed. "There's another mark on top and over on the upstream side." Ryder raised his large camera and snapped a photo. He walked to his left and snapped another from a different angle.

"Looks like there was a scuffle, all right," said Captain Harold Bray. The chief investigator was a tall, husky, capable man with thinning hair, who'd served during World War II and joined Naval Intelligence after the war. "That would explain the cap and hat in the creek. The two likely banged against the rail during a fight, and the cap and hat went flying into the creek. I know Ad, and he'd never back away; he'd fight for his life."

Bray stepped down the rocky creek bank and scanned the eight-foot-wide, one-foot-deep stream. He then ordered Verne Soucie, an investigator for the sheriff's office, to go back to the office and bring the diving gear. "You can use it to get on your hands and knees or lie down to see if there's anything under the water."

When the young Soucie returned around four o'clock, one of the deputies had discovered that the creek's flow could be diverted to an irrigation ditch farther upstream. Soucie assisted in shutting the floodgate, and after a few minutes, the flow of water beneath the bridge slowed to a trickle. Without the continuous rustle of shallow flowing water, the area grew quiet except for the sound of the gusting wind and distant voices of officers. Soucie and others scoured the banks and the creek, wearing rubber boots and carrying rakes or sticks. Pools of water dotted the creek bed lined with stones and boulders, fallen tree trunks, tree branches, clumps of mud and grass, old scraps of clothing, part of a garden hose, bottles, and rusted buckets and cans long tossed into the creek, now stuck to its bottom. The men forged along, slowly walking four-abreast, bending down and moving objects with their rakes and sticks, some kneeling and swatting the ice-cold water from pools to peer beneath the surface. The sun glaring down on the creek sludge soon began to produce a pungent odor. After a few hundred feet, they were back at the bridge. They'd found nothing on the upstream side.

Soucie walked about halfway on the bridge to rest a moment before he began searching downstream. He lit a cigarette, leaned against the railing, and glanced down. There, on a portion of a water-soaked scrap of cardboard, lay a pair of eyeglasses, just sitting on top as if someone had placed them there. They were about three feet from the bridge and only a few feet upstream from where Ad's cap and the unidentified fedora had washed against the creek bank.

"Dale! Come here and see this!" yelled Soucie.

Ryder joined Soucie, carrying his large camera strapped on one shoulder, and saw the eyeglasses below. He snapped a photograph from the bridge before the two men walked down and traversed the rugged creek bank. Beneath the bridge, Ryder stepped over the glasses and snapped another photo.

"Look," said Soucie, picking up the glasses and holding them toward the sky. "The left lens is cracked, right in the middle, straight up and down. Could've been a punch in the face that broke 'em. But the frames don't seem bent or nothing."

Ryder took the eyeglasses, placed them in a plastic bag, and showed them to Captain Bray. Bray saw Bill Coors standing near the Travelall, watching the men search for clues. Bray asked Ryder to come along as he approached Bill to speak with him.

"Excuse me, Bill," said Bray. Bray actually had been a friend of Ad's since childhood. "One of our officers located these on the creek bed directly below the bridge near where the hats were found. Are they Ad's?"

Bill took the bag and looked at them through the cellophane. "They do look like Ad's. Same color and shape. I can't be a hundred percent certain, though."

"His wife would recognize them, wouldn't she?" Ryder interjected.

"I wouldn't bother her now unless you absolutely have to."

Four days later, Bray contacted the optometrist. The store's name was on the inside of one of the temple pieces.

"Yes, I made those for Ad Coors," said Dr. O. E. Maring, a Denver optometrist. "I made an identical pair with the same prescription only with colored lenses. Those are Ad Coors's eyeglasses. No question about it."

"Why hasn't someone called? Shouldn't we have heard something by now?" Mary removed her hand from the drapes and turned away from the window toward Joe. "Maybe you should go back over there."

"They'll let us know when they find him," said Joe. "Bill will, for sure. Rest and take the other pill like the doctor said. He said to take two."

Mary sat in her chair and folded her hands in her lap. "I want to have my wits about me. I don't want to fall asleep."

"You should. All you're doing now is worrying."

Mary stood and walked to the window again, pulling back the same drapes. She stared in the direction of Turkey Creek Bridge that lay just beyond the ridge north of her house, though she couldn't see it. *How can this be happening? Everything was fine this morning. Why couldn't today be like every other day and Ad be at work?* She left the window and walked down the hallway toward her bedroom.

"That's good. Go lay down. I'll let you know if I hear anything."

Mary didn't wish to lie down. She viewed the photos on her bureau instead. A photo of the family from one of last summer's vacations. A wedding picture. She opened Ad's closet and lifted one of his jackets from the hanger bar. It smelled like Ad. Mary began to cry. She fell across the bed and touched Ad's side. She lay there, motionless, tears in her eyes. *Please let him be all right.*

Mary exaggeratedly inhaled and exhaled trying to calm herself. The attractive forty-four-year-old was no helpless wallflower. Her family had settled in Colorado when it was only a territory, and they had helped the drive for statehood. She was the granddaughter of Colorado's third governor, James B. Grant, who was born affluent and then made a fortune in mining. Her grandmother was often referred to as "a pioneer in [Denver's] cultural and social life." Mary's father, James Grant Jr., a prominent Denver attorney, had been educated at Yale and Harvard Law School, and her brother, James Grant III, who attended the same schools, was an attorney in New York City. Her uncle was a physician, and her cousins were prosperous and powerful members of not only their communities but of the state of Colorado. Her family had given to the community, and in return, community leaders named streets, parks, and schools after them.

Like them, Mary was intelligent and independent thinking and was naturally sociable, believing it to be her civic duty as a Grant and a Coors to join clubs, support charities, and volunteer when and where needed. She also enjoyed a good cocktail, an occasional smoke, and golf—something Ad's father, who believed women were born to obey their husbands and rear children, didn't appreciate. She'd graduated from the Kent School for Girls and the exclusive Vassar College in New York. She spent a winter in London after college and continued to travel abroad as a young woman. She'd learned fashion and etiquette, and knew how to be a lady, even if she had taken a back seat to her husband and lived on a ranch.

Yet she didn't mind so much, because she was married to Ad. She loved him, and he loved her. "I know I don't say this as often as I should, but you know I couldn't be happier. We've got each other, the kids are doing great. I'm a lucky man," Ad told Mary often over the course of their twenty-year marriage.

On that dark, cold Tuesday afternoon, Mary thought of Ad's words as she lay on the bed, holding back the tears, terribly afraid for herself and her children of the possibility of bad news. *Oh, Ad, my darling. Where are you?*

By late afternoon, newsmen began arriving at Turkey Creek Bridge. Word quickly spread of the possible kidnapping of Adolph Coors III, chairman of the Adolph Coors Company and firstborn grandson of its founder. Local newspaper reporters wearing suits and ties with pads in hand crowded about, mingling with radio announcers tethered by long microphone cords, as crews set up cameras and lights powered by loud generators while slick-haired television newscasters jockeyed for the best viewpoint around the bridge. Reporters were free to walk around, even to ask deputies questions and speak to Bill Coors. They captured images of the bridge, the investigators stirring about, and those on horseback trotting by. The images and headlines would be splashed across Colorado newspapers and picked up by newspapers and television channels all across the country and even internationally.

Others from the press tried to access Mary at home, but were prevented by deputies guarding the residence. Still others tried to gain access to a Coors at the brewery, but were stopped by plant security. In contrast, those assigned to the Jefferson County jail were welcomed into the sheriff's office and invited to set up lights for their cameras. Wermuth removed his eyeglasses, combed his hair, slipped on his jacket, and posed as newspapermen's cameras snapped and TV cameras hummed.

"I'm afraid he's been kidnapped," Wermuth said. "No, the family hasn't received any calls or ransom notes yet. . . . Because the evidence points in that direction. I can't say more. . . . Yes, we'll start the search again in the morning about six. . . . Some of the mounted posse and jeep patrol are still out there. . . . The Civil Air Patrol will send a helicopter and maybe a plane tomorrow to scan the area from the air."

A secretary informed him that someone from the FBI was on the telephone. Scott Werner, special agent in charge of the FBI's field office in Denver, introduced himself. Although Wermuth was pleased to receive assistance from the FBI, Werner couldn't assign any field agents to assist in the investigation for twenty-four hours, under the Lindbergh Act. If Ad Coors didn't show up by morning, the FBI could legally presume he was transported across state lines.

Still, Special Agent Werner wanted to send over a group of agents in an unofficial capacity to act as liaisons, so the FBI would be fully prepared if Ad Coors was still missing in the morning. Wermuth filled him in on what they had found so far, including the blood on the ground and on a bridge rail.

"The blood should be analyzed as soon as possible," said Werner, who also asked that samples of the blood and the railing be flown to the FBI Laboratory in Washington.

The sheriff and FBI agent coordinated further, anticipating the worst the following day.

Around 4:30, Captain Charles Morris, a large, heavyset man, arrived at Turkey Creek Bridge. He approached Captain Bray with a disturbing report. "Hey, Harold. Found more blood on Kipling Street south of the Bear Creek School. One of the kids said he saw it there about 8:30 this morning."

"Why would blood be on the bridge here and on a street way over in Morrison without a body at either place? Doesn't make sense." Nevertheless, Bray assigned Dale Ryder to go with Morris to Kiplinger Street in his 1959 Ford Edsel patrol car and secure some photos and samples of the blood there.

A cold northwesterly wind was gusting, and darkness was settling in. The headlights of Art Schoech's tow truck shone on investigators and deputies looking about, reporting their findings to Captain Bray, who relayed them to Sheriff Wermuth.

Bill Coors, having refused to leave, stood with a cup of hot coffee provided by the sheriff's office and watched his brother's Travelall hitched to the tow truck and the railing with scratches and blood spatter placed in the back. As it pulled slowly across the bridge, the tow truck's yellow fog lights and orange roof lights eerily revealed boulders, barren trees, and searchers in the darkness with each passing flash.

"Okay, wrap it up, boys!" Bill heard Captain Bray yell to the other investigators. "The sheriff's called us in till morning."

Bill walked to where Captain Bray was coordinating the search. A large generator and portable light were placed at the bridge, now lined with flaming smudge pots puffing black smoke into the cold night air. Men had built campfires on the ground and in barrels with twigs and scraps of wood to provide a little warmth on the cold evening.

"You calling off the search?" asked Bill.

"No, sir," said Bray, looking up at the six-foot-two Bill Coors. "The search is continuing. I'm calling only the investigators off till morning. Hard to spot clues with just flashlights. We've gathered about all the evidence we can anyway."

"I told my men to keep their long johns on. Nobody from the state patrol is goin' home tonight," said Chief Carrel.

"Plus," continued Bray, "we have about twenty jeeps that'll keep up the search tonight, and a bunch of the mounted posse is gung-ho to stay on. There's still a few on foot."

"That's fine, thank you. My family appreciates all you men are doing," said Bill.

A *Denver Post* reporter spotted the tall, lanky Bill talking with the two lawmen.

"Excuse me, Mr. Coors. Can I have a comment about your brother's disappearance for *The Post*, sir?"

"This is all so incredible, but it's obvious that someone waylaid him," Bill calmly told the reporter.

"Do you know who might have done this?"

"I don't think he had an enemy in the world. And he carried very little money. The family is baffled. All we want is Ad's return, and we will appreciate anything that anyone can do to bring this about. That's all."

CHAPTER 7

Mary had been dreading this moment. Joe's wife, Holly, and Coors security guards picked up the children from school, and they were on their way home. All they'd been told was their father was in some kind of trouble and their mother needed to speak with them. Mary walked into the living room and sat down.

The living room of the ranch home was her favorite room. It was paneled on three sides by European chestnut wood, and the fourth wall was entirely formed of windows facing west toward the Colorado Diamondback with the Front Range and Pike National Forest in the distance. The floor was made of wide French mahogany planks, and a fireplace flanked by chestnut bookcases provided a comfortable yet elegant touch. The house was nothing like the two-story brick Georgian-style home she'd left in Denver. The rustic exterior of the four-thousand-square-foot ranch home was painted brown with a red-shingle roofline broken by a lone brown brick chimney and French gutters. The interior was decorated Victorian-style, with antiques, candlesticks, high-backed chairs, mahogany tables, and lavish rugs.

But today, none of that mattered. The living room of her beautiful home was simply a place that made her feel secure.

Mary heard the youngsters coming into the house. Their entry was much quieter than usual. She met them as they entered. They placed their books and satchels on the counter, but didn't sit. Mary could see from their faces they were expecting bad news.

Mary did not want to tell them. Her heart was breaking, and she hadn't spoken a word yet. It would be much easier to take another pill or pour another drink and crawl into bed to let someone else tell them, but she knew they needed to hear it from her. She drew a deep breath.

"I have something to tell you. Now, it'll be okay—everything will be okay. It's something we have to go through for a few days, and then everything will be back to normal."

"What is it, Mama?" asked Brooke.

"Your father is missing."

"Missing? What do you mean, Mama? How can Daddy be lost?"

"Your father's car was discovered on a bridge near here. The sheriff and his men are trying to find him. . . . I have to tell you, though, they think he may have been kidnapped." Mary's voice began to crack.

"Kidnapped!"

For some, the seriousness sank in immediately. For others, it seemed too remote, like it was on television, not really happening.

The girls hugged their mother and tried not to cry, but couldn't help it. Sadness overcame the boys, who drew closer to their mother and older sisters.

"Okay, now stop this. Your father is a strong man. He'll be okay. If he's been kidnapped, the kidnappers will get their money and let your father go."

Holly waited in the den, out of sight. Her heart was breaking as she overheard Mary and the children. Joe stepped outside.

"Aunt Holly is going to take you to her house and then to your grandparents' for a few days when they get back from Hawaii. I've packed some clothes for you. Brookie, you and Ces may want to take along some other things. Spike and Jim, if there are some toys or games you want to take, set them out."

Holly was good to Mary's children. She was an attractive, sandy-haired, educated Philadelphia debutante who was fun and gregarious and a good mother who knew how to make her nieces and nephews feel loved and comforted.

"When are we going?" asked Brooke.

"You need to go in a few minutes. The kidnappers could be watching the house. There'll be policemen. It's better if you're not here."

"How long do we have to stay at Grandpa's?"

"Until your father comes home. Maybe tomorrow, maybe this weekend. I don't know for sure, but it won't be long, I hope. I'll call you every day and visit when I can."

"What about school?" asked Brooke.

"We've already talked to your schools. They understand. You can keep up with your homework at your grandparents'. They'll see that you get your assignments."

"Daddy's going to be okay, isn't he, Mama?"

Mary suddenly felt dizzy and tired. Maybe it was the sedatives, or the gin, or the worry. She became befuddled and upset.

"I hope so, honey, but we may never see your father again. We have to be prepared just in case."

"What do you mean, Mama? I thought you said everything is going to be okay."

"Oh, Brooke, you know what I mean. He might be, your father may be . . ."

Mary passed out, falling to the floor. Fainted in front of her children, just after telling them their father might not ever be coming back. She'd meant to be strong, to protect them from the pain and sadness.

"We had an ideal family and were living the American dream," Spike recalled as an adult. "We had the home in the mountains, wealth, social success, and parents who loved us and took time to let us know their love. My life was almost everything a boy could want. Then on February 9, 1960, our world was ripped apart."

The door opened with a jerk and slammed shut. Corbett twisted the night latch, locking the door behind him. He glanced at the windows and rushed to pull the cord along each side, closing the blinds. He poured himself a beer and hurried into the bathroom, where he crammed his clothes in a laundry bag and showered.

With the room completely dark, he stretched out on the couch to calm himself. When that didn't work, he sat up and switched on the television set. The glow of the picture tube lit up the room and reflected off his eyeglasses. It was too late for the evening news telecast, so he reached for his transistor radio and began thumbing the dial.

> . . . near his home in Morrison. FBI Special Agent-in-Charge Scott Werner says the FBI will enter the case in the morning. According to the Jefferson County Sheriff's Office, blood discovered at the scene is en route to the FBI Laboratory in Washington, D.C., to be analyzed. Adolph Coors III is the grandson of the founder of the Adolph Coors Company in Golden, Colorado. Established in 1873 . . .

Corbett turned off the television set and lifted one of the blind's metal slats. He watched for several minutes. A few cars drove by, and three or four people walked past on the cold night.

He plopped on the couch and sipped his beer as music played on the radio. He stretched his legs, and without intending to doze off, did. Nearly two hours passed. Corbett awakened, took a sip of warm beer, and ambled to the kitchen table, where he'd placed a blanket. He unfolded it to reveal a pistol inside. He pulled the clip and emptied the chamber. Slowly, he raised the barrel to his nose. The smell of spent powder filled his nostrils. The gun was dirty and gritty, powder residue formed a film around the tip of the barrel, and the stock was covered in mud and perhaps more.

He returned to the couch with a clean towel from the bathroom and a small can of machine oil. He switched on the television once again and began cleaning his pistol. He'd pour a little oil on a towel and gently rub the oily cloth along the barrel and around the chamber, intensely observing his handiwork.

Soon he got up for another look out the window. Peeking under the blinds, he saw only a car pass and then a truck. And then—

A draw on a cigarette glowed red inside a car across the shadowed street. Corbett watched for several minutes before he sprang from the couch, spilling a half-filled beer glass on the floor.

He grabbed a cloth from the bathroom to soak up the mess. His movements were jerky, in bursts, darting here and there.

A suitcase stuffed full of clothes already stretched across the floor. Empty drawers were pulled from a small chest lodged in the closet. Grocery sacks and empty liquor boxes scattered about the floor were filled with clothes, books, pens, and papers.

He opened the refrigerator and cupboard doors and dumped the foodstuffs into paper sacks—frozen TV dinners, a loaf of bread, crackers, frozen strawberries, fresh bananas. He carried the bloated sacks down the hallway and dropped them into a garbage chute.

After he'd emptied the refrigerator and freezer, he continued with the pantry. Everything had to go. But he was drawn to the window and peeked out once again.

Still there, just sitting. What is he doing?

Corbett grabbed cleanser from beneath the kitchen sink and began wiping door handles, cabinets, lamps, light switches, even the toilet seat and tank handle. Finished with one object, he'd search the room for another to wipe. He caught himself trotting from one object to the next, pausing long enough to brush his sweaty face with the back of his forearm. He was cleaning the metal lever on the window when the urge to peek out struck again. He switched off the light.

Where is he? He's gone! Good. . . . Wait a minute. There he is. Corbett sighed. *Why would he move his car three parking spots and just sit there? He's gotta be on a stakeout, watching me.*

Corbett stepped away from the window and exhaled. He picked

up his pistol beside the couch, cracked the blinds with the tip of the barrel, and peered out again into the darkness. His secret plan was unraveling, and so was he.

Captain Bray and Undersheriff Hawley drove to Ad and Mary's house with Bill to interview Mary and apprise her of the latest on the search and investigation. Sheriff Wermuth was on his way from Golden to meet them. The headlights of Bray's patrol car shone up the gravel driveway as the car came to a stop. The two investigators stepped out of the patrol car with Bill just as Wermuth pulled up the drive.

Joe met them outside. The eave lights lit up the sidewalk. "Anything?"

Bill shook his head and glanced past Joe toward the house. "How's she doing?"

"She's holding up pretty well. The doctor came by and gave her something. But she's worried sick."

"Is she able to talk to us?" asked Wermuth.

"I think so," Joe replied.

"You call Father?" asked Bill.

"Yeah. He's mad as a hornet. He and Mother are flying out tomorrow morning. It's three hours earlier there, so they should arrive in Denver tomorrow night. Said they'd try to call when they land in Los Angeles."

The men entered the house. Mary recognized Sheriff Wermuth in his mackinaw and Stetson, and Captain Bray, a longtime friend of Ad's, in his county uniform, something he rarely wore. She didn't know Lew Hawley, who was wearing a salt-and-pepper tweed coat over his suit with a dark green alpine hat that he had removed.

"There's still no word from Ad," Joe said before Mary could ask. "This is Sheriff Wermuth and Undersheriff Hawley. I think you know Harold Bray. They'd like to talk to you."

"Yes?" said Mary, deflated by the lack of news.

"Please sit down. We want to tell you what we've found and ask you a few questions," Wermuth said.

"I want to help any way I can," said Mary, who then stood. "Would you gentlemen like some coffee?"

The lawmen reluctantly accepted the kind offer.

Mary entered the kitchen. She gripped the edge of the counter and steadied herself. She felt woozy, like she could faint again. She inhaled and exhaled deeply a few times and then retrieved mugs from the cupboard and poured from the same percolator Ad had used that morning, though that morning seemed like a lifetime ago. Mary was determined to put on a good face for her guests. She handed them cups of coffee.

Bill sat on the couch beside Mary while Joe leaned against a wall as Sheriff Wermuth began. "Mrs. Coors, first, I want you to know we're doing everything we can to find your husband." He informed her about how the investigation had gone that day, and he summed up by saying, "It seems to me like your husband was forcibly removed from the area."

Mary gave no reaction. She didn't cry. She didn't scream. She and Joe had already discussed that possibility. "You mean he's been kidnapped?"

"Yes, ma'am. I'm afraid so," answered Sheriff Wermuth, a bit surprised by Mary's calmness, though he'd been told she was taking sedatives. "I know this sounds strange, but the way I figure it, a kidnapping can be a good thing in this situation. It's gonna fall well below freezing tonight. The kidnappers have your husband in some kind of shelter, with a stove and blankets. They probably have—"

"You say *they*. Do you know how many?" interrupted Mary.

"No, ma'am. I don't. It could be a single kidnapper, but usually there's more than one. Again, I can't even say for sure it's a kidnapping till you're contacted, but that's the theory we're working under. It makes the most sense."

"Excuse me," injected Captain Bray. "I think there's only one kidnapper, because knowing Ad like I do, he might've fought one man, but if there'd been more, especially with a gun, I think he would have been smart and gone along with them."

"Joe says it looked like the kidnappers may have hit Ad and dragged him to their car," said Mary. "Is that what it looked like to you?"

Bray and Hawley glanced at each other.

"Could be," Bray said. "We don't know anything for sure right now."

"You got to think the kidnappers planned this and didn't hurt your husband bad enough to miss out on the ransom," said the sheriff. "I'd expect the kidnappers to call tonight or tomorrow. We'll need to hook up a recorder to your telephone, and I'll post two deputies to spend the night and listen in case they call. Is that all right?"

"Of course. But they may call Ad's office, or his father, or Bill or Joe."

"We've thought of that," said Captain Bray. "We're gonna set up recorders on all telephones used by Ad's father and his brothers, whether at their homes or the brewery, just in case. But before we do that, I need to ask you a few questions to help us in our investigation. It won't take long, I promise."

"Ask me whatever you need to," Mary said.

Captain Bray scooted to the edge of his seat and leaned toward Mary. "Okay, first, what time did Ad leave home this morning?"

"It was after the kids went to school. A little before eight o'clock. The news was on when he left, so I'd say closer to five till. My husband is always punctual and leaves the house about the same time every morning."

"I see. How was Ad feeling this morning? I mean, did he seem nervous or troubled like something was on his mind? Did he say anything that made you think he might be in some kind of trouble?"

"No, he was fine. Same as always. He exercised, showered, and ate breakfast. He was cheerful, in a good humor."

Hawley took notes as Bray continued questioning Mary.

"What was your husband wearing when he left home?" asked Bray, who decided to use a more professional appellation and stop using the more personal "Ad," despite being his friend.

"He has on a white shirt with green check stripes and a buttoned-down collar."

"Was the shirt monogrammed?"

"No."

"Go on," said Bray.

"He's wearing a dark blue necktie he bought at the Aspen Country Store. He usually wears a silver ski-shaped tie clasp with his initials on it. I believe he was wearing it this morning. I'm not sure. It was a gift for ushering at John and Vivian Sweeney's wedding. Oh, my, what else?" Mary paused to think.

"It's okay. Take your time," added Bray.

"He wears brown high dress shoes, size 10½ AA. They're Wright Arch Preserver brand. He had on a pair of Hickey Freeman slacks I bought him, they're gray, with a plain brown belt. Oh, yes, he wears a Patek Philippe Genève silver wristwatch with a brown leather strap."

"How do you spell that?" Bray asked.

Mary obliged.

"What else?" asked Bray.

"He carries a silver key chain with a small penknife on it. I bought it for him last November as an anniversary present at the 14 Karat Shop in Cherry Creek Shopping Center. I had it engraved with his initials 'AC III.' He keeps his car key, house key, a key to the safe, and keys to the plant and the barn on it." Mary paused again. "It was an anniversary gift."

"Yes, ma'am. Anything else?"

"A navy-blue windbreaker with gray quilted lining. It's Abercrombie & Fitch. It has a wide waistband and zips up the front. He wears it almost every day to work. And a pair of white deerskin gloves from Gokey he usually wears in the winter. I think he took those this morning. And a brown belt. Oh, I think I said that already, didn't I?"

"Does your husband wear eyeglasses?" Sheriff Wermuth intervened, already knowing the answer. Bray glanced at Wermuth, and Bill gave him a look of concern.

"Yes, he does."

Wermuth reached inside his coat and withdrew a plastic bag. "Are these your husband's glasses? It says 'Paul Weiss, Optician' right here."

"That's where he goes, but Ad can barely see without his glasses."

The sheriff handed Mary the bag.

"They look like his. One of the lenses is . . . broken," said Mary, looking up. "Did you notice? The left lens is cracked!" Mary said, her eyes filling with tears.

"They were in the creek. They—"

"They probably cracked when they fell," Bray snapped, interrupting his boss.

Mary was stirred by the sight. A soft whine could be heard as she raised one hand to her face. Her shoulders shook.

The room grew silent.

"Excuse me," said Mary as she stood and rushed out of the room. "I'll be right back," she said as she hurried down the hall.

"I had to ask," the sheriff said to the others.

Bill stood. "I'll go check on her."

Bill found Mary in her bedroom's bathroom, crying, trying to stop the tears by placing tissues against her eyes.

"I'm sorry, Mary."

"Oh, Bill!" Mary bawled as Bill uncharacteristically, but gently, reached his arms around her. At the moment her emotions reached their lowest, Mary caught a glimpse of herself in the mirror. *Pull yourself together*, she thought. *Ad wouldn't want you falling apart like this. And the children . . .* Mary released Bill and straightened. She wiped her eyes and then looked at Bill. "Ad's going to be okay."

"Of course he is," said Bill.

"No, I mean it. Ad is going to make it through whatever this is. He has to . . . for the children's sake. And when he walks through that door, I don't want him to hear about how the mother of his children wilted on the vine while he was away. Now, go and tell them I'll be right out."

Though Mary and Bill weren't particularly close, Bill admired her strength and dignity at times. That evening was one of those times.

"Okay," Bill said and rejoined Joe and the sheriff and his two investigators in the den. "She said she'll be out in a minute." As soon as Bill spoke the words, a composed Mary strode down the hallway.

"I'm sorry, gentlemen. I'm fine now. Please continue."

"Are you sure?" asked Joe.

"Yes, please. I'd like to help if I can . . . please."

"Okay," said Captain Bray. "Does your husband carry a lot of money with him?"

"No. I'd expect he had less than twenty dollars in his wallet."

"And what kind of wallet?"

"Oh, I don't know. Just a brown leather one."

"Thank you. One more question, Mrs. Coors, and we'll let you rest. Was your husband acting strangely the past few days, or did you notice anything odd or see anything out of the ordinary?"

"No, like I said before, my husband was the same as always. We'd just gotten home late Saturday from a brewers' convention in Miami. Ad was here Sunday working about the place, taking care of the horses, riding. The children and I went hiking, but Ad didn't come along."

"Okay. Thank you, Mrs. Coors. I guess that—"

"There was this one thing."

"Yes?"

Mary nodded toward Joe. "I told Joe about it this afternoon. I don't think it was anything, but I've seen men in a yellow car driving up and down the road. They parked not far from the house. I saw them two or three times in January." Mary's recollection garnered the lawmen's attention.

"How many men? Can you describe them? How about the car?"

"No, they were too far away. Sometimes it was one man, other times two. Once, one of them had a rifle, because I saw it sticking out the window toward some deer on the ridge. Ad saw them once, too, and said they were probably deer poachers and he was going to have a talk with them next time he saw them. This is a game preserve, and there's no deer hunting even during deer season, but we still have a problem with poachers out here a lot."

"Did your husband speak with the men?"

"No. He was going to, but I don't believe he got the chance. Leastways, he didn't mention it to me."

"And the car?"

"It was yellow. Thelma Coffman—she's our maid—she saw it, too, and I believe she said it was a Lincoln—no, I mean a Mercury. But there's been other cars and trucks out here, too. I know one was a gray Ford. The other was dark green. I think. I don't know the kind. You can ask our ranch hand, Bill Hosler. He probably knows."

"Thank you, Mrs. Coors. We will. Thank you very much. That's all we need for now," Captain Bray said as he stood.

"Yes, Mrs. Coors. We know this is difficult for you, and we appreciate you talking to us tonight," said Sheriff Wermuth.

"I only want to find my husband. That's all I care about."

"That's all we care about, too, ma'am—that and catching whoever's done this," Wermuth said. "You get some rest, and we'll contact you as soon as we find out anything."

"What about the FBI?" asked Mary. "Joe said the FBI will be finding Ad, too. Are they? Working on it, I mean?"

"Yes, ma'am. We're in contact with the FBI office in Denver. They've already sent some men, and they'll be out in full force in the morning. Probably will come by to interview you tomorrow."

"Okay, good. Thank you, gentlemen," Mary said as she stood. "Any more coffee before you go?"

"No thanks."

Bray and Hawley began walking slowly toward the door accompanied by Joe. Mary and Bill followed with the sheriff.

"Well, good night."

"Good night."

The two investigators stepped outside while the sheriff talked a bit longer.

"Hey, pooch," said Hawley to Ad's bluetick hound, approaching with tail wagging.

"I'll say it again. That's the hardest part of the job," Bray said. He lit a cigarette and released a puff that was more of an extended sigh. The wind was cold, but it felt good to him.

"It's peculiar," Bray noted. "Ad's brothers thought he'd only been blackjacked. Just hit over the head. I don't get that. Wishful thinking, I guess. And they took the news of the kidnapping like cool customers."

"It's that rich blood, I guess," said Hawley. "Keeps 'em calm under pressure."

There was a pause as Bray smoked.

"So, why didn't you tell her?" Hawley asked. "Somebody's got to tell her."

"The FBI will take over the case tomorrow," said Bray. "Ever work with the FBI on a case?"

"No."

"I have. The sheriff won't like it. The FBI runs the show. Usurps all authority and treats the locals like flunkies. Always need to know what you know but never tell you what they know," said Bray, who nonetheless had a decent working relationship with Special Agent Werner.

The men got into the car and shut the doors. Bray turned to Hawley. "So let them tell her about all the blood."

That same evening, Jefferson County lab technician Dale Ryder suggested to Undersheriff Hawley that he and Captain Bray travel to the Denver Police Department Crime Laboratory to compare the blood discovered on Kipling Street in Morrison with that retrieved from Turkey Creek Bridge. There was some question whether the Kipling

Street sample was even blood. So far, county investigators had centered their search at Turkey Creek Bridge, but wondered if it should be expanded to Kipling Street. Around 6:30 that evening, Ryder and Bray met up with Lieutenant Joe Moomaw of the Denver Police Department.

Moomaw switched on the laboratory lights and stepped up to a counter. "Let me see what you got."

Ryder opened the lid of a pasteboard box. He reached inside and removed clear plastic bags and glass jars containing blood, soil, blood smears, and two small pieces of wood blotted with specks of blood.

Moomaw reached up and clicked on an overhead light. He slipped on rubber gloves and opened the two glass jars that contained samples from the bridge and Kipling Street. Using tweezers, Moomaw lifted a tiny piece from each container and placed the specimens on separate petri dishes, probably made at Coors Porcelain. Then he applied drops of alcohol with an eyedropper, followed by a few drops of phenolphthalein and a few drops of hydrogen peroxide. The samples immediately turned pink.

"They're both blood, all right," said Moomaw. "But I can't say if they're human or not, or from the same person, but they both contain hemoglobin. I'd have to use more of the samples to determine if they're human and their type, but it's my understanding these samples are headed to the FBI Lab."

"Yes, they are. Okay, well, that's something, I guess," Bray said. "We'll have to wait for the feds to tell us more tomorrow."

Captain Bray phoned Hawley and told him what the test revealed. Hawley instructed Bray to meet him at the entrance to St. Anthony's Hospital and bring Ryder, Moomaw, and the collected evidence. Hawley had already spoken with Special Agent Werner to coordinate his flight to Washington, D.C.

Around ten o'clock, the four men stood outside their cars in the St. Anthony's Hospital emergency parking lot and smoked. The temperature had dipped into the twenties, and a tempestuous wind made it feel even colder.

"I hope Coors is somewheres warm," said Moomaw.

The shivering men all nodded, and someone grunted, "Yeah, me, too."

Ryder handed Hawley the pasteboard box tightly bound with string, containing the blood specimens, the small pieces of railing, and the cap, hat, and eyeglasses discovered at the bridge.

Hawley placed the evidence in his car and headed to the airport to catch a 1:40 a.m. United Air Lines flight to Washington, where the samples would undergo analysis in the FBI Laboratory. He hoped they'd have some answers tomorrow.

Earlier that night, at nine o'clock, Corbett walked to the back door of the Perlmor Apartments and reached into his pants pocket. No key. He checked his other pocket and then those in his coat. Amid all his nervous activity, he'd left the key in his apartment. The wind was cold as he cautiously trotted around to the front of the building and rang the buzzer connected to his landlady's room, trying his best to remain in the shadows.

"Yes?"

"It's Walter Osborne," he whispered into the intercom. "I forgot my key."

The door lock clicked open, and Corbett hurried to his landlady's room near the front door.

"I'm sorry, Mrs. Merys. I know it's late," Corbett said, doing his best to appear calm.

"Oh, that's okay. Hold on one second while I grab the master key."

Soon the two stood outside the door to room 305, and she unlocked it.

"There you go," Mrs. Merys said.

"Thank you."

"No trouble at all. Good night," said the landlady, turning to leave.

"Mrs. Merys? I need to talk to you about something," said Corbett, looking up and down the hallway.

"Yes? Is it your heater? No hot water?"

"No, the room's fine. It's just that . . ."

The landlady and her tenant stood in the hall and talked for a few minutes. That was the longest Mrs. Merys had ever conversed with her reclusive tenant. As she went down the stairs to return to her room, she was surprised by what he'd told her.

A   Adolph Herman Joseph Coors III. *(The Denver Public Library, Western History Collection)*

B   Adolph Herman Joseph Coors III shortly before his death. *(The Denver Public Library, Western History Collection)*

C   Mary Urquhart Grant Coors. *(The Denver Public Library, Western History Collection)*

D   One of the "No Hunting" placards posted around Ad Coors's ranch. The irony is obvious. *(The Denver Public Library, Western History Collection)*

A Primitive Turkey Creek Bridge: The scene of the attempted kidnapping that ended in murder. *(Federal Bureau of Investigation)*

B Jefferson County Mounted Posse and Jeep Patrol gather at Turkey Creek Bridge to search for Ad Coors. *(The Denver Public Library, Western History Collection WH 2129 RMN)*

C Jefferson County Sheriff's Jeep Patrol examines a map of the area surrounding Turkey Creek Bridge. *(The Denver Public Library, Western History Collection WH 2129 RMN)*

D Three posse riders cross Turkey Creek Bridge on the night of the kidnapping. *(The Denver Public Library, Western History Collection WH 2129 RMN)*

Mrs. Coors:

Your husband has been kidnaped. His car is by Turkey Creek.

Call the police or F.B.I.: he dies.

Cooperate: he lives.

Ransom: $200,000 in tens and $300,000 in twenties.

There will be no negotiating.

Bills: used / non-consecutive / unrecorded / unmarked.

Warning: we will know if you call the police or record the serial numbers.

Directions: Place money & this letter & envelope in one suitcase or bag.

Have two men with a car ready to make the delivery.

When all set, advertise a tractor for sale in Denver Post section 69. Sign ad King Ranch, Fort Lupton.

Wait at NA 9-4455 for instructions after ad appears.

Deliver immediately after receiving call. Any delay will be regarded as a stall to set up a stake-out.

Understand this: Adolph's life is in your hands. We have no desire to commit murder. All we want is that money. If you follow the instructions, he will be released unharmed within 48 hours after the money is received.

A   Undersheriff Lew Hawley boards a plane on his way to the FBI Lab. *(The Denver Public Library, Western History Collection WH2129 RMN)*

B   Ransom note mailed by Joe Corbett to Mary Coors after Ad Coors's murder. *(Federal Bureau of Investigation)*

C   Jefferson County's Captain Morris points out a bloodstain on Ad Coors's Travelall's front seat. *(The Denver Public Library, Western History Collection WH2129 RMN)*

D   Joe Corbett's 1951 Mercury sedan burned in Atlantic City, New Jersey. *(Federal Bureau of Investigation)*

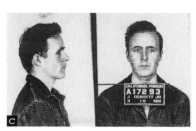

A FBI Wanted Poster issued six weeks after the kidnapping, on March 22, 1960. *(The Denver Public Library, Western History Collection WH1625)*

B California arrest record of Joseph Corbett Jr. shows that he escaped prison on August 1, 1955. *(California Dept. of Corrections & Rehabilitation)*

C A young Corbett following his arrest for the murder of USAF Sergeant Alan Lee Reed in 1951. *(California Dept. of Corrections & Rehabilitation)*

D Jefferson County Sheriff Arthur Wermuth (left) escorts Joseph Corbett Jr. from the Denver Jail following his extradition. *(The Denver Public Library, Western History Collection WH2129 RMN)*

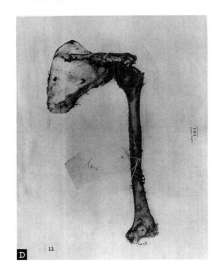

A Joseph Corbett Jr. awaiting a hearing in Golden, Colorado.
(Douglas County History Research Center, Douglas County Libraries)

B Joseph Corbett Jr. in the Jefferson County Jail following his extradition from
Canada. *(Douglas County History Research Center, Douglas County Libraries)*

C Jefferson and Douglas County authorities inspect the crime scene.
(The Denver Public Library, Western History Collection WH2129 RMN)

D Ad Coors's right shoulder blade: The two fatal shots are visible.
(Federal Bureau of Investigation)

A   Ad Coors's bloody jacket: Two bullet holes are visible on the right. *(Federal Bureau of Investigation)*

B   Ad Coors's bloody shirt: Two bullet holes are visible on the right shoulder. *(Federal Bureau of Investigation)*

C   Ad Coors's bloody undershirt: Two bullet holes are visible on the right shoulder. *(Federal Bureau of Investigation)*

D   Douglas County Coroner Doug Andrews and Sheriff John Hammond view Ad Coors's skull in a box. *(The Denver Public Library, Western History Collection WH2129 RMN)*

A   Ad Coors's skull and lower jawbone discovered at the dump site. *(Federal Bureau of Investigation)*

B   Joseph Corbett Jr. escorted to court by Sheriff Arthur Wermuth. *(The Denver Public Library, Western History Collection WH2129 RMN)*

C   Barney O'Kane, Ronald Hardesty, Joseph Corbett Jr., and Malcolm Mackay at a pretrial hearing. *(The Denver Public Library, Western History Collection WH2129 RMN)*

D   Joseph Corbett Jr. with one of his attorneys, William H. Erickson, during the Coors murder trial. *(The Denver Public Library, Western History Collection WH2129 RMN)*

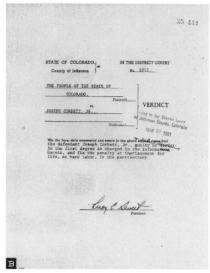

A Left to right: Defense attorney Malcolm Mackay; prosecutors
Ronald Hardesty and Richard Hite; and defendant Joseph Corbett Jr.
listen with the jury as the judge reads the verdict. *(The Denver Public Library,
Western History Collection WH2129 RMN)*

B Jury's verdict: Guilty of first degree murder.
(Federal Bureau of Investigation)

C A convicted Corbett in Colorado state prison at Cañon City.
(California Dept. of Corrections & Rehabilitation)

D An older Corbett upon his first parole from Colorado state prison at Cañon
City. *(California Dept of Corrections & Rehabilitation)*

CHAPTER 8

Golden is located on the Colorado Front Range, the first upwelling of the Rocky Mountains from the Great Plains. Founded in 1859 as part of the Colorado gold rush, the mining town became the first capital of the Colorado Territory and the seat of Jefferson County. After the gold panned out, German, Swedish, Italian, and Chinese immigrants stayed to make Golden their home. From 1860 to the 1950s, the population seesawed between 1,000 and 2,500 before swelling to more than 8,000 residents by 1960.

Residents of Golden enjoyed a traditional Western way of life. Men and women in boots and cowboys hats walked along sidewalks shared by those in suits and fashionable dresses. On Washington Avenue, the main thoroughfare, automobiles shared the road with horses and an electric trolley. Few communities can boast the picturesque scenery that surrounds the valley town—a river rushing through the middle called Clear Creek, Lookout Mountain to the southwest (where Buffalo Bill is buried), North Table Mountain on the north side, and to the south, South Table Mountain with its Castle Rock casting a crown above the Coors brewing and porcelain companies. And if its citizens wanted a change of pace from the serenity, Denver awaited only fifteen miles to the east.

On the morning of Wednesday, February 10, the citizens of Golden awoke to headlines on the front page of *Rocky Mountain News*: ADOLPH COORS III FEARED KIDNAPED! and *The Denver Post*: ADOLPH

COORS III DISAPPEARS; FBI ENTERS SEARCH. They were stunned. It seemed unfathomable to them. The outpouring of concern and kindhearted remarks by the townspeople filled the airwaves and print.

"I don't know of anybody who didn't like Ad Coors," said Walter G. Brown, Golden city manager.

Kriss Barnes, assistant vice president of Golden's First National Bank, told reporters, "I can't understand how anybody in the world would have anything against Ad Coors. He's reassuring, mild-mannered, and considerate."

"Ad is kind and generous," said Pete Puck, who worked at the Coors Porcelain plant and helped out on Ad's ranch. "This disappearance is a terrible thing, a terrible thing."

Ad's ranch manager, Bill Hosler, agreed. "He's just as nice as can be."

Many people in town knew Ad. They'd gone to school with him, hunted, skied, or transacted business with him. Many had a genuine affinity for the eldest Coors brother.

"He'd always smile and call me by my first name. Just a real nice guy," said Louis Kubat, who played softball with Ad in the Arvada League when Ad played first base for Golden years earlier.

Almost anyone asked would say he was a good man. Good, despite the fact he was rich. But Goldenites couldn't begrudge him that. He wore his wealth humbly. That was one of the things people liked most about the Coors family: their humility.

"Nicest guy you'd ever meet," said Arthur Jensen, the chief brewer in the Coors kettle room. "Always wore a smile and said hello and called you by your first name, and let you call him *Ad*, not *Mr. Coors* or whatever. He always seemed interested in what I was doing, and I liked that about him."

"Everyone in town knew my father," Spike recounted as an adult. "He was just like Grandpa and Great-Grandpa, a complete workaholic, a financial success, active in the town, and respected by everyone."

That's why townspeople were in disbelief. At gas stations, taverns, and beauty and barbershops all around town, everyone was talking about the disappearance. To many, an attack on a Coors was an attack on Golden and everyone in it. Coors was Golden, and Golden was Coors.

Who would do such a thing? That was the question of the day at establishments all around town. Anyone who dared denounce a Coors now did so at his peril. Even a person who had no beef with a Coors could become a suspect just because he was peculiar. For instance, Jack Peters, in charge of Coors plant security, heard from a guard that a man named Robert Everhart should be checked out. Peters telephoned Captain Bray and told him that although he couldn't put his finger on anything specific, there were "suspicious and odd circumstances surrounding Everhart, too numerable to mention." He was investigated and eliminated as a suspect.

Others were more specific in their charges. Anyone who'd ever harbored ill feelings toward a Coors was suspected. Anyone in a dispute over property rights years earlier, or someone Ad may have cut off in traffic, or an employee that had been fired by a Coors, any kind of run-in was enough to raise suspicion. The theories and suspects abounded that morning and throughout the day. One possibility in particular made everyone in town a bit nervous: could it be a union man?

"Both major Coors industries have been embroiled in labor strife during the past few years," reported *Rocky Mountain News* that day. "Colorado unions, in recent months, have placed an unofficial boycott on Coors products because of what they term unfair labor practices at Coors. . . . Bill Coors, however, did say Tuesday night that he discounted any beliefs his brother's disappearance stemmed from labor difficulties at the Coors firms."

"Ad was never a part of the difficulty at the brewery," Walter Brown said.

Union leaders especially hoped a member hadn't committed this crime. If he had, the news would drive a stake through Local 366 once and for all.

When asked about the possibility, Joe Coors scoffed. "All we want, all the whole family wants, is Ad's safe return." When pressed by a reporter, Joe said, "Ad's received no threats from anyone, particularly labor. We are completely baffled. Bill and I are very strong in the feeling, however, that this has nothing to do with the labor movement."

That same morning, a motorcade of four dark, unmarked sedans drove down Washington Avenue, passing beneath the famous banner that stretched across the street:

Howdy Folks!
WELCOME TO GOLDEN
WHERE THE WEST REMAINS

The FBI was officially on the case. Code name: *COORNAP*. Each sedan carried FBI field agents as unmarked as their cars—dark suits, ties, starched white shirts, fedoras, trench coats, trimmed hair, shaven faces, and sunglasses or eyeglasses. That was the directive from J. Edgar Hoover in Washington, D.C., the agency's director since 1924. Another fifty officers of the FBI Western Kidnap Squad were combing a thirty-mile radius. Hoover stamped the case top priority. He'd given Mr. Coors his private assurances. A quick resolution of the high-profile case would also give the agency a gold star just as the motion picture *The FBI Story* was playing in theaters around the country.

One of the bureau-issued sedans dropped two agents at Mr. Coors's house and Joe's home to man the telephone surveillance and recording devices that had been set up by Denver undersheriff A. S. Reider and Denver Police chief Walter Nelson, with the help of Golden Telephone Company employee Carl Horblett. Other agents stopped in Golden to question persons in town. The remaining agents stopped at the Adolph Coors Company to question anyone who might have useful information, particularly Bill and Joe Coors, who had returned to work that day.

Similar cars with agents headed to Bill Coors's house in Denver to operate the telephone recorder and to Ad's home near Morrison to question Mary and relieve the county deputies who were conducting surveillance inside and outside her home, watching for kidnappers who might be staking out the ranch to drop off a ransom note. One agent joined deputies standing on the road in front of Ad and Mary's house, stopping all passing cars and trucks and questioning their occupants. Other agents drove to the sheriff's office to question deputies and investigators, and to Turkey Creek Bridge to question anyone who lived nearby who might have seen or heard anything Tuesday morning.

Agents arriving at the bridge site were met by newsmen from Denver, Golden, and other Colorado towns, and by correspondents from national news services who'd flown into Denver the night before. Reporters in turn were met with a curt "No comment." All questions were referred to Special Agent in Charge Scott Werner at the FBI office in Denver. "The FBI will maintain complete silence until the release of the victim," said FBI special agent Edward Kemper. "Our interest is the safe return of Mr. Coors." The FBI also instructed members of the Coors family not to speak to reporters.

County investigators had completed their collection of evidence at the bridge the day before the FBI's arrival. The remaining task for the sheriff's office at Turkey Creek Canyon was to find Ad Coors. Volunteers arrived early that morning and set up tables near the bridge with pots of hot coffee, doughnuts, sandwiches, and water for those men in the mounted posse and jeep patrol who had spent the entire night searching and for those who'd arrived at sunup to join or relieve them.

An H-19 helicopter sent from Lowry Air Force Base outside Denver hovered above the lifting fog, trying to spot a man stranded or hurt, or anything that appeared out of the ordinary among the rocky hills and ravines. US Air Force C-45 and C-47 airplanes and Civil Air Patrol Piper Super Cubs were standing by to take off if needed.

Despite all the manpower, horses, jeeps, and aircraft, there was no sign of Ad Coors. "We haven't been able to find a thing," said Captain Morris of the sheriff's office. "We're as baffled now as we were yesterday."

The FBI took a different tactic. Agents, along with some county investigators, visited all houses in the Turkey Creek Canyon area and interviewed their residents. One was Mrs. Rosemary Stitt:

It was about eight o'clock, right after I sent my kids off to school, about twenty minutes after. The bus picks them up around twenty till every morning. First, it sounded like somebody hollered down at the bridge. I can hear people talkin' down there pretty plain most times. Hear their cars crossing over. I live only 'bout a quarter mile away. But yesterday the wind was blowing really hard so I couldn't hear so plain. I was sittin' in front of my sewing machine by the window. It sounded like one or two words is all. It was two different people, I think. Then I heard a cracklin' noise like lightnin' striking a tree. As a little girl, I heard lightnin' split a tree in half right next to the house. That's what it sounded like. I looked out the kitchen window to see if a tree fell down out back but didn't see nothin'. So it was then I got to thinkin' it might be a gunshot. Just one shot. Or, it coulda been two really close together.

I talked to Bill about it last night, that's my husband, and he asked if it sounded like a .22 that him and my son shoot at rabbits or like a .38 they shoot ever once in a while at targets they set up in the hills. I said it sounded more like the .38 'cause it sounded like lightnin'. The shot came about a minute or two after I heard the hollerin'. I thought it might be poachers shootin' game on the preserve. We've had some trouble with hunters up here. Or maybe some surveyors I seen workin'. I didn't hear nothin' else, so I went back to doin' housework. . . . Later on in the mornin', though, about ten thirty, eleven o'clock, I heard summore hollerin' and a horn honkin'. About fifteen, twenty minutes after that, the milkman showed up and told me about a car blockin' the bridge down yonder. He asked to use the telephone, but we ain't got one. So he left and said he'd telephone the police at his next stop.

Mrs. Pauline Moore, who lived with her husband, Cloyce, two and a half miles from Turkey Creek Bridge, told the FBI a similar story:

Right around eight o'clock yesterdee, I was hangin' the wash on a clothesline out back. The wind was blowin' real hard. I could barely get a clothespin on 'em. Then I heard a shot in the canyon real clear. I usually work on Tuesdays cleanin' folks' houses in Denver, but my boss called the night before and told me not to come in. The shot I heard was a far-off shot, not a close up, but a far-off shot, towards the bridge.

After hours of exhaustive interviews, the FBI learned that no one in the area had actually seen Ad Coors or his abductors on the bridge. No one could tell how many kidnappers there were. No one reported seeing a struggle or a shooting. No one saw the abductors' car leaving the scene. Several did, however, report seeing suspicious vehicles at or near the bridge during the days before the disappearance. There was only one problem. They saw too many.

Mrs. Stitt told the FBI, "My husband said he seen a 1954 blue-green Ford parked on the bridge the week before, once with the doors open and lights on, but nobody around. Coulda been a 1955 or '56, he said."

Ranch hand Bill Hosler and Mary Coors's maid told the FBI they'd seen an older-model green Dodge with red-and-white license plates parked near the ranch on Monday. Both said they saw at least two men in the car that appeared to be watching the ranch for at least an hour. One was tall and thin, and the other was short and stocky with a dark complexion. Hosler said the same car had been there the week before. They also stated they'd seen a yellow car there on more than one occasion.

Hilton Pace, who leased and worked a uranium mine near Turkey Creek Bridge, said he'd seen a man driving a white-over-gray Ford in the area a few times. He'd even spoken with him one day.

Janette Erickson, who lived less than a mile and a half from the bridge, said she'd seen a yellow car near the bridge on that Sunday. Viola Ranch said the same thing. Other witnesses said they saw a car resembling a 1951 Mercury in the vicinity. Three said it was yellow; one said cream. Two said it was a solid color; two said it had a black top. Viola Ranch said it had a green cloth top.

Former Morrison town constable James Cable, a caretaker at the uranium mine leased by Hilton Pace, said he and his wife, Margaret, saw a yellow 1951 or '52 Mercury near the bridge several times, including at eight o'clock Monday, the morning before the disappearance, about a hundred feet from the bridge. That was the morning Ad took a different route, driving to Denver before going to the brewery.

Miss Nadene Carder said she'd seen a yellow car parked near the bridge three consecutive days when she was on her way to work at the Colorado School of Mines the week before the disappearance. That was while Ad was in Miami.

Jim Massey said he often saw a yellow Mercury near the bridge. He told the FBI he'd seen it around 5:30 p.m. on Sunday, with a man standing beside it wearing a brown hat and eyeglasses. His wife said she'd seen the car around 1:00 p.m. on Monday, a mere nineteen hours before the disappearance.

The one thing all eyewitnesses did agree on was that none had seen any of the cars since the disappearance.

But James Cable saw something no one else had. When interviewed, he gave the FBI a clue so important that without it the case may never have been solved. He had a partial license plate number. "It was a 1960 Colorado-style plate. Read *AT-62*," he said. "It may have been *AT-6205*. I'm not a hundred percent sure about the last two numbers." *A* was the county designation for Denver.

Agents hoped the plates weren't stolen.

When newspapermen asked about rumors of car sightings the evening after Ad's disappearance, FBI agents said, "Refer all questions to Special Agent in Charge Scott Werner at the Denver office." When Bill was asked what he knew, he replied, "The FBI has requested that we make no further statements." Sheriff Wermuth, however, was happy to oblige.

"We're looking for two, possibly three assailants in a green Dodge that's been seen parked near Ad Coors's home," the sheriff said to reporters. "That's the strongest lead we've got in the case at the present time. . . . I believe we'll have a break in the case by noon Saturday. . . . I'm basing that on studies of other kidnap cases. The crucial time in other reported cases is thirty-six hours to four and a half days after the abduction is made. . . . Yes, it's my belief that Ad Coors is alive and held somewhere in the state. . . . According to a witness, the green Dodge had red-and-white license plates, which means it's an out-of-state car, possibly Utah, Florida, or Ohio. . . . We believe they've split up. One of the three men is a good suspect centered around Denver. We're anxious to check his movements. . . . I can't tell you that right now. The other two are believed to be somewhere southeast of Golden."

Reporters continued barking out their questions to the sheriff.

"No, I haven't positively identified the blood yet. Lew Hawley telephoned me from Washington to tell me the blood found on the bridge is group A, but we haven't located any medical records that show Ad Coors's blood type. . . . No, the blood on Kipling Street was canine. That's right, just a dog hit by a car. No connection there. . . . The tan cap and eyeglasses have been identified as belonging to Ad Coors. . . . No, we'll keep the mounted posse and jeep patrol out there through tomorrow and then I'll decide whether to suspend the search depending on the snowstorm they're calling for late Thursday. . . . Yes, group A. Okay, that's all I got for now, fellas."

Amid the barrage of questions, Wermuth told reporters that Mr. and Mrs. Coors were due to land at Denver's Stapleton Airfield that night. They had boarded a plane very early that morning to make the long flight home. Despite the earliness, reporters were waiting for them as they boarded.

"Mr. Coors! A few words about your son, sir! Please!" one of the correspondents asked, holding a pad and pencil.

The Hawaiian sun beamed on the tarmac at the Honolulu airport. Mr. Coors had telephoned FBI director J. Edgar Hoover, who assured Mr. Coors he would personally oversee the investigation into catching the kidnappers and bringing Ad home safely.

"I am dealing with crooks who are in business," Mr. Coors replied. A hot gust of wind almost blew the gray fedora from his head. "They have something I want to buy—my son. The price is secondary."

"So you've been told your son's definitely kidnapped?"

"No, but logic tells me he has been kidnapped. It's a matter of now waiting for an offer. It's like any other business transaction at this point."

"You're treating the kidnapping of your son like a business deal?"

"That's what it is. Besides, I cannot be emotional about this."

"Any idea who'd want to kidnap your son?" asked a different reporter.

"The union?" asked another.

"I don't know. No, we don't have any enemies in Golden. Excuse us, we have to board now."

"Good luck, sir!"

FBI agents assigned to coordinate the exchange of evidence with local law enforcement were about to finish up around the bridge site. They'd walked the creek bank on both sides and in the middle. They'd scoped the typography and investigated a pit silo and a cave directly across the state road from the bridge. They dusted for prints, including inside and outside the Travelall, took additional soil samples and bridge scrapings, and reviewed the deputies' reports. Dale Ryder had shown the agents where the Travelall was found by the milkman and where the cap and hat, eyeglasses, and blood had been discovered. He showed them sketches that county detectives had etched out using precise measurements that revealed the exact locations of the cap, hat, blood, scuff marks, and tire tracks. The last thing was to view the crime-scene photos. The two agents leaned on the hood of their sedan and observed as Dale Ryder flipped through the crisp black-and-white photos he'd taken the day before, one by one.

"The splash pattern was in that direction? Toward the southeast?" The agent nodded in a southeasterly direction as he asked about the blood spray.

"That's correct," said Ryder.

"I don't know. That's a—" The agent stopped as he spotted Bill walking up to the bridge. He was on his way back to Mary's after work and saw the officers standing round and decided to stop.

"Go ahead," said Bill. "Go ahead with what you were saying. I don't want to interrupt."

The agent introduced himself. "Now this is just my opinion, you understand, not the official FBI position." The agent paused.

"Go on," said Bill.

Mary held a ransom note in her hands. She put on her glasses, fearful of what the letter might say, but grateful to have it at all. She began to read:

```
Mrs. Coors:

Your husband has been kidnaped.  His car is by Turkey Creek.

Call the police or F.B.I.: he dies.

Cooperate: he lives.

Ransom: $200,000 in tens and $300,000 in twenties.

There will be no negotiating.

Bills: used / non-consecutive / unrecorded / unmarked.

Warning: we will know if you call the police or record the serial
numbers.

Directions: Place money & this letter & envelope in one suitcase
            or bag.

            Have two men with a car ready to make the delivery.

            When all set, advertise a tractor for sale in Denver Post
            section 69.  Sign ad King Ranch, Fort Lupton.

            Wait at NA 9-4455 for instructions after ad appears.

            Deliver immediately after receiving call.  Any delay
            will be regarded as a stall to set up a stake-out.

Understand this: Adolph's life is in your hands.  We have no desire
to commit murder.  All we want is that money.  If you follow the
instructions, he will be released unharmed within 48 hours after
the money is received.
```

Sitting in her chair in the den she enjoyed so much, Mary rested the letter in her lap, removed her glasses, and looked up at the FBI agents standing round. Her eyes were weak from lack of sleep and the dulling effects of sedatives. "Ad's still alive," Mary said. "He's alive. All they want's the money."

FBI agents in their dark suits and ties said nothing. It was Wednesday. Ad had been missing almost two days.

Mary didn't appreciate their silence. "It says right here," she said forcefully, holding up the note. "'We have no desire to commit murder.'"

"Yes, ma'am."

Bill spoke up. "Sure he's alive. That's the only way the lousy kidnappers collect."

"Of course he is," said Gerald Phipps, who'd joined Mary with his wife, Janet, to provide comfort and support on that terrible day. Gerald and Janet were close friends with Ad and Mary. They had hosted a wedding shower for Ad and Mary twenty years earlier, and they traveled in the same elevated circle of affluent Coloradans. Gerald Phipps's father had been a US senator and an executive at Carnegie Steel. Janet's father was the head of US Rubber. Also visiting were the elder Mrs. Coors's brother, Erle Kistler, and the well-to-do Kenneth and Sheilagh Malo.

Mary reached for her gin and tonic on the side table and rose from her chair. "We've got to get the money ready. Bill? Joe? How do we do that?" Mary said, ignoring the agents. "Will you two deliver it?"

Donald Hostetter, special agent in charge of the Detroit field office and head of the Western Kidnap Squad, interrupted. "May I please have the letter, Mrs. Coors? Thank you." He handed it to another agent. It was a copy. The original was on its way to the FBI Laboratory. "You're correct, Mrs. Coors. Your family should begin making arrangements to obtain the money immediately. We will assist you and your bank in coordinating the selection of denominations and recording the serial numbers. I'll have two agents make the delivery. We don't want anyone else in harm's way."

"But the letter," said Mary. "It says if we call the police or FBI, or if you mark the money, they'll hurt Ad. I'm sure we can find some friends or someone at the brewery to deliver the ransom."

"The kidnappers already know the sheriff and FBI are involved," Joe said. "It was in the papers this morning."

"But . . ." Mary placed her drink on the table. "Oh, I don't know what to do." She lowered her head and shielded her face with one hand.

"Don't worry, Mrs. Coors. That's why we're here. We do know what to do," said Hostetter. "All kidnappers say don't contact the authorities. Most victims' families do because it's the proper thing to do. The kidnappers had to have known that by leaving your husband's car on the bridge, law enforcement would become involved. And there's no way they'll know we've recorded the serial numbers. It's scare tactics."

"That's right," said Joe. "How would they know something like that?"

"Not possible," replied Hostetter. "Now, when the time comes, my agents will handle the drop-off. We'll dress them like ranchers or choose men who resemble your husband's brothers. I haven't exactly decided yet, but believe me, we'll do whatever it takes to procure your husband's safe return. That's priority number one. Apprehension is always secondary in these cases."

"I don't know. I know you men are professionals at what you do," began Mary, "but to tell you the truth, I don't care about the money or if they're caught. I just want Ad back. What do you think, Bill?"

"I think you have to trust the FBI," replied Bill. "But I will say this: I agree with Mary that the main thing is getting Ad back. The family doesn't want anyone, and that includes the FBI, doing anything that jeopardizes Ad's safe return."

"We don't either," said Hostetter.

Jefferson County investigator William Flint had intercepted the ransom note at the Morrison post office that Wednesday at 9:40 a.m. and immediately turned it over to the FBI, which dusted the envelope and letter for prints and made copies. Postal employee Joe Murphy said, "With the 3:00 p.m. Denver postmark on the envelope, the letter had to have been mailed in Denver on Tuesday, between 1:45 and 2:15 p.m."

Agents were pleased to have the letter. It represented the first piece of physical evidence, other than the brown felt hat, belonging to the kidnappers. Agents in Denver would receive a report from the FBI Laboratory in Washington two days later detailing the lab's findings:

> In the lower left-hand corner of the envelope was typed the word "PERSONAL"; in the center of the envelope the words "Mrs. Adolph Coors III, Morrison, Colorado," and on the upper right-hand corner of the envelope were typed the words "SPECIAL DELIVERY." The envelope bore a postmark "Denver, Colo, 2 1960" on the outer circumference of the cir-

cular postmark and in the center of the postmark the letters and numbers "FE 9 3 PM" . . .

The envelope and note were treated for fingerprints by the use of triketohydrindene hydrate and silver nitrate. No latent impressions of value were found . . .

The typist is experienced and made no errors in punctuation or spelling; double spaces after a period, which is taught in typing schools; but does overuse colons and uses only one space after a colon rather than two as is the approved practice in typing.

The author is reasonably well educated; writes well . . .

The letter was typed with either a Hermes or Royalite portable typewriter; both are sold extensively in the United States. . . . The Royalite has been on the market for less than three years. It is an inexpensive machine sold in large drug and department stores. Inquiry was made at the Royal McBee Corporation, manufacturer of Royalite typewriters, to determine retail outlets in the Denver area that sell the Royalite and the serial numbers of typewriters shipped. A representative of the manufacturer advised that two businesses sell the Royalite portable typewriter. They are the Denver Dry Goods Company, 16th & California Streets, and the May-D&F Company, 16th & Tremont. . . . This particular machine has a defect. The letter "s" is defectively applied. It is struck lower than all other type in the letter. . . . The typewriting on the envelope and note were compared with those in the Anonymous Letter File and the National Fraudulent Checks File. No matches were realized . . .

The envelope measures 4.24 inches in width and 9.37 inches in length. The paper has a substance weight of 20, measures 8.42 inches in width and 10.94 inches in length. Both contain the watermark, "EATON'S DIAMOND WHITE BOND BERKSHIRE COTTON FIBER CONTENT," and are sold by the Eaton Paper Corporation, 75 South Church Street,

Pittsfield, Massachusetts. A code mark under the first "E" in "BERKSHIRE" indicates the envelope and paper were manufactured in 1959. A representative from the manufacturer advised subject envelope and paper were shipped in reams and boxes after February 10, 1959, to five businesses in the metropolitan Denver area. Only two stores sell both the paper and the envelopes. These are the Denver Dry Goods Company, 16th & California Streets, and the May-D&F Company, 16th & Tremont. Dates and amounts of purchase have been recorded. Interviews of sales clerks at each store to follow.

As Agent Hostetter left Ad and Mary's home, he instructed two of his agents to relieve those who'd manned the recorder the night before. "I want to remind everyone not to say anything to reporters. If pressed, tell them the FBI told you to remain silent. Not only do leaks about our evidence, suspects, and theories compromise the investigation, more importantly, they put Mr. Coors in added jeopardy." He would relay the same message by telephone to the foremost offender, Sheriff Wermuth.

More than a year later, Mary testified in a crowded Jefferson County court, "I felt a little bit relieved because the ransom note gave us hope that Ad could still be alive."

CHAPTER 9

Corbett sat on a log beside a small river, stretching his legs. He'd been driving for hours. He unrolled some wax paper and bit into a bologna-and-mustard sandwich he'd picked up at a filling station along with a bottle of Pepsi. The man behind the counter had cut the rag bologna thick like Corbett asked. It was a dime more, but Corbett thought he'd splurge. He was hungry, having missed breakfast and dinner the day before.

He just sat there, rested, and ate, watching the cold water rush by with dead eyes. Those who knew him in his youth would never have guessed he'd be sitting on that log with little money and even less of a plan, a fugitive from justice soon to be suspected of another crime.

Corbett's homelife had been normal enough, although he had an older brother who died in 1927 at the age of six. The little boy had run into the street, chasing an errant ball, when he was struck and killed by a passing automobile. Corbett, born twenty months later and oddly named Joseph Corbett Jr. after his deceased brother with the same name, was left with a stepbrother and a young Alaskan boy named Russell Mallott that his parents had taken in at nine but later relinquished at age sixteen when his father was released from prison.

"I knew the family well," said an elderly woman who lived on the same street as Corbett's parents. "I'd see the boy playing out on the sidewalk. I remember him as a good boy; never heard of him being involved in any juvenile mischief. I'd talk to his mother when she came out on the back porch. Seemed like a fine woman. I didn't speak to his father other than to wave or say hello."

Yet Corbett would grow up to consider his mother "strange" and his father lacking moral fiber. "He oozes selfishness. He gambles and is an alcoholic. Taken the cure one or two times at AA," Corbett told friends. Nevertheless, his father was an intelligent man and a stable employee. He'd set type, written columns, and edited at *The Seattle Post-Intelligencer* almost all his working years. He was well respected by his coworkers and had been elected to the board of trustees of the Seattle Press Club.

Corbett had been an exemplary student. At Bryant Elementary School in Seattle, he had several friends and earned straight As. Though there were instances when he didn't focus on his studies at Roosevelt High School, he was in the debate club, German club, and science club, played soccer and softball, and worked after school. At seventeen, he submitted an essay entitled, "Why a Merchant Marine?" in a National Maritime essay contest sponsored by the Propeller Club of the United States. His was the winning entry and earned him a $50 war bond. He graduated eighty-eighth in a class of 455 students. Many thought he could have finished first had he been more interested in his studies.

"He was president of the Bryant Boys Club in 1942," recalled Scott Cassill Jr., a salesman for Graystone, to a reporter. "I was vice president. He was a darn nice guy. As close as we were, I really can't remember anything about him after the middle of our high school days. He matured much faster than the rest of us. He was a head taller than I when we graduated from Bryant and must have been six feet tall when we got out of elementary school."

"Did you stay in touch afterward?" asked the reporter.

"No, I lost track of him in high school."

"Everyone says he kept to himself, didn't talk to anyone, that he was a recluse," said the reporter.

"If that happened, it was much later," continued Cassill. "I remember him as a reasonably extroverted type."

"Was he a good student?"

"If he turned into a bookworm, as some news accounts say, it was much later than when I knew him."

After high school, Corbett entered college, the University of Washington in his hometown, an uncommon path for young men in the 1940s who weren't entering under the GI Bill. He'd scored 91 out of 99 on his admittance exam when 50 was an average score. He joined a fraternity of twelve physics majors called the Quantum Club. He ran a typing business on campus for students and also maintained a part-time job at American-Marietta Company, testing adhesives.

He seemed to have a bright future, working his way through college with a genius IQ. He had his eyes on medical school. Perhaps his brilliance, part-time jobs, and resultant lack of free time accounted for his dearth of socializing that others thought odd; perhaps not.

"When Joe left the plant at night, it was as if the doors had shut behind him," said Henry Preusser, technical-service manager for American-Marietta Company. "He had no friends from the company . . . he never attended our parties, didn't bowl with our team . . . he took no part in our extracurricular activities. It was almost as if he was trapped in the building and just accepted it and felt forced to take part in the discourse that went on inside the plant. . . . On his last day, it was the darnedest thing. He left early, about three o'clock, to avoid a going-away party we were throwing for him. We bought him a bright sports shirt to go with those drab khakis he always wore. One of our employees delivered it to him the next day after he didn't show."

Clearly, Corbett already had developed a penchant for solitude. Then on the morning of June 7, 1949, Corbett was enjoying his summer vacation from the University of Washington when his mother, Marion, a Democratic precinct committeewoman and founder of the women's auxiliary of the American Newspaper Guild, plunged from a kitchen balcony onto an iron well grate. No one saw her fall. Corbett found his mother on the well cover in the yard, he said. She died after lying unconscious in a Seattle hospital for five days.

Corbett was devastated. He failed to return to college in the fall, merely one year shy of graduation. Instead, he moved to San Francisco and worked at odd jobs while he withdrew even more, refusing to make friends, eventually quitting work entirely.

And then he did the unthinkable. Four days before Christmas 1950, he murdered a man. Alan Lee Reed, a twenty-year-old sergeant from Ligonier, Indiana, stationed at Hamilton Air Force Base north of San Francisco, was found dead from two bullet wounds, one behind each ear. His lifeless body had been dumped at Larkspur in Marin County, California, like a piece of garbage, leaving behind a three-mile trail of blood that led to the site of the shooting.

Corbett was arrested in Beverly Hills driving a stolen car and carrying a .32-caliber revolver and a .38-caliber automatic pistol. Ironically, Corbett was captured because his father, who was worried about his son because he had not heard from him in days, called and asked the police to check his son's Kensington Park boardinghouse to make sure he was all right. When police arrived at Corbett's boardinghouse, they found his bags packed sitting in the middle of his apartment. His landlady, Grayce Fahey, described a car she'd seen him driving for several days and even provided the license plate number. The plate matched that on a stolen vehicle that had been the murder car, filled with blood from the crime, ditched a few miles from the shooting.

Corbett's attorney, Albert E. Bagshaw, argued it was self-defense. He said Corbett admitted stealing the car, but that on the way back from target shooting, he picked up Reed as a hitchhiker, and an argument ensued because Reed insisted on going out for a night of drinking and gambling. During the quarrel, according to the lawyer, Reed went for Corbett's gun, and Corbett had no choice but to shoot him.

"Joe Corbett kept very much to himself and was regarded as reticent," Fahey recalled in 1951, soon after her tenant shot and killed the air force sergeant. "Generally, he stayed home nights and had no friends that I know of. He paid his rent regularly and didn't smoke or drink. . . . He read a lot and owned quite a few guns; always cleaning them."

"He showed considerable interest in short firearms," said a former boardinghouse roommate. "He spent quite a bit of time cleaning them."

Corbett's father stood by his son. "I'm completely satisfied that Joe is innocent," said Mr. Corbett shortly after his son's arrest. "And I'm convinced he is a victim of circumstances that point a finger of suspicion at him for something in which he had no part at all."

There was one problem with the father's account and that of the lawyer's. They were wrong. After Corbett was arrested in Beverly Hills in another stolen car, he told police he wasn't involved. When police recovered Corbett's blood-sprayed hat in his boardinghouse room, size 7⅜, he changed his story to one of self-defense. The police didn't believe that either. The evidence pointed to a robbery gone bad, since the sergeant's watch and wallet were missing. Deputy district attorney William Weissich believed the cause had more to do with primordial temper or simply plain meanness. Any way it went, he knew it was impossible for Corbett to explain how he defended himself by putting two .38-caliber bullet holes into the back of the sergeant's head.

When Corbett was arrested, local police didn't find the murder weapon, but did uncover seventy-five books in his room, which included books on physics, mathematics, psychology, and criminology. When the deputy district attorney asked Corbett if the shooting had been accidental, the well-read twenty-two-year-old correctly replied, "Well, even in an accidental shooting in the course of robbery, it's first-degree murder, isn't it?"

The young Corbett was offered and accepted a deal from prosecutors whereby he'd plead guilty to second-degree murder in exchange for a five-to-life sentence that was later fixed at ten years. Because Corbett's answers to interrogators were inconsistent and because there was no trial, the true facts of the case were never known.

After he was sentenced and sent to San Quentin, an optimistic Corbett told reporters he'd complete his education and obtain his master's in physics while in prison. He didn't.

A stunned Joe Corbett Sr. told the Seattle papers that his son hadn't shot the sergeant but, "If he did it . . . somewhere along the line something had snapped inside him."

Indeed, something seemed to have snapped. "Something was bothering the boy," said officials at the University of Washington.

"Friends and associates in Seattle recalled him as a brilliant student at the University of Washington whose personality changed after his mother died," *The Seattle Times* reported.

Corbett's father hired psychiatrist Dr. Joseph D. Catton to "leave no stone unturned" in trying to uncover some explanation for his son's strikingly altered behavior after his mother's death and his murder of the air force sergeant. Unfortunately, the doctor was unsuccessful.

"The crime I committed in California," Corbett later told an FBI agent (who hadn't asked), "I shot the guy. There was a fight, and I shot him. It was a terrible thing, but I pleaded guilty. It was due to my guilt complex that became a punishment complex. My mother was a very strange person. . . . I feel partly responsible for her death because I procrastinated in repairing the railing around the second-story porch where she fell and was killed. . . . I would have been greatly relieved if my father and stepbrother had said something, that they didn't believe I was to blame, but they made no effort to console me. For that reason, I retained the guilt complex and eventually decided to go to California. Both of them are responsible for my decision to leave home."

Corbett left the agent with a macabre thought: "It's only natural for children to have a desire to kill their parents," Corbett continued, "and from time to time I've had that desire. . . . But I did not kill my mother."

There was no evidence to prove otherwise. His mother languished unconscious for five days before breathing her last, never able to tell exactly what happened.

Dr. Robert N. Smith warned in his psychiatric notes from the California Medical Facility at Terminal Island:

> Joseph R. Corbett Jr. is markedly schizoid. He continually fails the social-fitness test, says he admires Nietzsche, saying, "Might makes right. Look at Nagasaki. The only thing that was important was the result of the bomb." He's a four-flusher or blowhard, always trying to impress others with his superiority, always thinking he's correct and those who disagree with him are wrong, always "going back to college." The thing that makes him most dangerous is he habitually represses emotion, maintaining a placid appearance to those who see him, but if something breaks through that reserve, he can burst into violent, uncontrolled emotion.

Another psychiatrist, Dr. W. A. Drummond Jr., who examined Corbett at San Quentin in 1951, wrote this:

> Corbett is a 22 year old man convicted of murder 2nd and referred for psychiatric examination because of the nature of his offense. He is a blond young man, tall and thin. His behavior is entirely proper, includes the usual social graces, and reflects his background of adequate good breeding. The most noteworthy thing is his reserve. Though quite cooperative in giving facts about his family and himself, he is obviously in uncomfortable territory when asked to describe personality characteristics. His descriptions along this line all closely approach usual concepts of "normality." One would suspect he has tremendous need to maintain his internal equilibrium by avoiding the contemplation of even ordinary deviations, and that the bringing of emotional factors offers great threat to him. The inadequacy of his personality in this respect is significant in relation to his crime. Excessive restraints against

emotionality when broken down, probably changed to violent uncontrolled emotionality, the personality having no facilities for dealing with it.

He describes his family history in terms of such stereotyped normality that very little is learned. Both parents had been married previously, the mother bringing to the second marriage a son who was three years older than Subject and who grew up with him. When Subject was about nine, an Alaskan boy was brought into the home as a foster son, for reasons not made clear. One is struck by the undercurrent of violent incidents in the family, though no details are brought out; mother's first husband was killed in an auto accident. One of father's two previous wives was killed in an auto accident. Child of one of father's previous marriages was killed in an auto accident. Father of foster brother was in prison.

He describes himself minimally. He "gets along well;" he is interested in engineering physics; he enjoys athletics. He utters such information with evidence of considerable disturbance. He does not, of course, admit to emotional disturbances since doing so would be contrary to his defenses.

Descriptions from others and observation of him make it seem clear that he is introverted, not very sociable, and consumed in interest with activities of internal importance. He must find great danger in introverted life, however, and resorts to a sterile though proper sort of extroverted behavior which denies his autistic preoccupations. Extroverted behavior falling short, and emotional factors finding no outlet, explosions become possible. The murder for which committed is probably the great example in his life of full expression of aggressive emotion which neither he nor others find compatible with the stirrings he allows himself to be aware of. He is not at all psychotic, but his defenses conceivably could allow the development of psychosis. The powerful motivations which his bland thinking is apparently guarding against could quite possibly be fantasies of omnipotence.

IMPRESSION: Character disorder with schizoid and asocial tendencies.

Not only prison doctors noticed Corbett was different. "I remember him as a quiet boy . . . a little withdrawn . . . maybe even an introvert," a shop owner near Corbett's boyhood home recalled.

Dr. Philip Huffman was a childhood friend of Corbett's, but didn't have fond recollections:

> Joe was proficient at shoplifting when he was eight or nine years old. He always stole scientific goods, such as electrical switches from dime stores and laboratory equipment from the chemical laboratory at the University of Washington. He had a small chemical set in his basement and replenished his supply from the University. . . . He took pride in his ability to evade apprehension. He was daring in his escapades, climbing the vines on the outside of the buildings at the University and on the elevator cables between floors.
>
> When we were twelve or thirteen years old, Joe said he wondered what it would be like to kill someone. That was typical of Joe's interest in new and different things. He was a lone-wolf type who always went ahead with whatever he planned even when the rest of us backed out.

Though he'd held promise as a youth, perhaps folks back in Seattle would not be surprised, after all, if they knew Corbett was sitting on a log, eating a sandwich in the cold, hiding from the law for yet another crime.

Regardless, Corbett didn't have time to reflect. He jumped back into his Mercury and spun loose gravel by the roadside. He had to keep moving.

CHAPTER 10

Stephen H. Hart, Ad's personal attorney, couldn't believe the news. A year earlier, February 19, 1959, he'd overseen Ad sign his last will and testament. No one in the room could ever have envisioned that the healthy man of forty-three years seated before them could be dead in less than a year. The attorney hoped the will wouldn't be needed for years to come, but just in case, he removed the will from the firm's fireproof vault—and read it.

Ad Coors has never been involved in any of the labor negotiations at the plant," *Rocky Mountain News* reported. "Bill Coors has headed the sometimes bitter labor management talks at the brewery and Joe Coors has handled the same at the porcelain plant."

Reporters located Bill and Joe at the brewery that Wednesday. Word of Ad's apparent kidnapping the day before had spread throughout the plant early that morning. Employees were surprised to see the brothers working and walking about instructing employees like it was any other day. Some had expected a company meeting that morning to inform the employees of Ad's disappearance. After all, the Coors brothers often called meetings to discuss labor concerns or their views on various issues. Ad's disappearance seemed worthy of at least a few words from his brothers.

The brothers temporarily divided Ad's duties between them while handing off other matters to those who'd worked with Ad for years.

Of course, they wished for Ad's safe return, but until that day arrived, someone had to perform his duties. The Adolph Coors Company must continue brewing and making porcelain products.

Bill and Joe did think about their brother during work. If they forgot for one second, there was Ad's empty chair at his desk near theirs, just as it had been for years. They made sure they could easily be summoned if a telephone call came in from Mary, the sheriff's office, or the FBI. They'd already received word of the ransom note and rushed out to meet FBI agents, returning to the plant that afternoon. They'd be traveling to Mary's house again in the evening to be with her should the kidnappers call.

During the workday, they'd accept an "I'm very sorry" from employees with a nod, though they took calls from only their closest friends. To Bill and Joe, all that was Coors family business, and therefore it was none of the employees' business. There'd be no announcement, conversation, or prepared statement. Just work as usual.

While everyone searched for Ad Coors and his kidnapper in Colorado, Corbett was continuing to travel east in an automobile. Along the way, he in all likelihood kept up with news from Denver on the radio and in the newspapers where he would have read an article like this:

> Sheriff Wermuth called off the organized search yesterday after saying every bit of broken country between the Coors home and the brewery and porcelain plant at Golden, about ten miles to the north, had been thoroughly covered. . . . The elder Coors said, "It is a matter now of waiting for an offer." . . . Money was no object said Coors Sr. . . .

He also would have read news of a snowstorm approaching from the west, passing over Denver and across the plains, that would hamper lawmen's search for Ad Coors and clues as to his disappearance.

Corbett would later tell a reporter about leaving Denver in a rush, "I had some trouble in my past and had been in that area. I figured the police would come knocking."

Whatever the truth, Corbett had left Denver in a hurry. Where he was going, only he knew at that time. One thing was for sure: he wasn't carrying a bagful of money.

Landing lights on the Continental Air Lines Viscount flooded the runway as the commercial airliner touched down at Stapleton Airfield in Denver that Wednesday at 9:00 p.m. Reporters stood ready to storm Mr. and Mrs. Coors when they disembarked the plane. As the reporters checked their cameras' bulbs and tested their recorders, four propellers pulled the passengers swiftly past as the plane taxied beyond its scheduled gate to the Continental hangars, where Mr. and Mrs. Coors stepped down the plane's ladder and Bill whisked them away in their private car, a courtesy extended only to the ultimate first-class passengers at the fifth-busiest airport in the country.

Bill informed his parents that there had been no further communication from the kidnappers yet, though the FBI was pretty confident about the case. They had helicopters, undercover agents, dogs, all kinds of electronic gadgets. "The meeting about the ransom note is tomorrow morning, eleven o'clock at Ad's house," said Bill. "Mary has to stay near the telephone, just in case."

"What do you think about the note, son?"

"Joe and I read it yesterday with Harold Bray and an FBI agent at the big house. Based on it being postmarked before 3:00 and there weren't any press releases until 5:00, we think it has to be a valid note." (The 22-room Queen Anne house built by Adolph Coors in which Mr. and Mrs. Coors then resided was nicknamed the "big house.")

Mrs. Coors asked Bill how Ad's children were faring, and expressed her desire to pick them up from Joe and Holly's house now that she had returned from Hawaii. Mrs. Coors also asked about Mary and if anyone had called May Louise, Ad's sister.

It was a quiet drive the rest of the way home. Mr. Coors glared at passing house lights, and Mrs. Coors's glove-covered hands gripped her purse tightly. They were worried, but Mr. Coors refused to show it.

The following morning, Bill picked up his father and mother at the big house and returned to Mary's, where Joe was waiting with FBI agents and Harold Bray.

Mr. Coors walked up to Mary, patted her on her arm, and said, "Be brave for your young ones." While Mrs. Coors stayed to comfort Mary, Mr. Coors went into the living room, where FBI agents were posted.

"Who's in charge?" asked Mr. Coors, bringing the meeting to order as he looked about the room.

One of the men stepped forward. "Hello, Mr. Coors. I'm Scott Werner, special agent in charge of the FBI field office in Denver. Director Hoover extends his regrets and wishes to assure you that he is using the full resources of the Department of Justice and the FBI, sir, to secure your son's release unharmed."

"Thank you. Any idea where my son is being held?" asked Mr. Coors.

"No, sir. But if I may, I'd like to brief you on where the investigation stands."

"Go ahead," Mr. Coors said, taking a seat near the fireplace.

"We contacted your bank in Boston and arranged to have the ransom money flown to Denver tomorrow morning, subject to your order to proceed. We've recorded all serial numbers and marked several of the used bills."

Mary Coors protested that the kidnappers wrote not to do that. Werner assured Mr. Coors they could do it without detection. "Go on," said Mr. Coors.

"Your sons and I discussed whether this is a genuine note," Werner said, who then explained that it had been received before news broke of the kidnapping. "So, unless the writer is clairvoyant," Werner continued, "it has to be real."

The FBI chief went on to explain that the classified ad spelled out in the ransom note had already been arranged to be placed in *The*

Denver Post Sunday to signal the kidnappers that the money was ready. The ad would run for a fortnight. "We have men operating recorders on your home telephone and those of your sons and at the brewery. We'll also attempt to trace the call when it comes in, but if they're smart, they'll know that and won't talk long."

"What about the ransom drop?" asked Mr. Coors.

"We have two good men with experience in kidnappings who are standing by to deliver the money. One's Tony Redder. He's a pro at this type of thing," Werner said. Tony Redder was a retired FBI agent currently serving as Denver County undersheriff and jail warden. He had been the liaison in several past kidnappings around the country. Werner explained how typically one kidnapper stayed with the hostage while the other secured the ransom money, and that once the one with the money was safely away, the other would release the hostage, and then the two would meet at a prearranged location to divvy up the loot. "But we'll stay on the one with the money in unmarked cars and a helicopter. We'll grab him and the money as soon as your son is released. Once he's in custody, he'll snitch on his partner. That's the way it usually plays out."

"I know about the blood. Tell me, how bad is the boy hurt? Is he dead?" asked Mr. Coors, who rarely minced words.

Mary bowed her head.

Special Agent Werner glanced at Mary and then looked at Bill.

"Come on, Mary," said her brother, James Grant III (Jim), who had flown in from New York that day to stay with Mary awhile. "Let's go to the basement for a bit."

"Mother, why don't you go with Mary," said Bill. "I'd like Jim to stay up here in case any legal questions come up."

"Come on, dear," said Mrs. Coors, taking Mary by the elbow.

Werner nodded to Mary as she passed. He waited until he saw the door leading into the basement close before continuing.

Mary and Mrs. Coors, whose name was Alice May, sat on the couch in the basement and talked. They rarely did.

"I remember when Ad was a baby," Mrs. Coors began. "He was

the fattest little thing with a headful of curly blond hair. Can you imagine Ad with curly blond hair?"

"I've seen his baby pictures," said Mary. "He was very cute."

"I remember the paper telephoned and asked if they could borrow one of his photographs for a piece they were doing on little children, babies really, one or two years old, who belonged to the more respectable families."

"Spike's baby pictures always remind me of Ad's," said Mary.

"Yes . . . I can see that. They do favor."

Mary and Mrs. Coors sipped coffee and continued talking about Ad's childhood. Upstairs, Mr. Coors continued his board meeting.

"Well, is he alive or dead?"

"I'll be frank with you, sir," Werner said. "There was a great deal of blood at the scene caused by at least one gunshot, maybe two. There was a pool of blood on the ground as round as a washtub and saturated pretty deep. There was blood spatter on the Travelall's bumper, the windshield, the front seat, and along the driver's-side window as far back as the rear fender. There also was blood on a section of bridge railing and even on some logs twenty feet away along the creek bank."

Mr. Coors dropped his head. He didn't know there'd been that much blood. Neither did Bill or Joe.

"All the blood is group A," Werner continued. "That means in all likelihood, the blood came from one person. As yet, we've been unable to locate your son's blood type, so we can't be positive who the blood actually belongs to."

"I'm not sure I even know what mine is," said Mr. Coors, standing and stretching his hands out to feel the warmth of the crackling fire. "Do you boys know yours?"

Bill and Joe shook their heads.

"But one of your men said yesterday the blood could have come from a kidnapper Ad shot," Joe said, interrupting Werner. "'Cause he'd have fought like a wildcat. You can depend on it."

"It is possible he shot a kidnapper. His wife said he sometimes carried a pistol in his car, and we didn't find it in the Travelall, but we've since located it in this house, so it wasn't his gun that fired the shot. Still, he could have wrestled for a kidnapper's gun and shot one of them. If he did shoot one, he'll be in even more danger, but then again, it's better than if it's his blood because—"

"Yes?" asked Mr. Coors, turning to look at Werner.

"I'll tell you straight away, Mr. Coors, it would be nearly impossible for whoever got shot to survive after losing that much blood, even if taken to a hospital, which we know didn't happen. He would have bled to death not long after he entered the vehicle, if not before."

Mr. Coors sat. All eyes converged on the family patriarch, awaiting his response.

"Damn." There was a long pause as Mr. Coors sat stoically. "All right, then. Go ahead and get the money ready, but we don't pay until we know the boy's alive. And if he is, though you're saying he's probably not—"

"It's possible he's alive," interrupted Werner. "We have to operate under that assumption."

"Don't try to sugarcoat this like you do for that one in the basement," Mr. Coors said, gesturing with one hand toward the floor.

Before Werner could say anything, Mr. Coors continued, "Look. It's simple. I want my son if he's alive. If he's dead, I want his body, and I want his murderers executed. And if you have to give them the money, I want every penny of it back."

The next morning, Steve Hart's legal secretary knocked and entered the office. "There's a telephone call for you from Bill Coors."

"Thanks. Close the door behind you."

Steve Hart was a good friend of Ad's, and his wife had been a bridesmaid in Ad and Mary's wedding. In his early years, he'd worked for Mary's father, James Grant Jr. He'd chosen the law firm of Lewis & Grant over that of his own father, who was a prominent attorney in Denver, as was Hart's grandfather. Hart now practiced law in his own firm.

"Hi, Steve," said Bill. "Jim Grant and I would like to see you today. It's about Ad. You free?"

It was Thursday. Two days after Ad's disappearance.

They made the appointment for two o'clock.

After the three men had convened in the law office, Steve Hart's legal associate, Bruce Buell, joined the triangle of old friends. Buell was twenty-eight years old, good looking, tall, and thin, and was establishing himself as a respected estate attorney in town.

As they took seats around a conference table, Steve Hart knew Mary's brother, Jim, also a lawyer, though his practice was in New York City.

"Like I said on the telephone, we're here to discuss Ad's affairs," said Bill. "I guess you could say I'm representing the Coorses' interests, and Jim is representing Mary's interests."

"Have you received word of Ad's death?" asked Hart.

"No," said Bill.

"No," joined Jim. "It looks exceedingly bleak. Of course, we're maintaining all hope Ad will return safe and sound, but—"

Bill interrupted and explained that there was an awful lot of blood at the bridge. He told of his conversation the night before with an FBI agent at the bridge who told him that the bloodstain was not droplets, as Bill and Joe had initially perceived, but was substantial, covering an area twelve by nineteen inches, soaked in the dirt three inches deep, and the length of the spray was more than twenty feet down to the creek bank.

"So I asked if Ad was dead. I remember the agent rested his hands on his hips and looked down. 'I'm sorry, Mr. Coors,' he said. 'It seems cut and dried to me. Your brother never left this bridge alive,'" continued Bill. "And this morning at Ad and Mary's, Denver's FBI chief confirmed the same bloody details. So it looks like Ad's gone, I'm afraid, absent a miracle. That's why Dad wants me to make sure Ad's affairs are in order and there's nothing that might pop up, you know, from a company or personal standpoint that might be embarrassing to the family. Jim can speak to making sure Mary's taken care of. And the kids."

Buell felt the entire meeting was premature, perhaps a little cold. Though he'd been practicing law only three years, he'd never seen anyone talk about an estate before the person was known dead, especially only two days after he went missing. But then again, there was all the blood at the scene.

Steve Hart assured Bill that Ad did not own any stock or assets in Adolph Coors Company, Coors Porcelain Company, Coors Container Company, or other Coors-owned company. He then proceeded to recite the dispositive provisions of Ad's last will and testament that bequeathed most of Ad's assets to Mary, with some passing in trust for his children.

"Well, that sounds fine to me," said Bill. "But before we go any further, we need to know—Dad wants to know—there's nothing else— no kept woman, no blind trust for a bastard child, or anything like that."

"Absolutely nothing," Hart said without hesitation. "Ad was— is—a straight-up fellow. He hid nothing from Mary or his family, at least that I'm aware."

Jim went on to say that Mary would need access to Ad's assets very soon. The checks from the brewery were made out to Ad, so when the next one came in, she wouldn't be able to cash or deposit it. She needed an interim administration of Ad's estate to keep receiving money and paying the bills so she wouldn't be forced to access the Grant trust fund for her benefit.

"We can help her gain access to Ad's checks and assets, at least to some extent," said Hart. "The only problem is that Colorado doesn't allow for administration of a person's estate until that person is proved deceased, and in this case, at least so far, Ad is only missing two days. There's no body, no murderer, nothing."

"If Ad's dead, his body could be at the bottom of Soda Lakes for all we know," said Bill. "He may never be found."

"Colorado hasn't enacted any legislation to provide for the administration of an absentee's estate?" asked Jim.

"No, it hasn't."

"Anything you can do in the local courts? Seems to me it would behoove the judge to bend a few rules since it involves Ad and Mary. Is the judge an old friend of Father's?" asked Jim.

"It'll be Judge Roscoe Pile. Tell you what, I'll give him a call after we break up," said Hart. "He'll bend the law as far as he legally can to accommodate Mary and the Grant and Coors families. Of course, it's too early for an actual court administration, but I'll talk to the judge and see if we can get some concessions so Mary's hands won't be tied."

"That sounds good," said Bill, standing from his chair.

"And I'll be praying for that miracle, gentlemen," said Hart as he walked Bill and Jim to the door.

The snow and winds that had been predicted all week hit after five o'clock Thursday evening with lows reaching the teens, dumping several inches of snow in the foothills. Sheriff Wermuth temporarily halted the search for Ad. The storm forced Mary's doctor to park at the bottom of the drive and walk up the steep hill through the deepening snow. It had been one of the worst winters in years, with snowstorm after snowstorm.

The snow did not delay the plane carrying the ransom money from a Boston bank, however. It arrived early Friday afternoon. The FBI placed the used bills totaling $500,000 (more than $4 million today) and weighing seventy-five pounds in a footlocker and delivered the locker to Ad's house so when the time came, the kidnappers, if watching, would see the money loaded into the vehicle that would drop off the ransom. The footlocker creepily sat on the kitchen floor like a metal coffin.

Despite the bad weather, the FBI and county investigators continued interviewing possible witnesses and began focusing on two of the automobiles seen in the area before Ad's disappearance: a green 1946 or '47 Dodge sedan and a 1951 or '52 yellow Mercury.

Mary was crazed with worry, dozing in and out of consciousness, heavily sedated and distressed to the point of being physically ill. Late Friday morning, she awakened and walked to the kitchen, where she found her brother. He was seated at the kitchen table, reading documents he'd brought along from his New York office.

She walked into the den and gazed out the window at the melting snow. She saw deputies outside, lots of them. Standing, sitting, in cars, on cars, some huddled together near the house, on the road below, smoking cigarettes, or drinking coffee from thermos caps. She even saw one laughing as if telling jokes to his fellow deputy. Her grief turned to anger.

"No wonder the kidnappers won't contact us. Would you look at them out there?" Mary motioned for her brother. "The kidnappers said don't call the police, and look at them standing in the open. I want them gone. I want them out of here! Now! Call that FBI man or the sheriff or whomever you have to call, but get rid of them." Mary stormed away toward her bedroom.

Later that day, a statement was released to the newspapers. They were told it was from Mary Coors, prepared and released through the Denver public relations firm William Kostka and Associates, which represented the Adolph Coors Company.

> I am requesting Sheriff Arthur Wermuth of Jefferson County to withdraw all guards on duty, and men and equipment used in road-blocks near my home. I am also requesting that no one interfere with any steps which might be taken to effect my husband's safe return. The safe return of my husband is my only concern. Our entire family is deeply appreciative of the cooperation we have received from all officials and the concern that has been expressed by all our friends. I am grateful for the understanding of the press and hope that it will continue to exercise continued understanding of our position.

"We will jail anyone on complaint of trespassing that we receive from the Coors family," Sheriff Wermuth told reporters.

Wermuth had little else to say. He was being squeezed out by the FBI, a situation that was fine with the Coors family. They wanted the more experienced and professional federal agents heading the kidnapping investigation. He'd joined the many reporters waiting for word along the corridors of the Jefferson County Sheriff's Office. Wermuth taped a sign written in crayon on a door leading to the inner offices that read, "Law officers only beyond this point." When asked if contact had been made with the kidnappers, Wermuth said with frustration, "I'm not aware of any contact. I've had no communication from the Coors family."

The newspaper, television, and radio journalists respected Mary's plea and stayed away from the Coors ranch home. That was a rarity. Even reporters admitted they couldn't recall a time when they didn't look for personal beats on a story.

More snow fell on Friday.

"Well, I remember the snow very well," Mary Coors would tell jurors later. "It began to snow hard and steadily, and that again gave us a little hope that possibly whoever had taken Ad was not able to contact us. And it gave us hope, and yet again it was bad because we knew that he had been hurt and possibly he was somewhere where he could not get medical attention. I just remember snow and wind and very bad roads."

Special agents checked the records of the Denver Police Department's Auto Theft Bureau. One of the witnesses near the bridge, James Cable, had given the FBI a partial plate number. "*AT-62*, perhaps *AT-6205*," he said. Agent Leroy Green discovered only four Mercury automobiles in Denver had been assigned a license plate with the prefix *AT-62*.

AT 629 registered to CLARENCE GADE, 1479 South Wolff, Denver; 1951 Mercury coupe.

AT 6243 registered to **VANCE JOHNSON**, 4225 East Jewell, Denver; 1951 Mercury coach.

AT 6271 registered to **CLAIRE GUTHRIE TRAYLOR**, 836 Steele Street, Denver; 1956 Mercury station wagon.

AT 6203 registered to **WALTER OSBORNE**, 1435 Pearl Street, Denver; 1951 Mercury sedan.

Agents now knew one of these four automobiles had carried a driver either alone or accompanied by one or more unidentified passengers to the area surrounding Turkey Creek Bridge and Ad Coors's ranch on several occasions, including the Sunday and Monday before the disappearance, and hadn't been seen since. All agents had to do was check each of the four Mercurys to determine if one was yellow. That wouldn't take long.

Since it was a weeknight, the four suspected vehicles should be parked at their owners' residences.

"Come in, 31. Over."

"This is DN31. What you got? Over."

"Negative on Steele Street yellow. Repeat, Steele Street not yellow. Two tone, white and blue. Registration says ivory and turquoise. Over."

"Roger," said Agent Paul Casey. "Over and out."

A few minutes later, the same message came in from two agents checking out the Mercury belonging to the owner on South Wolff Drive. It turned out to be pale green.

Agents in squad car 31 drove along Pearl Street, then headed into the alley behind the Perlmor apartment building. They didn't spot a yellow Mercury.

"You get out here and go up the side. Meet me out front," said Agent Casey.

"Right," replied Agent Art Baier.

The black sedan parked in the darkness between streetlights on Pearl Street. The Perlmor apartment building was across the street.

"DN56, this is DN31. Got a match on the yellow Mercury? Over."

"DN31, just making visual. Negative. Color is dark blue. Over."

"Roger that. Over and out."

The agent stepped out of the car as his partner crossed the front lawn in the shadows and rejoined him.

"Got a negative on the third Mercury. This has got to be our man. You cover the back. I'll go in the front."

Agent Baier trotted across the front and along the side to the alley and positioned himself at the rear door.

Agent Casey walked up the steps and buzzed the manager. The door lock clicked, and he entered casually so not to raise suspicion. He knocked on a door near the lobby stenciled with the word MANAGER.

The door opened, and a woman about fifty with glasses and graying hair appeared.

The agent introduced himself, showing his identification. "We're looking for a man whose automobile is registered to this address. His name is Walter Osborne."

Mrs. Merys said, "Oh, yes, Mr. Osborne in 305."

"Is he in his room now?" asked the agent, pulling his suit coat back to reveal an FBI-issued .38-caliber revolver in a leather holster strapped to his shoulder.

Soon Agent Baier came inside, and the two agents with guns drawn stood on each side of the door to room 305. One knocked. "Open up. FBI." No response. The agent knocked louder and longer. "FBI! Open the door!" Nothing. The agent motioned for Mrs. Merys to reach around and unlock the door with the master key hanging from a safety pin stuck in her dress. "Step back." The agents shoved open the door and rushed in, pointing their revolvers about an empty room.

"I told you he'd moved out," Mrs. Merys said.

The agents surveyed the one-room studio apartment. Only a couch and kitchen table and chairs remained. One opened the closet. Empty. Another checked the bathroom. Nothing.

"Radio this in," said Agent Casey to his fellow agent. "The subject has fled. And get the forensics unit over here to dust the apartment for prints."

The agent walked with Mrs. Merys down the stairs to her apartment. Soon, he was joined by Agent John Goodwin, who carried out the questioning. "Tell me exactly when Walter Osborne left and what you heard and saw."

"Like I told you, he left Wednesday morning."

"That would be Wednesday the tenth?"

"That's right. He buzzed me the night before, about 9:00 p.m."

"Tuesday night the ninth?"

"Yes, and he told me he'd locked himself out of his room and needed me to let him in."

"Did he seem nervous or disturbed?"

"No, he was the same as usual. Polite, nice. He apologized for having me come up to let him in. He was the same as always. That's when he told me he was moving out and had some things he wanted to give to Goodwill. I was so surprised he was leaving."

"Why's that?"

" 'Cause he's lived here almost four years. Plus, we require a month's notice to terminate, and he'd already paid his February rent in full. I told him I'd have to keep the rent, though I'd try to let his apartment before the end of the month and mail him a refund."

"Did he leave a forwarding address or tell you where he was going?"

"No, he didn't seem worried about the money. All he said was, 'I'm going back to school, to the University of Colorado in Boulder. I guess I'm kind of old for that.' And I told him, 'No, not necessarily. But I'm sorry you're going. You're such a good neighbor.' "

"Did he leave that night?"

"No. Harry saw him about 8:30 the next morning around back carrying out some of his things."

"Harry?" asked the agent, scribbling notes.

"He's my husband, Eugene Harry Merys. He's an electrician and helps out with the management in his spare time."

"Anyone else see Osborne or his car?"

"Viola Borch said she saw him about 7:30 that morning loading belongings into a dirty car parked on East Colfax, which is around the corner. We both thought it was strange because Mr. Osborne's car was always neat and clean. Always real shiny. He was out there cleaning on his car twice a week. But Viola said this car was spattered with mud along the sides and even up on the windows."

"Do you know the color?"

"Viola only said it was muddy. You can ask her. She's in room 304, across the hall a bit from Mr. Osborne's old room. She did say the front and rear door handles were both in the middle of the car if that helps any."

"So the color wasn't yellow?"

"I don't know. She just said muddy."

"Ever seen him in a yellow Mercury?"

"No. He's had . . . oh, my . . . Mr. Osborne's owned a bunch of cars since I been managing the Perlmor. He had a blue-and-white Chevy, a blue Ford wagon, and a gray-and-white Ford, but nothing yellow that I've seen."

"Go on. Anybody else see anything?"

"One of my tenants said she saw him at 5:30 that morning carrying stuff out to his car. Almost bumped into him."

"What's the tenant's name?"

"Vivian Cherveny. She's in 306."

"What was Osborne's room like when he left?"

"The room was clean. Mr. Osborne always kept a clean apartment. I was surprised, though, at the amount of dust on the floor."

"See anything left behind? Did you remove anything?"

A buzzer interrupted. Mrs. Merys shooed the tenant at her door away with a quick answer.

"Sorry. Okay. You asked if I took anything out of the room? I did. Was that wrong? I didn't know he was in trouble. I cleaned the room for the next tenant."

"Can you tell me what you removed?"

"Well, he left behind that chrome table and chairs you saw in there.

I took out a floor lamp and a portable television set. It's a GE. And there were two metal poles in the closet. I took them down to storage. And there were some very nice polished boxes in the trash chute along with a lot of frozen food. I pulled the boxes out and didn't incinerate them. He had some stuff in storage, too. It's still there."

The agent asked Corbett's former landlady to take him to the basement. The agent inspected the items in a storage locker made of wooden slats and chicken wire marked 305. Behind the wire were two aluminum tent poles, a small black-and-white television set, a fan, a gasoline can, and a twelve-piece aluminum picnic set.

"Did you ever see a typewriter in his room?"

"Yes. I try to check my tenants' apartments every quarter to make sure they've not made a rat's nest out of them. I do remember seeing a typewriter. It sat on the kitchen table."

"Was it a portable or upright?"

"I can't remember. Might've been an upright. It was covered."

"See any guns in the room?"

"Oh, yes. They were in gun cases about the same size as Harry's rifle and shotgun."

"See any pistols?"

"No, I don't remember seeing a pistol."

After Agent Goodwin finished examining Corbett's storage space, he asked to see the trash chute and incinerator. Mrs. Merys showed the agent the boxes she'd pulled out of the chute but didn't incinerate. Goodwin was very pleased. They weren't boxes. They were polished black leather cases for four sets of handcuffs. *Monte Carlo* was engraved on the back of each case. She also showed Goodwin a Benjamin Moore five-gallon bucket full of metal chain her husband had found behind the apartment building.

While Agent Goodwin continued to interview Mrs. Merys, other agents began arriving. Corbett's apartment, the trash chute, the incinerator, the garbage bin out back, and the apartment's storage room were all dusted for prints. They ransacked the place, searching for store receipts, shell cartridges and casings, blood, paper, envelopes, used typewriter ribbons, stamps, maps, photographs, spent film, a diary, anything that might provide a clue. But the only piece of evidence retrieved was a single fingerprint on the Benjamin Moore paint bucket storing the metal chain. Corbett had done a thorough job wiping away all signs of his existence, with the help of a tidy landlady.

The agent ordered that the print be checked not only with driver's license records but with criminal records, too.

The tedious process of visually comparing thousands of fingerprints against those on the driver's license application of Walter Osborne and the bucket could take months. There were nearly 150 million prints on file in the FBI's national repository. Fortunately, it didn't take long. The FBI headquarters in Washington would discover a match in just three weeks.

CHAPTER 11

The signal was sent. On page 31 of Sunday's edition of *The Denver Post*, set to hit newsstands at 5:00 p.m. on Saturday, in the small-print classifieds devoted to farm implements, lay the tiny message, an ad without a telephone number:

> **JOHN DEERE. 1957 model 820, 69**
> **h.p. tractor for sale. King Ranch,**
> **Fort Lupton, Colo.**

At long last, Mary thought, *they'll call. Maybe they'll let me talk to Ad or at least hear his voice.* She'd been falling in and out of sleep brought on by sedatives all day. But starting at 5:00 p.m. sharp, Mary spent the hopeful evening in the den accompanied by cups of coffee, substituting cigarettes for sedatives as she anxiously awaited a telephone ring. Bill and Joe had joined her, all hoping the kidnappers would be anxious to initiate the exchange despite the bad weather.

Mary's friend Cecily Kendrick arrived around seven o'clock, bringing dinner with her. She and Mary talked late into the evening. It was nearing 10:30, and Cecily was about to leave when—

The telephone rang. FBI agents clicked on the recorder and contacted the Golden Telephone Company to trace the origin of the call. Mary leapt from her chair and stood beside the telephone. She glanced at the two agents, who gave her the thumbs-up signal.

"Hello," Mary said softly, looking at Bill and Joe.

"Is this Mrs. Coors, Mrs. Adolph Coors III?" asked a serious voice.

"Yes, it is."

"Don't say anything. Just listen. I've got your husband. Don't try to find him. Only I know where he's hidden, so if you ever want to see him again, you'll do what I say."

"Is he okay? Is he hurt? Can I talk to him?" Mary asked frantically.

"I said don't talk. . . . Your husband is fine, for now. So listen carefully. I want $60,000. Old bills. All twenties. Put the money in a briefcase and leave it on the back porch of the old sawmill a half mile outta town on Tuesday, midnight. Don't tell the coppers or else. Understand?"

"You say you want $60,000?"

"That's what I said. Used twenty-dollar bills."

"$60,000? But your letter said $500,000."

An agent stood and shook his head. There was a short pause.

"Hello?" said Mary.

"Sure I did. This is only the first installment. On second thought, forget the installments. Let's stick to the original plan. I want the full $500,000 put in a briefcase and left at the old sawmill. You have until Tuesday, midnight. No tricks."

There was a click, and the line hummed.

"Hello? Hello?" A perplexed Mary looked at the agents.

"I'm sorry, Mrs. Coors," said the agent, clicking off the recorder. "Just a piggyback kidnapper who learned about the kidnapping in the news. A con artist trying to extort money out of you. I'm sorry. We'll have to keep waiting for the real kidnappers to call."

Mary let out a scream. "How sick can someone be? What monsters! Don't they know Ad's life's at stake? Don't they know what we're going through?"

She began to cry and hurried toward her bedroom. Cecily followed. They'd been friends since childhood. Mary fell on the bed, crying longer and louder than she had since the first day. Cecily didn't try to stop her. She rubbed Mary's back and patted her, saying nothing until Mary rolled on her side and spoke.

"Ad's not coming back, Cecily. He's dead. I know it."

"You've got to believe Ad is out there right now and he's coming home. The telephone could ring any minute and you'll hear his voice, just like that."

"Oh, Cecily, that would be so wonderful."

There were no other calls that night.

Special Agent Werner was busy following his new lead, Walter Osborne, and relaying information of the case's progress to J. Edgar Hoover in Washington. Hoover told Werner to keep pressing, not to let up. Find Osborne. Though Hoover was overseeing cases involving international criminals and Soviet and Cuban intrigue, COORNAP was unquestionably the most important domestic case to the FBI director at that moment. And that was a problem for Werner. He had no idea who or where Osborne was.

February is the coldest month in Colorado, filled with knee-deep snowfalls, blistering winds, and treacherous roadways. A strenuous, grueling time for humans and livestock alike. A month in which the blue grama grass has turned pale and brown, amid everything colorless and dreary save the scattered mountain pines. A month indicative of Mary's present situation. Yet rare beams of sunlight broke through the ashen clouds that Sunday morning as six inches of snow continued falling. Mary opened her eyes to a room filled with light. The night had been a long vigil.

The alarm clock beside her bed read eleven o'clock. *Why should I get up? Just another day of waiting, worry, and anguish*, she thought. On the dresser, she noticed a small package wrapped in red paper and a white bow beside an envelope containing a card. It was Valentine's Day. Mary had planned to attend a Valentine's Day dinner with Ad at the Denver Club the night before. The club would be decorated with red and pink hearts and white streamers and other papier-mâché creations. A tiny bouquet of roses would be the centerpiece of each table, covered with red, white, and pink tablecloths. She and Ad would share some wine and toast to each other, their children, their health, and their future. They'd exchange cards whose printed words eloquently expressed each other's love and appreciation. And there would be gifts and intimacy. Mary opened her eyes and saw her gift for Ad on the dresser.

She thought about Valentine's, Ad, and even their wedding. It would be their twentieth wedding anniversary that fall. *What a grand day that was*, she thought.

"Miss Mary Urquhart Grant is engaged to be married to Adolph Coors III of Golden," *The Denver Post* declared in September 1940. "This announcement, made Monday, tops the season's news of socially important events, for it heralds the union of two outstanding families and has long been anticipated by Denver's most exclusive groups."

At twenty-five, Mary was a beauty. Her photo in *The Denver Post* announcing her engagement witnessed that fact.

"Of primary interest to the city's most prominent circles is the news that Miss Mary Urquhart Grant . . . one of the loveliest members of the exclusive younger set is betrothed to Adolph Coors III," read *The Post*. "A radiant personality and quiet charm are combined in Miss Grant to make her one of the most sought-after members of fashionable society. She reflects the aristocracy that has marked her family through its many generations of service to Colorado."

Mary had tucked those newspaper clippings safely away with her wedding photos and scrapbooks. She hadn't flipped through them in a long time, but could remember many of their words, words written by family that left her embarrassed at the time. She especially remembered the parties. "Prenuptial parties for Mary Grant and Adolph Coors to enliven the season," *The Post* heralded. There were endless bridal parties. Mary remembered all the fun she had at the many "beautifully appointed" breakfasts, buffet suppers, dinners, cocktail parties, and other "smart entertaining" for the betrothed couple hosted by family and friends at private residences and country clubs. How she loved them; but Ad, he would have preferred a picnic lunch on a butte far away.

Their wedding day was November 15, 1940. Marie Lewis from Baltimore was her matron of honor, and Ad's brother Bill was his best man. Her six bridesmaids were dressed in velveteen gowns in a soft shade of copper with empire-style hats to match. She could still see them vividly. They carried bouquets of yellow calla lilies down the aisle while ushered by Ad's close friends. Her father took her arm and stood waiting for the music to cue her march to the altar, where she could see that Ad was so nervous, hoping not to stutter "I do," but he'd never looked more handsome.

They'd spent their honeymoon in sunny Bermuda, unable to go to Europe because of World War II. But Mary didn't mind. She was with her loving husband.

Mary raised her head from the pillow. Ad's bluetick hound was barking. Mary decided she should try to get out of bed. She was visiting the kids later for brunch to celebrate Valentine's Day at the big house. She slowly arose from her bedroom and entered the kitchen when she heard the side door open from the carport.

"Ready for some breakfast, dear?" asked Mary. She stopped short as soon as the words came out. Her mind was groggy, and for an instant, she thought Ad was coming in from the barn like he often did on Sunday mornings while the kids were at church. Instead, it was one of the agents stepping inside after a smoke.

"I'm so sorry," Mary said.

"Please, don't apologize. It was a rough night for everybody."

At noon, Mary drove over to the big house, where her children were staying with their grandparents. Two agents followed her in their unmarked sedan.

"Mama!" the kids shouted as she entered the big house. They hadn't seen their mother since Thursday. One by one, they handed Mary their valentines, some homemade with crayons and glitter, others store bought. They also gave her a box of chocolates and a single rose. Her eyes watered.

"We have cards for Daddy, too," said Jim.

Mary wiped away some determined tears with the back of her hand and stood. "When I get home, I'll set your cards on the mantel so they're the first thing your father sees when he gets back, okay?"

"Good idea."

"When is Daddy coming back?" asked Jim.

Spike elbowed him.

"Soon, sweetheart, very soon," said Mary. "I hope."

After lunch with Ad's parents and some other family members who'd dropped by, it was time for Mary to return to the ranch. It was not wise to stay away for long. The kidnappers might attempt to make contact. She hugged her children, who escorted her to the door with her valentines, chocolates, and rose. It was a sad parting.

Mary had not been home long when there was a knock. An agent, with his hand gripping a pistol strapped to his hip, opened the door. A deputy stood beside a man Mary didn't recognize.

"Delivery, ma'am. I was told to extend the store's apologies. Supposed to be delivered yesterday. Please sign here."

Mary stepped outside to sign for it. She entered the house carrying a dozen roses and a small box marked with a Cherry Creek jewelry store label. Agents had checked the delivery on the front steps. They stayed outside.

Mary read the card on the flowers:

> *Happy Valentine's Day sweetheart!*
> *You are and always will be my Valentine.*
> *Love forever, Ad*

On the night of February 17, eight days after the kidnapping, Corbett parked his car in a municipal garbage dump outside Atlantic City, New Jersey. He removed the license plate and stuck it in his travel bag. He then lifted a gasoline can from the trunk and poured its combustible contents across the front and rear seats of the car he'd driven 1,800 miles from Denver without detection. When the gas can was empty, he tossed it inside, lit a match, and ran. The windows of the car exploded, and a plume of black smoke rolled up into the orange-lit sky.

Corbett scampered for the cover of trees and tall spartina grass, escaping into the darkness, confident he'd erased all evidence inside the vehicle and all connection to him. Within a few minutes, the car would be nothing more than a burned-out hull.

He was a long way from home, pleased but also frustrated as his $400 car went up in flames leaving him on foot. Only twenty minutes from the famous Atlantic City Boardwalk, he cut through the pines along a path worn in grass-covered sand till he hit asphalt. Soon, Corbett was strolling along the brightly lit beach among throngs of people out on the warmer-than-usual evening. None would have surmised that the tall, thin man had torched his vehicle and was about to head out of town on US Highway 30 with only a few belongings and dwindling funds.

Before the flames reached their zenith, a man spotted the fiery automobile. The Atlantic City Fire Department arrived at 9:30. Within minutes, the firemen doused the inferno to a smolder. Those on the scene radioed for an inspection team to canvass the burned automobile. Battalion Chief James Evans soon arrived, as did two Atlantic City policemen, Charles Callender and Wilbur Johnson, to inspect the charred automobile.

"It's a Mercury four-door sedan," an officer told the battalion chief. "Early '50s model, maybe a '51 or '52. Pale yellow. No human remains inside." Though scalded, with only metal framing and cushion springs remaining inside, some of the paint remained visible along the front and rear of the car and its fenders. What was left of a spare tire filled the crumbling trunk.

The battalion chief wiped away the soot and located the car's serial number imprinted on the warm Mercury's body frame. "Write this down," he said, shining a flashlight. "51 LA 38766 M."

Police sent the serial number over the teletype and learned it was registered in the state of Colorado to Walter Osborne. He had no criminal record, but was wanted for questioning in connection with a kidnapping. The Atlantic City police contacted the Newark FBI field office to take possession of the blistered vehicle. A second inspection by the FBI confirmed the car was registered to Walter Osborne, the same man whose fingerprint had been lifted from a paint bucket in a Denver apartment.

Corbett thought he was being smart in his attempt to erase all evidence from his car, but all he had done was draw attention to his location on the East Coast. He'd even failed to eliminate all the evidence because the FBI still located something extremely valuable. It was as plain as dirt.

CHAPTER 12

The Denver Post reported on Friday, February 19, "The Coors family remained in seclusion Thursday while presumed negotiations went on for the release of Adolph Coors III."

When reporters asked Sheriff Wermuth how close they were to obtaining Ad's release, he said with annoyance, "I don't know anything about the progress of ransom negotiations. I haven't had any contact with the Coors family since I withdrew my officers a week ago."

Mary's brother, Jim, read the *Post* article to Mary, who'd quit reading newspapers and watching television news. She only *wished* negotiations were progressing.

Mary had heard nothing from the kidnappers. It had been ten days. Ten excruciatingly worrisome days. She'd been told that typically contact is made and the victim released within one to three weeks. *There's still time, but what could have happened?* Mary asked herself. The days kept passing without word from Ad or the kidnappers.

The thick-skinned Bill described the family's emotional battle in a courtroom months later. "We spent a lot of time mentally and emotionally conditioning ourselves for the worst."

Mary's conditioning, however, had failed dreadfully. Her mind focused on Ad every second of every day. By the end of each day, she was hollowed out and deeply depressed, yet sleep came with difficulty and then only if brought about by sedatives. She paced about, a prisoner in her own house, obsessing about the kidnapping. Her stomach was continually queasy, causing a loss of appetite. Worse, she increasingly found herself with a drink in her hand, needing alcohol and sedatives to make it through each day. She knew if she didn't hear from the kidnappers soon, Ad had to be dead. The evidence pointed to that conclusion. She didn't wish to face it, but there was the blood and no trace of Ad anywhere despite teams searching on the ground and in the air.

Prank calls had disturbed her sleep the night before, sleep that was difficult to attain, especially when awakened in the middle of the night. When sleep did come, she would be tormented by dreams both good and bad. But her tortured nights would not end soon. There'd be more than fifty ransom letters and telephone calls to come (intermingled with cards and letters from well-wishers). All were intercepted and read by the FBI.

More hoaxes came that day. *Rocky Mountain News* received and published a handwritten ransom note from a prankster presumably intended for Ad's parents:

> If you expect to see your boy alive do exactly like I tell you. Go to the Denver U.S. National Bank and deposit $1 million dollars to Paul A. Loveless and give book to Board of Directors. Then have President make it all into U.S. Savings Bonds with Paul A. Loveless name on each. To prove you have done this Tues nite at six o'clock you and President will meet on TV 9 and you will resight Humpty Dumpty and President will resight Little Bo Peep. President will put bonds in safety boxs at his bank and wear the keys around his neck at all times. You got nothing to loose. You got everything to loose.

Other fake demands were short like, "Put $50,000 in a suitcase. Wait for contact. Son is O.K. Be smart." Others were long ramblings. Most contained misspellings. Mary didn't have to read the letters because the FBI appropriated them at the post office. The FBI knew it already had the genuine ransom note, but still looked out for a follow-up note from the real kidnappers.

The phone calls were what tortured Mary. Day and night, prank or piggyback kidnappers called. If she was asleep, she was awakened. Friends and family were told not to call, so all calls made to the residence were treated as from the real kidnappers. And Mary had to speak to each one.

On Saturday, the twentieth, the FBI and the Coors family met with Special Agent Hostetter to receive an update on the investigation and to consider what could be done to encourage the kidnappers to make contact. Comments from everyone bounced about the room.

"If half a million dollars won't bring 'em out in the open, I don't know what the hell will," said Mr. Coors. "The boy's dead. Gotta be."

"Don't say that, Father. It's not the money. It's the fear of getting caught," Joe said.

"Perhaps we should offer a reward," suggested Bill.

"I wouldn't recommend that," said Hostetter. "It only brings the nuts out of the woodwork, taking up agent time chasing down false leads. We're not to that point yet. Let's put that off a while."

"It doesn't matter. Ad's dead," said Mary, who stood and walked to the kitchen window as if in a trance.

Mr. Coors slapped his thigh and nodded in agreement. Bill thought the situation was bleak indeed when his father and Mary agreed on anything. He believed his brother was dead, too. Everybody did. Yet there lingered a sliver of hope. And Mary didn't really believe her callous remark. She simply was angry and exhausted.

The sheriff and deputies had already been called off the case to make the kidnappers less wary. Mary wanted to go further. She wanted the FBI agents to go, too.

"I know it seems bleak, Mrs. Coors," said Hostetter, "but it's possible the kidnappers are simply extremely cautious. So why don't we try this: What if we release a statement to reporters that our agency has withdrawn from the case even though we really haven't?

The kidnappers won't know the difference. They're reading the newspapers like everyone else. Would you be okay with that, Mrs. Coors?"

In actuality, Hostetter was propounding a suggestion merely to appease Mary. Though he hoped he was wrong, he believed Ad was dead, too. No other reason for the blood and the delay made sense. Besides, he now had a suspect, Walter Osborne, who'd left town two weeks earlier, and it was doubtful he was taking Ad on a cross-country tour. But in Mary's house that day, Hostetter kept those dark notions to himself.

The Denver office of thirty FBI agents covering Wyoming and Colorado fought crime on three fronts as March 1960 neared. Bank robberies, bombings, fugitives, kidnappings, public corruption, espionage, and organized crime required investigating as usual. The unexpected kidnapping of Ad Coors required so many agents that J. Edgar Hoover sent additional men to Denver to handle the investigation. And consuming a great deal of fruitless effort were the extortionists—ransom notes and phone calls demanding money for Ad's safe return from persons who knew nothing of Ad's kidnapping other than what was reported in newspapers and on radio and television.

Letters poured in from all over the country: Pennsylvania, Ohio, Indiana, Texas, and, of course, Colorado. To the FBI, it didn't matter the sender's true intention or how little money was asked. Under the Hobbs Act, it is a federal crime to wrongfully employ the US mail to use fear of physical injury to any person to induce the victim's consent to give up money.

To assist the FBI, Mr. Coors, Mary, Bill, and Joe had signed authorizations for any post office receiving suspicious mail addressed to a Coors to be turned over to the FBI for analysis. Every letter mailed and every call made to the Coors family exacting a ransom were investigated. Most were quickly determined fraudulent and investigated as separate cases apart from the Coors kidnapping to gather evidence that would support federal extortion charges.

An example of the tenacity of the FBI came in the form of an investigation into a ransom note, postmarked at 1:30 p.m. on February 11 in Boulder, Colorado. The letter read:

The letter inside read:

> TO WHOM IT MAY CONCERN:
> WE WANT $8,000 BY
> THE 15TH OF FEB. TAKE IT TO THE INDIAN
> GRILL AT U OF C MEMORIAL CENTER.
> PUT IT IN A BRIEF CASE AND LEAVE IT BY THE
> CAST DOOR.
> DO NOT TELL THE COPS OR ELSE.

It didn't matter that the ransom was a measly $8,000 (about $65,000 today). The letter and envelope were sent to the FBI Laboratory in Washington, and a report was generated and sent to the FBI field office in Denver, detailing: the paper and envelope; they were made by the Western Tablet and Stationery Corporation in St. Joseph, Missouri and could be purchased in the University of Colorado bookstore; the print was uppercase block stenciled with a ruler of a type used by engineering students; owing to the nature of the printing, it was doubtful it could be matched with known handwriting samples; and five latent fingerprints of value were developed and processed through the single fingerprint file without effecting an identification.

The FBI spoke with the Boulder Police Department, the sheriff of Boulder County, and university security, but none had any suspects in mind, and all believed that whoever sent the note was a student pulling a prank and had no intention of collecting the money, only wanting to watch the drop-off spot simply for a thrill perhaps.

Agents appeared at the university campus and observed the Indian Grill, the location of its doorways, and its proximity to dormitories, postal drop-offs, and the area by the "cast door" designated as the drop site.

The agents interviewed the university psychiatrist, administrative staff, and faculty. Most agreed they knew of no suspects and the letter most likely was a student hoax. There were some, however, who identified particular students who'd sent angry or vile letters to faculty or staff in the past and others who were known troublemakers. The agents interviewed them all, even those who'd dropped out of school living as far away as Philadelphia. None turned out to be the mailer of the extortion letter.

"Youth must have respect for authority," said one special agent, "and for the victim's family. What he or she may think is merely a joke is actually impeding our kidnapping investigation, costing the American taxpayers, and worst of all, causing the Coors family more suffering. Our agency believes that the student should go before a federal judge and let him decide what to do with this so-called prankster."

The FBI would spend an entire year investigating what by all accounts was a prank letter from a college student asking for $8,000 he had no intention of collecting. The case was finally closed in March 1961.

Some notes seemed possibly related and were investigated as further contact from the real kidnappers. A note might be received stating, "We are ready to turn your son over," and provide instructions on delivering the $500,000 asked for in the genuine ransom letter. Upon analysis by the FBI Laboratory, those that contained "some significant similarities" were investigated, but none were ultimately found to have anything to do with Ad's kidnapping. All were discovered to be nothing more than extortion letters and treated as separate criminal cases.

Still, the FBI did have someone they wanted to question, and he was becoming more of a solid suspect: Walter Osborne. There was only one hitch. The FBI couldn't find him. Not a trace. Agents on the East Coast checked pawnshops and entered bars on snowy and rainy days and nights, but no Osborne. Banks and hospitals were alerted to be on the lookout for him, as were gun shops, optometrists, barbershops, and used car dealers. Since Osborne's burned Mercury was discovered near major port cities, the FBI feared he may have hopped a merchant ship headed for some faraway port like Singapore or Buenos Aires. Maybe he'd crossed into Canada or south into Mexico or the Caribbean. But while agents kept running into dead ends searching for Osborne, they were about to receive evidence that would break the case wide open.

On Monday the twenty-second, two weeks after Ad's disappearance, the Coors children returned to school and to their home. Like Mary, they'd been having a terrible time—worried, upset, crying, waiting for word about their father.

The children were escorted to school by armed guards provided by the Coors plant. While in class and at recess, the guards positioned themselves at all exterior doors and on the playground. It may have seemed to Goldenites that the Coors children were as closely guarded as President Eisenhower. The boys didn't play sports—no spring baseball. The girls didn't go out. None would join their father as a kidnap victim, that was for certain.

FBI QUITS COORS CASE FOR TIME TO AID CONTACT, read *The Denver Post* headline on the same Monday that the Coors children returned to school. Mary released a statement to the press later that afternoon:

> My family and I are anxiously awaiting word of my husband, Ad. I have asked all law enforcement authorities to withdraw from active participation in this case, which they have done. By this action, we are giving assurance that no effort will be made to interfere with attempts to communicate with us. We are ready to pay for my husband's safe return. I thank the people, the press, television, and radio for the kindness and understanding they have shown during the past several days.

The statement was prepared by the Coors publicist at the suggestion of the FBI, but the FBI's only suspect, Walter Osborne, didn't read it. He was more than 1,500 miles away.

Stomping snow from his feet, Corbett entered a boardinghouse at 47 Keele Street in Toronto's west downtown area. He walked upstairs to the second floor and unlocked the door to his room. Once inside, Corbett kept on his coat, gloves, and hat. It was cold, very cold. Though water and electricity were provided as part of his rent, he'd chosen not to connect the gas service. He had the money. He'd recently gotten a decent-paying job as a lab technician on Queens Quay West at the Inner Harbour, a trade he'd learned in prison and in which he'd gained a high level of skill. Yet the gas company required background information and references. He'd given the name Walter Osborne and a phony address and fictitious references to employers, but he couldn't give a phony address to the gas company. So he lived without gas heat in a city where subzero temperatures in February were common. His only means of warmth were a coat and an electric space heater he kept next to his chair and bed.

He also no longer owned a television set or an automobile. He kept up with the news with a small transistor radio, used newspapers from a café down the block, and a television sitting behind a local bar counter. Though he'd hocked most of his belongings, he still possessed his Llama 9 mm pistol, which he always kept near.

But with March approaching, Corbett believed things were looking up. Toronto was nice and quiet. It had recently completed a subway, allowing him to move around the city without an automobile. He'd located a clean room, a good job, and a metropolitan area of almost two million people among whom he could vanish. When he wasn't working, he took hikes, stopping in parks to read the comics in the local newspaper, laughing at their silliness. He boated on Lake Ontario, took in a hockey game, and even went target shooting on warmer days, as he'd done around Denver. With spring

around the corner, he was looking forward to fishing and more target shooting and minor-league baseball. He had no family, no
friends, and no female or male companions, but he didn't mind so
much. He'd lived in solitude most of his adult life and preferred it
that way.

"No comment," one agent told a reporter who'd asked the FBI
about its suspect's lifestyle while running from the law. "I will say it
is not a pleasant feeling for a criminal to know that he is the object
of a widespread and intensive search. Constant fear of recognition
and a necessity for keeping on the move are simply not good for the
nerves."

Corbett's nerves were just fine. So confident and comfortable was
he that he had not changed his alias of Walter Osborne or his appearance. He'd moved into the boardinghouse on February 21, just
days after Ad Coors's disappearance, and signed the lease under the
name Walter Osborne. He'd evaded the FBI and the state and local
police without really trying that much. And even if incarcerated,
he'd busted out of prison once before, and no one had caught up with
him for five years.

Perhaps Corbett recalled his escape from Chino while holed up in
Toronto. Perhaps it gave him solace when his confidence began to
ebb, if it ever did. For on August 1, 1955, after lights out at Chino,
Corbett tucked his California prison-issue shoes under one arm and
released the latch from the steel door that led into the prison laundry.
Inside, he tossed dirty linen from a cart and uncovered a pressed shirt
and slacks and polished dress shoes. He changed and stuffed his
prison garb deep in the cart's bottom.

Corbett also may have remembered how he slid through the open
ground-floor window with a small bag of belongings. How he
crouched in the darkness beside building 7, cloaked from the watch-
ful light cast on the prison yard, and then advanced slowly along the
wall that guided him past the prison dairy, mindful to stay clear of
the lights.

At the north fence, he unrolled a soiled rug from the laundry and tossed it over strands of barbed wire along the top of a chain-link fence. Chino had no twisted razor wire, no sentry towers manned with guns, no uniformed men gripping billy clubs. Guards were called supervisors, and the warden was the superintendent, in the considerate nomenclature of the state's progressive correctional system. Chino was a minimum-security prison—part of California's recent legislative effort of "moral rehabilitation and restoration to good citizenship."

Corbett may have recalled how he climbed the fence and stretched his torso across the rug and how he pulled himself over the fenced perimeter and sprinted into the shadows of thick brush, taking care not to snap branches that might later reveal the path of his departure. Beyond the glow of the prison lights, he reached an open pasture and scampered toward the hills. Dangers lay ahead, like deep ravines, thorns that could rip off a sleeve, and coyotes and mountain lions. Though the night was quiet, Corbett looked back one final time for searchlights or other signs his escape had been detected.

But Chino was still dark, and the dark was still.

Ontario, California, lay seven miles away. Growing tired of managing the rocks and furrows, Corbett decided to take his chances on the paved road. He removed his prison shoes and tossed them in a ditch, replacing them with the polished dress shoes that had been dangling around his neck.

He made his way toward the dimly lit town, continually turning to glance behind him. Once in Ontario, he located the bus station. It was nearing midnight when he stepped inside and canvassed the handful of patrons. No law enforcement. The coast was clear. He slipped into the men's bathroom, brushed dust and burrs stuck to his clothing, washed his hands and face, wiped his eyeglasses, and combed his brilliantined hair.

"Yeah, that's him," a ticket agent told a San Bernardino County deputy, pointing at a photograph of Corbett. "Came in last night. No baggage. Let me see . . . here it is. Says he caught the 12:20 to Los Angeles."

The ticket master was right. By one o'clock, Corbett was sitting near the rear of a darkened bus. Prison officials would be surprised when the sun came up.

"Corbett! Joe Corbett!" broke the morning stillness. A supervisor shouted the name again when Prisoner A-17293 failed to acknowledge his presence. He wasn't in the infirmary. A quick search of his cell revealed that some of his personal items were gone. When guards went to the laundry to see if he was already at work, a screen missing from an open window told them he'd escaped. A prison-wide alarm rang out. Supervisors mounted horses to scour the vast 2,600 acres surrounding the prison. Superintendent Kenyon J. Scudder telephoned the state police, sheriffs, and police chiefs at nearby Pomona, Ontario, Diamond Bar, and Corona. Others telephoned bus and train stations and taxicab companies. Radio, television, and newspaper offices were alerted, followed by wires of the fugitive's photo and description:

> White male; 26 years of age; 6'2," 170 pounds; medium
> build; brown hair; hazel eyes; fair complexion; wears brown
> horn-rimmed eyeglasses; mole under chin; line scar on right
> side of abdomen; wears heavy gold ring with plain round red
> stone; approach with caution.

Corbett's scheme had worked. He'd originally been sent to San Quentin, where a breakout was impossible. He knew a transfer to the minimum-security prison at Chino was his only way to escape.

The fugitive's sixty-year-old father was in disbelief, later telling a reporter, "My wife and I visited him Sunday. He told me he had hopes he would be paroled shortly and would return to Seattle and go back to school and lead a normal life. The next day, when I got home, I got a call from the warden at Chino that Joe had walked away. We haven't heard from him since."

Reaching Los Angeles, Corbett easily evaporated among five

million residents. He sought shelter for a few weeks with the Salvation Army, an "army" of Christian faithful who wished to help the wicked and destitute find repentance and inspiration. Corbett quickly wore out his welcome. He located a hotel in a run-down section of the city that rented by the hour, or for those of more ambitious intentions, the week. Days later, Corbett moved into a rooming house using a fictitious name. Although he needed money, he wasn't about to contact anyone, particularly his father, who would attempt to convince his fugitive son to capitulate and, when he didn't, might notify authorities where they could locate him.

Holing up in a flophouse, he found work at a factory storehouse, loading and unloading wooden crates. Not long afterward, he moved on and found office work at Adams Rite Manufacturing Company.

Soon Corbett left Los Angeles and moved into a slightly more respectable boardinghouse in Glendale and worked as a clerk in a hardware company, mailing invoices and filing records. He did his job quietly, refusing to mingle with coworkers until one day he vanished without a word.

"A fellow con told me about Colorado," Corbett would tell a reporter many years later. "So when I escaped, I thought, 'Heck, I'll go to Denver.'"

His inmate record card chronicled a new entry: 8-1-1955 ESCAPED. Of 250 escapees from Chino, all but ten had been apprehended, and after five years, Corbett was still one of those ten. If discovered in Toronto, he wouldn't be returned to Chino. He'd be sent to a California maximum-security prison like San Quentin or Folsom with no parole in sight . . . or he'd be imprisoned in Colorado for what he did at Turkey Creek, or worse, sent to the gas chamber if Ad was dead.

Perhaps Corbett didn't want to remember prison, after all. If caught, there'd be no escape for him a second time.

"This meeting of the board of directors of Adolph Coors Company is hereby called to order," announced Mr. Coors. He hadn't spoken those words in years. They'd been reserved for his eldest son and chairman, whose chair now stood empty.

Mr. Coors sat at the head of a large table inside the boardroom decorated plainly with Coors memorabilia. The lavish décor of mahogany-paneled walls and gilded carvings of many corporate boardrooms wasn't the Coors style. Like the brothers' shared office, the walls were lined with gray tiles made at Coors Porcelain, dotted with framed scenes of mountains and beer bottles and cans.

The elder Coors had first sat as chairman of the board in 1929 after his father jumped to his death from a hotel window. He last sat there in 1952, when he gave up the chairmanship to his eldest son and namesake, Adolph Herman Joseph Coors III. After Ad's retirement one day, Mr. Coors expected Spike to take over as chairman, and then Spike's future son, Adolph Herman Joseph Coors V, would do the same. But with each passing day in March 1960, it seemed to the old man that the Coors' family tradition might at last be broken.

After a few words about his son Ad, akin to a eulogy, Mr. Coors proceeded to the business at hand. "The president has the floor," Mr. Coors directed in accord with parliamentary procedure. "Bill?"

Bill discussed brewery business that included upcoming quarterly revenues, gas line extensions, and the soaring aluminum can business. He passed the floor back and forth to the treasurer and secretary, not once mentioning his missing brother other than to talk about those who'd assumed some of Ad's duties.

Though Bill was president of the company and was older than both Ad and Mr. Coors had been when they took over as chairman of the board, Bill would not be chairman for now. Mr. Coors reclaimed the chairmanship to hold Ad's seat for as long as it took.

As board members filed from the room after the meeting, Mr. Coors stopped and nodded for Bill and Joe to follow him. They walked into Mr. Coors's office, where he sat in the only chair. His sons stood.

"Our distributors are grumbling. Say the costs of cooling their warehouses and buying refrigerated trucks are hurting their bottom lines. And the retailers are mad about having to keep our beer in drink boxes. You sure about this cold filtering, Bill?"

"To hell with the distributors," Bill said. "Last I saw, they were making money hand over fist."

Mary felt that beer wasn't the only thing cold at the brewery. It bothered her that Ad's father and brothers continued working every day as if nothing had happened. She felt the plant should have shut down, at least for one day. They seemed more concerned with making sure Ad's responsibilities were covered than with the fact that Ad was still missing. But that wasn't true. That was simply the Coors way. Emotions took a back seat to duty.

Still, Mary could sense a wall rising, cutting her children off from the company and the rest of the Coors family. While Bill and Joe went to work and came home and talked to their wives, she had become isolated. No one talked with her about the Coors business or her children's future roles. She and the kids were secluded on their big ranch, miles and minds away from the rest of the family.

To make matters worse, Mary's brother, Jim, returned to his law practice in New York after comforting her for two weeks, missing Mary's birthday on the twenty-eighth of February, which passed almost without notice. Though separated by distance, Jim followed up with the FBI and sheriff's office regularly and maintained daily contact with Mary.

She voiced her concern with her brother. "If Ad doesn't come back, I'm afraid Spike and Jim will lose their rightful places at the brewery. Spike is fourteen, and Jim is only ten years old. By the time they're out of college or graduate school, somebody else will be running the company, like one of Joe's sons."

Bill's only son had died at fourteen months from choking on a chicken bone. He and Geraldine had three daughters, Geraldine (Missy), Margaret, and May Louise, but a woman running Coors was out of the question. (Bill would later have a son with his second wife, Phyllis Mahaffey, his former secretary.) Joe hit the jackpot in the male successor department with no daughters and five sons. Joe Jr. was already eighteen years old.

"You can't worry about that now," Jim said. "They'll have a place in the company. After all, Spike's name is Adolph Herman Joseph Coors IV."

But Mary was worried. She knew Mr. Coors and his dislike for her. If Ad didn't come back, her children might no longer have a birthright.

An agent in a white starched shirt and black tie strained his neck peering into a large magnifying glass affixed to a long rod. Through the lens, each of the fingerprints on file had their own stories to tell. He and other agents in the latent fingerprint section of the FBI Laboratory in Washington had been at this case for weeks. But this time, the agent withdrew a smaller lens and examined the prints again. He studied the subject print and then the comparison print. Unlike thousands of others checked previously, these two prints matched.

He stood and hurried down the hallway carrying two sheets of paper into the office of his supervisor.

"I got a match in the COORNAP case," said Agent Sebastian Latona.

Minutes later in Denver, another young agent hurried down another hallway's polished floor.

"Come in," said Special Agent Werner, hearing a knock.

"Washington says they have a match in the COORNAP case, sir," said the young agent. He handed the facsimiles to Werner, dressed in his oft-worn dark blue suit.

Werner read the memorandum dated March 5, setting out the lab's analysis of the prints. Opening a desk drawer, he removed a small lens from a leather case and placed it atop an opaque page. He scanned the one print and then the other, paying particular attention to the matching points delineated by arrows from the FBI Lab. He raised his head and smiled.

"He's the man, isn't he, sir?" the young agent said and grinned back.

The suspect revealed by the print comparison made sense now. Werner reached across his desk, opened a small wooden box, and removed a cigar. He pulled out an old lighter from the middle drawer of his desk and lit the cigar, puffing with satisfaction.

"This son of a bitch may've got the jump on us, but it's a long race, and like every two-bit criminal who thinks he's got it all figured out, he never will get away, and you know why that is, Agent?"

The young agent hesitated and then answered, "The FBI, sir?"

"You're damn right the FBI. Now get me the district attorney's office on the line, and let's catch this no-good son of a bitch."

What the agent in the FBI Lab had discovered was that the print on an application for a Colorado driver's license and another print affixed to a bucket outside a Denver apartment belonged to Walter Osborne, the man in the apartment who'd left Denver the morning after Ad Coors's disappearance and whose yellow Mercury was observed burning in Atlantic City. The problem was Walter Osborne seemed to have no family, no past. He was nothing more than a vapor, a mist hanging above Denver that drifted away the morning after Ad Coors's disappearance.

This lab report, though, cleared the mist and shone light on his true history. That was the reason the Washington agent hurried the prints to his supervisor. Not only did the prints belong to Walter Osborne, a man with no criminal record and little history, they also matched the alias's owner—Joseph R. Corbett Jr., convicted murderer and California state prison fugitive A-17293.

CHAPTER 13

Joe Corbett was now the strongest suspect, but the FBI believed he might have a confederate. After all, the ransom note did say "kidnapers" (the common spelling in 1960), and Corbett had sometimes been seen with another man in his car.

Arthur C. Brynaert was a twenty-five-year-old, five-foot-eight, 145-pound, brown-haired man with a shady past. Though young, he'd already amassed an arrest record that included felony warrants for passing bad checks and vagrancy. He'd also deserted his wife and three children just a year earlier and was heavily in debt to several loan companies. But that didn't interest the FBI.

The down-on-his-luck Brynaert had ascended to the top of the FBI's suspect list principally because he'd worked with Corbett each night at Benjamin Moore & Co. In fact, they had been the only two in the entire plant during the night shift. Not only had they been coworkers, they had been drinking buddies, frequently going out after work. But the most interesting fact (among all facts concerning Brynaert set out in the FBI's investigation report) was that on February 16, 1960, one week after Ad Coors's disappearance, Brynaert quit his job at Benjamin Moore and went into hiding for three days. Then Brynaert and his new wife and baby caught a 2:45 a.m. Greyhound bus to Omaha, Nebraska. The FBI understandably viewed his movements as suspicious. His car, a 1946 Chevrolet, resembling a Dodge that had been spotted near Ad Coors's house and Turkey Creek Bridge, had also disappeared.

The FBI caught up with Brynaert and his new family in Omaha on March 17. Brynaert was at work at the Peter Pan Market when agents interviewed his wife, Frances, at their residence in the Chief Hotel.

"What kind of car does your husband drive?"

"He did drive a 1946 four-door Chevrolet that he bought back in January."

"Where is it now?"

"I don't know. Art said it blew up and wouldn't run."

"When was the last time you saw it?"

"Let me think back. It would have been on Monday, the fifteenth of February, the day after Valentine's. He called me the next day and told me it'd blown up on 'im."

"Would your husband have loaned it to anyone?"

"I don't know if he did, but he would, I think, if somebody needed it."

"Did you notice anything unusual about the car the last few times you saw it, like was it muddy, did it have stains on the seats, an unusual odor, anything?"

"No, I didn't."

"Can you account for your husband's whereabouts after the fifteenth?"

"No, 'cause he was hiding out from collectors, especially the Liberty Loan Company that was looking for him. They came by once, so he left home."

Brynaert's wife went on to explain how her husband frequently gambled his Benjamin Moore paycheck away, which caused them to fall behind in their payments to various finance companies. He'd also written two bad checks in February and was behind on the rent. They'd skipped out on their Denver landlord in the middle of the night when they absconded to Omaha.

"Did your husband ever mention Adolph Coors III or anything about the Coorses?"

"Just that he thought the Coors man probably had run off with a woman or something like that."

The FBI also interviewed Brynaert that March and again in April. He didn't try to run and was cooperative. His car checked out to be just as his wife had described—no longer running. Most exonerating was that Brynaert was given a lie detector test and passed. So despite the suspicious circumstances, he was no longer considered a suspect but a witness, someone who could tell them all he knew about Corbett and his whereabouts. Brynaert provided plenty of information about Corbett's habits, his guns, and his talk of pulling a big job. But unfortunately for the FBI, Brynaert had no idea where Corbett might be.

Agents stood around the burned hulk of the yellow '51 Mercury of Walter Osborne—or more correctly, Joe Corbett Jr.—at a garage in Atlantic City as soil, rock, and paint samples were scraped from the undercarriage and fenders.

"Careful! Make sure it goes in the bags!" shouted FBI Agent Emanuel Johnson of the Newark field office. "Check under the bumpers, too!"

Samples were coded and placed in marked cardboard boxes for shipment to the FBI Laboratory in Washington, D.C.

In Colorado, Agent Doug Williams and other agents scoured the countryside taking what they called "alibi soil samples." Areas around Denver, Turkey Creek Bridge, Pikes Peak, and the Dakota Hogback near Ad's house in Morrison were visited, and scoops of soil were collected and placed in marked containers. Another example of the thoroughness of the FBI. A total of 457 samples were collected, plus several others from Atlantic City, along with a cross section of earth and debris attached to the undercarriage of the burned car, and were delivered to the FBI Laboratory. The lab's initial response: "Please don't send us any more samples."

Soil scientist Richard W. Flach was the chief forensic geologist for the FBI. Flach had assisted establishing the forensic geology unit within the FBI Laboratory years earlier.

The chemistry and geology sections of the FBI Lab began their tedious work. Color, texture, and mineral deposits were analyzed with microscopes, chemicals, and other modern processes, such as spectrographic analysis, identifying four distinct layers beneath the charred yellow Mercury. The outermost layer consisted of sands, silts, paper fibers, cinders, glass wools, and black slags that generally were rounded and marine, exhibiting the characteristics of that located around Atlantic City. The next layer was embedded with pink feldspar, sharp and fresh, peak granite, the light-gray quartzose sands of the Dakota Hogback and the varicolored sandstones, limes, and clays of the lower and upper levels of Pikes Peak, where Ad possibly had been taken. The next layer contained the usual mineral characteristics indigenous to Morrison and the Coors ranch. The innermost layer was unremarkable, just deposits from the general Rocky Mountain area. Interesting, however, was a sprinkling of yellow paint and asphalt between the Pikes Peak and Atlantic City layers. The yellow paint matched that used by the Colorado Highway Department. The undisturbed particles of asphalt suggested a long highway drive. Little had Corbett known he'd been writing his itinerary on his car's undercarriage and the FBI geologist in Washington, D.C., was its reader. That chapter must not have been in Corbett's copy of *The FBI Story*.

Ten days later, the FBI placed Corbett on its Ten Most Wanted List distributed nationwide and in bordering Mexico and Canada. He was the 127th criminal to make the list. The Ten Most Wanted List changed the game for any criminal on the run, including Corbett, who was designated as FBI No. 605 861 A. His aliases were listed as Walter Osborne, William Chiffins, William Osborn, Charles Osborn, James Barron, and W. William Osborne. Aliases not listed included Michael Dean Brent, Ian Bolme, Michael MacLean, Ian N. McIntosh, and Thomas C. Wainwright.

When asked by reporters, who'd noticed the recent interest, if Corbett was a suspect in Ad Coors's kidnapping, FBI agents answered, "No comment."

The official crime listed was "unlawful interstate flight to avoid confinement after conviction for murder," referring to his escape from Chino that California law enforcement had left unsolved nearly five years earlier. The unofficial "crime" not listed was being the only suspect in the Coors kidnapping.

The first batches of 1.5 million "Wanted by FBI" flyers were immediately posted by law enforcement in post offices, train and bus stations, at YMCAs and Salvation Army mission homes, and in business establishments around the country that Corbett might visit looking for a job or to pawn property.

J. Edgar Hoover also made a statement:

> Mankind knows no crime as base and vicious as kidnapping. It is an offense all the more savage because it pits brute force against the innocent, the unsuspecting, the helpless. . . .
>
> The [Ten Most Wanted] program continues to represent an extremely effective weapon of attack against the criminal element. Since the institution of the program in 1950, a total of 114 criminal fugitives have been apprehended, forty-five as a direct result of information provided by alert citizens who recognize the fugitive from publicity concerning them. . . .
>
> Joseph R. Corbett Jr. is now on that list. He is the most wanted man since John Dillinger. Escape is impossible. He *will* be apprehended.

After the list's release, people began spotting Corbett everywhere: Denver, Las Vegas, Reno, Hot Springs, Wichita, South Dakota, Wyoming, Nebraska, Texas, California, Mexico, and even Australia. The ubiquitous Corbett was in none of those places. He was discreetly living and working in Toronto.

The average criminal thinks he can outsmart the FBI, but he is apprehended 178 days after hitting the Ten Most Wanted List, according to Hoover. Corbett had one day behind him. How many would he go?

"I thought it strange that these teams of FBI agents started coming around all of a sudden since it has been five years since he fled prison in California," Joe Corbett's father told a *Rocky Mountain News* reporter just after the FBI issued its Ten Most Wanted List. "Then the other day the Coors case came up and I knew what it was all about. We haven't heard from him since the day before his escape from Chino. . . . I don't know why he took Walt's name," Corbett's father said of Corbett taking the name of his stepbrother, Walter Osborne Corbett. "Walt is an engineer and he's ready to leave for Brazil to take a good job, and I hope to God this doesn't hurt him any."

Unlike Joe Corbett Sr., the FBI simply provided a curt "No comment." Sheriff Wermuth and his undersheriff, Lew Hawley, who'd just called up another search in the surrounding mountains for the missing Ad Coors, also provided no comment, not because the sheriff was uncharacteristically withholding information from the press but because he still knew nothing. The FBI and the Coors family had cut him off long ago. "It's all news to us," said Hawley when asked about Joe Corbett Jr. being the principal suspect in the Coors kidnapping case. "But it's obvious the FBI figures it has something hot."

Hawley was correct. Though the FBI wouldn't say, Corbett was more than a hot suspect. He was the bureau's only real suspect. His photo had been shown to everyone in the Coors family, but none recognized him. A painstaking search of personnel records at all Coors facilities failed to indicate Corbett, Osborne, or any of his other aliases had been employed. Local 366 membership records were scoured. Nothing. One person, however, did recall seeing Corbett at a Coors facility: the Coors Rifle Range in Golden.

The following morning, Wednesday, March 30, almost eight weeks after Ad's disappearance, the FBI finally released word that Corbett was sought in connection with the kidnapping of Ad Coors. Goldenites woke to newspaper headlines that read: ESCAPED KILLER SOUGHT AS TOP COORS SUSPECT; FBI SEEKING FUGITIVE IN COORS CASE; SUSPECT IS UNKNOWN TO COORS FAMILY. Photos of Corbett accompanied the articles. Now citizens had a face. Before, FBI agents had conceded

Corbett would be difficult to spot. "He looks like a college professor, speaks like a cultured, educated man, and no one meeting him would associate him with a criminal background," one FBI agent said. It didn't matter now. His photo would be everywhere.

Folks in Golden were relieved to learn the FBI was interested in an escaped convict from California who wasn't a union man or one of them. People filing into the post office could see the FBI Ten Most Wanted poster. Another was posted in the bus station and one in the train depot. They'd seen the three photos of his face and his fingerprints published in the newspapers, but seeing it posted in public, printed by the US government printing office, made it more ominous.

Mary had seen the kidnapper's face for weeks in her dreams and during the quiet of the day. The face was always changing and a bit fuzzy. Like a vapor drifting in the darkness, it would form the shape of a man's face she didn't recognize. Other times, it would shine in the sunlight distinctly, always dimming before drawing near. It was only Ad's face she saw clearly in her nightmares—his eyes, his hair, the strain of a struggle, and she heard his words as he lay in a pool of blood: "I love you, Mary. Tell the kids I love them. Goodbye, sweetheart."

Those were only Mary's dreams and imagination, but holding the newspaper on March 30, she saw the actual face of the suspected kidnapper. It wasn't what she'd expected. His face was plain, common, nonthreatening. She'd expected more. A rough-looking character, with maybe a beard and a scar and angry eyes. That she could understand. This man had attended college, was a Fulbright Scholar, the paper said, and had been a premed student at Berkeley. How could an intelligent, educated man commit such a brazen, horrific crime? He wasn't even from Colorado, but Seattle. None of it made sense to her.

Beneath the headlines and photographs, local newspapers were flush with articles about the release of the black-and-white Most Wanted poster.

A 31-year-old murderer is being sought for the kidnapping of Adolph (Ad) Coors III, reported the *Rocky Mountain News*. . . . The FBI said Corbett fled Denver on Feb. 10—the day after the millionaire Golden brewery firm head disappeared en route to work. . . . An intensive search of the area by sheriff's officials and volunteers failed to disclose any trace of the missing man. . . . Corbett's yellow Mercury sedan which answers the description of a car seen near the home before Ad Coors' disappearance was located Feb. 17 by the FBI near Atlantic City, NJ . . . burned and gutted.

Despite all the interviews, quoted statements, maps, photos, and prognostications, the information glaringly absent from the sweeping news coverage was what citizens wished to know most: Where was Ad Coors and his kidnapper?

CHAPTER 14

With April came an early spring, and life returned to the Colorado mountains and river valleys. Buds bloomed and grass in the foothills began to green. April also delivered Cecily's seventeenth birthday without her wish being granted. The month of May brought even warmer temperatures, and animals could be seen in the warmth and sunshine. With June came tourists and July brought a celebration of Independence Day (and a new US flag with fifty stars).

Things in Golden and even at the Coors plant had returned to normal. Everyone had their own lives to lead, and the subject of Ad's disappearance came up sparingly. But none of those passing months brought any information about the whereabouts of Ad Coors or his suspected kidnapper. All believed Ad to be dead, except possibly Mary, whose hopes now seemed more fantasy than genuine. Still, until authorities presented her with physical evidence that Ad was dead, she could cling to the hope that he might return, no matter how unlikely that possibility.

The FBI didn't sit still during the change of seasons. All over the Denver area, agents continued searching for clues. They interviewed landlords, gas station attendants, store clerks, doctors, nurses, dentists, convicts, coworkers, and the library where Corbett checked out textbooks on chemistry, physics, and other technical subjects. They also searched all along the Upper East Coast.

The world-renowned law enforcement agency had collected, analyzed, and cataloged all forms of evidence during their investigation. Yet with August approaching, there were still loose ends to be tied.

A mysterious fingerprint lifted by the FBI from inside Ad's Travelall didn't match Corbett's. That troubled the FBI. It troubled the district attorney more. The FBI fingerprinted everyone who might have had contact with the Travelall, including the milkman who'd moved the vehicle, law enforcement, family, friends, and employees who had access to Ad's car, and of course, compared it to Corbett's. But none matched. That would have been the strongest evidence connecting Corbett to Ad and to Turkey Creek Bridge on the day of the disappearance. Without it, the FBI had to build a circumstantial case for the district attorney, whose case against Corbett would have to work around the unexplained fingerprint inside the Travelall. Prosecutors knew the defense attorneys would bring up that fingerprint repeatedly as belonging to the "real" killer.

Yet one link might be established. "That typewriter has to be found," said Special Agent Werner during a morning briefing of his Denver field agents. "It's the key to the case. Find that typewriter; it will match up with the ransom note, and that's direct evidence linking Corbett to the kidnapping."

Almost immediately, the FBI had a lead. Agents learned Joe Corbett purchased a Royalite typewriter from May-D&F department store in October 1959. Discovering that fact required painstaking work. The FBI had contacted the Royal McBee Corporation and learned the Royalite portable was sold in Denver at only two locations: May-D&F and Denver Dry Goods Company. Agents requested store managers to sift through hundreds of sales slips at both stores to locate buyers of Royalite portable typewriters.

Armed with the list of serial numbers, the FBI set out to visit the homes of the Royalite purchasers.

"Hello. We are searching for a Royalite portable typewriter purchased in Denver since February 1959. Do you have such a typewriter?"

The agent knew very well the homeowners had purchased the typewriter. He had a copy of the receipt in his suit pocket. He asked only to hear their response. The married couple took the agent into their teenage son's bedroom, where the typewriter sat on a night table. The agent lifted the typewriter and read the serial number beneath the carriage. He checked off the serial number from his list, made a sample of its typeface, and led the couple into the kitchen.

"I would like you to look at photographs and tell me if you recognize any of these individuals." The agent laid four photos side by side on the kitchen table like tarot cards. One was Corbett's driver's license photo. The husband and wife sat and stared at the photographs. "No, we have never seen any of these men."

The agent picked up the photos, thanked the couple, and departed, on his way to the next address on the list, where he conducted the same inquiry without success. Eventually, he had one serial number remaining: RL 3663901. The Royalite purchased with cash and carried from the store. He already knew that was the one. The checking of the others had been mere routine procedure. Jerry Davis, a young clerk at the May-D&F department store, had already given the FBI what it needed.

"I remember the sale well. It's the only typewriter I've ever sold for cash," said Davis. With an agent present, Davis examined the store's 1959 typewriter customers' book and on page 60 identified his own penciled handwriting showing he'd sold a Royalite portable typewriter on October 8, 1959, serial number 3663901 for $66.55 cash-and-carry, to William Chiffins, 1735 Pennsylvania Street, Denver, Colorado.

"Are you sure that's the correct name?" asked the agent.

"Yes. I remember I asked him to spell it."

"Can you describe the man who bought the typewriter?"

"Yes . . . he was about thirty-five, tall, over six feet, maybe 160 pounds. He wore glasses. They were horn-rimmed. I remember he tried out the display machine before he bought one."

"Take a look at the men in these photos," said the agent, spreading the photographs of four men side by side.

"That's him," said Davis. "That's Mr. Chiffins." The clerk pointed out Joe Corbett.

Just to be sure, Agent John Broughton checked for anyone named William Chiffins in the area. He checked apartments, houses, businesses. He checked telephone directories, library cards, driver's licenses at the Department of Motor Vehicles, voter cards at the election commission, marriage licenses, death certificates. He checked hospitals, military installations, credit unions, social clubs, retail associations. Nothing. There was absolutely no record the FBI could find of any person named William Chiffins having ever lived or died in the entire state of Colorado. But a man named Arthur John Cheffins had been imprisoned at San Quentin during Corbett's incarceration there, and Corbett knew him. In addition, *William* was a popular alias of Corbett's.

The FBI also discovered that 1735 Pennsylvania Street was the address for a building converted into a two-residence boardinghouse. One room had been rented to Eloise Bissett since February 1958, and the other had been vacant for two years. The boardinghouse just happened to be around the corner from Corbett's old room at the Perlmor.

Their legwork told the agents that Corbett had to be the purchaser, and if agents could locate the typewriter, there'd be absolutely no question Corbett was guilty. Special Agent Werner's office mailed hundreds of letters under his signature to department stores, typewriter dealers, pawnshops, and thrift stores in the Denver area.

In connection with an official investigation, this office is attempting to locate a Royalite portable typewriter, Serial Number RL 3663901, which may have been sold, pawned, traded in on another machine, or otherwise sought your attention since October 8, 1959. Your assistance is requested in checking your records to determine whether this typewriter may have been in your business establishment.

Despite an exhaustive probe, the FBI could not locate the typewriter. It was probably at the bottom of a mountain lake. Without the typewriter, they couldn't match it to the type on the ransom note, which meant the FBI still had no direct evidence. They resumed building a circumstantial case.

Agents hoped to tie Corbett to the type of paper used for the ransom note. Though Corbett had left behind paper in the chicken wire storage at the Perlmor Apartments, the watermark didn't match that of the ransom note. That was disappointing. Agents could only attempt to connect Corbett to purchasing paper with the identical watermark. Flimsy evidence on its own, but when viewed collectively with other evidence gathered, it might help close the gas chamber door on Corbett.

Paper used to type the ransom note was traced to the manufacturer Eaton Paper Company and to the Cherry Creek Store branch of the Denver Dry Goods Company. There, Ann Thompson, a college student working as a clerk during December break, told an FBI agent, "I'm nearly positive he's the one who purchased the typewriting paper. I'm an art student at Denver University, and I noticed his facial bone structure and slanted teeth." She pointed at Corbett's photograph. "See, it's a salient feature. We're taught to notice those things in art class."

Agents were pleased. They had collected evidence showing Corbett purchased one of the Royalite typewriters sold in the area, giving a future jury the opportunity to conclude that Corbett's Royalite was the one that typed the note, especially in light of the evidence that Corbett purchased typewriting paper from a store that sold paper of a variety that matched the ransom note. The FBI continued gathering evidence. They needed more.

But FBI agents weren't the only ones working the case. Colorado Department of Game and Fish director Tom Kimball inspected hundreds of hunting and fishing licenses in an attempt to locate Joe Corbett, Walter Osborne, or any of his other aliases, with the hope of determining what areas he frequented. Perhaps he was holed up somewhere in the mountains or he'd left behind evidence in a cabin or at a campsite. Maybe he could be connected to a place where he may have taken Ad . . . or hidden his body.

The weeks crept by for Mary Coors. She'd held out hope, but by July, all hope seemed lost. Everyone believed Ad was dead, and now the last holdout, Mary, resigned herself to the fact that her husband was gone forever, too. She drifted through each day like a sleepwalker, medicated and drinking more. The alcohol calmed her nerves and distracted her endless obsessions and memories, and all the *what-ifs* and *should'ves* she played and replayed in her mind. She tortured herself with guilt for not giving Ad a hug and saying more meaningful words, but how was she to know that morning would be her last seeing him?

Her conversations with friends often turned to Ad. Mary was not only depressed but fraught with hatred. It seethed behind her every thought. As well-meaning as friends were, it was natural for some to tire and drift away. Many grew weary of her morose disposition. Those that once entertained with Ad and Mary as a couple began to view her as the odd woman out. Even so, a few friends wouldn't leave her.

During a luncheon, she was invited to accompany a friend and her husband to Bermuda in the fall. When Mary initially demurred, her friend pressed her to give one good reason why she couldn't go.

Mary hesitated and then blurted out, "Ad and I spent our honeymoon there."

She had been dating and married to Ad for more than twenty years. Everything reminded her of Ad. There were few places she could go for a change of scenery. No place to run, except to the bottle.

Mary pulled away from Joe's wife, Holly, who had become a fundamentalist Christian. Holly's often spoken words of faith and statements of God's will fell hollow on Mary. Mary had never been much of a believer, and seeing Holly clutch her Bible angered Mary all the more. How could God take away a loving husband and a wonderful father?

Her sister-in-law Geraldine wasn't much comfort either. She had her own problems. She was an alcoholic, smoked three packs of cigarettes a day, and her marriage with Bill was in serious trouble.

Mary had never had much of a relationship with Ad's sister, May Louise Tooker. She'd moved to Greenwich, Connecticut, many years earlier, and they rarely spoke, except at occasional family gatherings.

And Ad's father and mother were pulling away or so it seemed to Mary. Not that they'd ever been that close. She spoke to them on the few occasions her kids stayed over, which were becoming infrequent. Mary never thought Mr. Coors cared for her. He'd made his feelings pretty clear each Sunday when all the children and grandchildren gathered at the Queen Anne mansion for Sunday dinner. Maybe it was because she was a Grant and didn't need the Coors name or money, and like Mr. Coors, she could be indomitable. She was intelligent and didn't tremble whenever Mr. Coors raised his voice. She and Mrs. Coors had gotten along fine, but Mrs. Coors had taken Ad's loss hard. After all, he was her firstborn child, and she didn't want to talk about Ad. If Mary brought up his disappearance, or even Ad himself, Mrs. Coors often changed the subject. Perhaps Mary reminded Mrs. Coors of her son too much. It didn't matter; Mrs. Coors didn't contradict Mr. Coors. Whatever the problem was, a rift was growing between Mary and Ad's parents and, worse, was spreading to Mary's children.

As for *The Denver Post* and *Rocky Mountain News*, their articles about Ad's disappearance were becoming fewer and fewer until they almost fizzled out altogether. One bizarre article that did appear added only embarrassment to misery.

MYSTIC DETECTIVE ARRIVES IN DENVER, the *Rocky Mountain News* headline read in July. The self-styled "telepathic detective," Peter Hurkos claimed to have extrasensory perception and to have solved twenty-seven murders in seventeen countries. He was said to have acquired his ESP powers after falling from a ladder. "I see pictures in my mind like a television screen. When I touch something, I can then tell what I see."

He made appearances on British television and *The Tonight Show Starring Johnny Carson*. Several said he really did have ESP. Others said he was merely a showman. Still others called him a charlatan. When he claimed his powers helped detectives solve actual crimes, police often refuted those claims.

Reporters and cameras had been bad enough, but with the self-professed mystic's arrival, the Coors family believed the circus had at last come to town. When asked if the Coors family hired the paranormal crime fighter, the Coors spokesman fired back an emphatic "No." Mercifully, Hurkos and his wife moved on to Pueblo, Colorado, to "investigate" another missing person, leaving the Coors family in peace.

What reporters didn't know was Bill may have actually contacted a psychic soon after his brother's disappearance. Not Peter Hurkos but Florence Sternfels. According to Ms. Sternfels, Bill secretly flew to her home in Edgewater, New Jersey, carrying a photograph and one of Ad's favorite belt buckles. The elderly Sternfels had gained some notoriety as being what she termed a "psychometrist," who receives mental pictures of someone by handling an object that belonged to that person.

"I see a pool of blood on a bridge," she said, rubbing the belt buckle in one hand. Of course, everyone knew that, Bill thought. It had been in all the papers. "Here, I'll draw a picture of it. I hate to tell you this, but I see your brother near this." Photographs and diagrams of Turkey Creek Bridge also had been in the newspapers. "I see your brother was followed on his way to the factory." Again, in all the papers and on television. "Oh, my head feels like there are two bullets in it." That could have been a reference to Corbett's shooting victim in California who had been shot twice in the head, or to the witness account of hearing two shots (again in the newspapers and television). "His body will be found at the end of the summer." At last, a statement by the gray-haired prognosticator that was original, but still could be a simple guess, Bill supposed, who left New Jersey thinking he'd wasted a trip.

As the first days of August came to pass and summer was nearing a close, the FBI and Jefferson County Sheriff's Office were no closer to solving the crime than they had been in March when Corbett's identity was first discovered. Mr. Coors told reporters he was convinced his son had been murdered, and he'd already abandoned hope his missing son would ever be found. Yet the end of the summer was quickly approaching, and Ms. Sternfel's only prediction would soon be put to the test.

CHAPTER 15

It was a beautiful fall day. The September skies were clear and blue. The smell of autumn was in the air. Edward Greene took full advantage. Sunday was his day off from his delivery job at Original Pizza Crust Company, so he grabbed his .25-caliber pistol and headed off to the Elephant Rock area near Devil's Head Peak to enjoy what he and many Coloradans enjoyed—target shooting, hiking, and solitude.

Greene pulled his truck across a small ditch near the entrance to a dump in Douglas County. It was a secluded area, difficult to reach, off a more dirt than gravel road winding up a mountainside to its summit, fifteen miles southwest of Denver. No Trespassing signs warned visitors like Greene to stay away, but it seemed no one was ever around to enforce them. The pizza deliverer didn't hesitate. He entered the property identified by a large sign: "Shamballah Ashrama—The Brotherhood of the White Temple." The private dump was scattered with myriad objects that made perfect targets for his new pistol. He began to scrounge around for bottles to shoot. "Usually, I go with somebody else. But this time I went alone," Greene would tell reporters. "But yesterday, I had a creepy feeling, kinda made the hair stand up on the back of my neck."

The garbage was smoldering from its last burn, and smoke was hanging low that cool afternoon. Greene continued along one of two parallel paths worn by tires of vehicles belonging to those of the commune. He took a trail around the dump on his way down to a creek at the base of a steep hillside behind the dump. Hiking along the dirt path, scattered with fallen limbs, vines, and clumps of bushes, Greene descended the slope through thick overhanging pine and aspen amid massive boulder formations.

Greene grabbed limbs and pushed loose brush aside as he made his way along the steep, overgrown ravine. About six hundred feet down, he spotted a pair of leather dress shoes among the pine needles, leaves, and twigs. As he stepped past them, he thought they looked like a new pair, though one was unlaced and the other was full of spiderwebs.

A few feet farther along the path, he spotted a pair of gray flannel pants with a brown belt. They appeared new, just as the shoes did, except for having a tear down one leg. He kicked the pants to launch them off the path. They jingled. Greene kicked them again. He heard a rattle once more, so he reached down and picked them up. As he did, out spilled several coins—a quarter, dime, nickel, and three pennies—forty-three cents. *Nice*, thought Greene. He stuffed the coins into his pocket and rummaged through the pants. Inside was a pocketknife stamped *MIAG* and a key chain with eleven keys. Greene counted them as he considered what they might fit. And there was a penknife. *This is my lucky day*, Greene thought. *Looks like silver.* He flipped it in his hand and noticed some writing on it, an inscription. He strained to read the script in the shade of the enveloping trees. He read it once . . . and then again. "Holy shit!" Greene shouted, shattering the serenity of the deep woods.

The young Greene wasted no time hurrying up the steep hill to his truck. He set out for home, puffing hard from the climb and excitement. Greene later described his swift exit to a reporter: "Before I hightailed it out of there, I thought I saw some other things but thought I'd better report what I'd seen as soon as possible."

He stopped at Johnson's Corner and ran into a service station to borrow the telephone. He called his mother and told her what had happened at the garbage dump. "Inside the pants pockets was Adolph

Coors's key chain. It's got his initials on it—*AC III*." Greene's mother told him not to get mixed up in the matter and to come straight home. (Amazingly, Greene's brother had discovered a dead body a year earlier while fishing near Aspen.)

On the way home from the gas station, Greene stopped to speak with Charles Riddle, an Englewood police officer and friend. He handed the monogrammed knife to Riddle, who immediately called the FBI field office in Denver.

Forty-five minutes later, two carloads of agents arrived at Riddle's house. By 4:30 p.m., they were at the dump.

Greene led the agents along the narrow footpath. Not long into their sweep, near where Greene had kicked the pants from the path, agents began to spot other pieces of clothing. The exploration continued for two hours until it became too dark to see. Most of the items discovered during the search were located in more or less a straight line heading down the slope to the bottom of a ravine, about a one thousand-foot stretch.

Agent Raymond Fox contacted Bill Coors and drove to his house in Denver, arriving around 6:30 p.m. Mary was there when he arrived.

With Bill's wife, Geraldine, by Mary's side, the agent began handing Mary the discovered items. Each item had been collected in a separate plastic bag. She identified the penknife with Ad's initials. She could not identify the pocketknife bearing *MIAG*, but Bill did. An identical knife had been given to each Coors brother from a German company that sold grinding and milling equipment to the brewery: Mühlenbau und Industrie Aktiengesellschaft. A gray ballpoint pen also could not be identified, though it most certainly was Ad's.

"Now, Mrs. Coors, I'm about to hand you items of clothing that we believe belong to your husband," began Agent Fox. "What we'd like you to do is tell us if each piece of clothing was worn by your husband that last morning. I must warn you some clothes are stained and weather-beaten, and others are torn. But we really need to know if they're his."

"I understand," Mary said. The sight of Ad's personal items had not made her emotional. When she saw the bags of clothing, however, her mood changed.

"Can you do this?" asked Agent Fox. "If you'd like to wait until—"

"No, I've waited seven months," said Mary.

The agent showed her a dress shirt that had been found 250 feet from the pants. It was stained with deteriorated blood and torn in several places. Both sleeves had been ripped. It smelled like it had lain in a musty fruit cellar.

Mary hadn't expected the clothing to be so disgusting. "Yes, that looks like what he wore that morning."

"And this tie?"

"I don't know. It looks like his, I suppose."

"This tie clip was dangling from it . . . shaped like a ski."

Mary balked. The sight of the tie and the ski clip together made it more personal. She felt sick. "Yes, that was his. It was a gift from the Sweeneys." Bill agreed the tie clip was Ad's.

"You all right, Mrs. Coors?" asked Fox.

"I'm feeling a little queasy."

"You need something to drink?"

Geraldine jumped up and retrieved Mary a glass of cold water.

"Thank you," Mary said and sipped.

"We can take a break if you need to," said the agent.

"No. Let's go on and get this over with."

The agent continued. "And the socks?" he asked, holding a bag with a pair of dirty, torn blue socks.

"I'm not sure."

The agent continued until each remaining piece of clothing—a white undershirt torn in three places, ripped pants (a label inside read, "Expressly for A. Coors, III"), shorts, belt, and a glove—had been tagged as either identified by Mary or Bill or not. Then the agent handed Mary the last item. It was stuffed in a grocery bag. "What about this blanket?"

Mary's eyes widened. "No!" She yanked her arm back and turned her head. "Take it away," she directed loudly. Mary knew what the blanket had been used for, and now so did the agent.

When leaving to return to his Denver office, Agent Fox asked Bill and Mary not to reveal the discovery until agents had more time to explore the area. If word got out, the site could become crowded with souvenir seekers and the curious who would contaminate or remove evidence and slow the search.

The following morning, Fox traveled to the dump site to rejoin fellow agents searching for bones and clues. Before long, Fox and other agents spotted a three-pawed bear rummaging about and called for a deputy to shoulder a rifle just in case the bear approached. The bear wandered away, agitated by all the activity.

Special Agent Werner had amassed twenty-six agents to scan the woods surrounding the garbage dump. Rope stretched across areas canvassed the day before as part of a search grid. Each discovery brought Special Agent Robert Nelson with a large camera to snap photos and local pathologist Henry W. Toll Jr., M.D., to examine the find and document it, after which Agent Nelson would place it in a bag and stake a crude flag at the site. Numbered flags soon dotted the hillside indicating where discoveries had been made, such as a rib or a vertebra or a wristwatch with a dangling brown leather band.

The scattered bones discovered at the site were ushered in secret to Dr. George Ogura, chief pathologist for the Denver City and County Coroner's Office at Denver General Hospital. He also operated under a cloak of silence. This allowed the FBI to circumvent the Douglas County coroner and the sheriff's office with the goal of keeping the lid on their search.

Fox again visited Mary to show her additional items discovered that day. He met her at the home of David and Mary Jean Pate. It would be her last experience identifying Ad's belongings until the trial.

When reporters learned of the search two days later, on Wednesday evening, their newspapers' carried photos of Ad Coors with large bold headlines. The front page of *Rocky Mountain News* flashed:

Skeleton Unidentified
COORS CLOTHES FOUND BY FBI
A skeleton believed to be that of Adolph Coors III, missing
Golden business executive, has been discovered in Douglas County

Mr. and Mrs. Coors were staying at their vacation home at the Point in Nantucket, and no family member had telephoned to tell them the news. They heard it from a *Denver Post* reporter, who called to hear their reaction. "That's news to me," Mr. Coors said coldly.

Bill Coors was asked if the finding at the dump meant the Coors family at last had given up hope. Bill told the interviewer, "You never give it up. Until you have definite proof, there's hope. And you hope."

"Do you consider this definite proof?" asked the reporter.

Bill hesitated and then answered. "I would say . . . yes."

Two weeks earlier, Corbett, still using the alias Walter Osborne, stepped out of his Bathurst Street apartment heading to work at McPherson Warehousing Company. He picked up the newspaper lying outside his door on his way to catch a bus. Corbett boarded with his lunchbox and the newspaper stuffed under an arm. Though always circumspect, Corbett had grown comfortable in Toronto. It had been fairly easy hiding in Canada.

Corbett unfolded his newspaper and eventually reached the local news. When he read the headline, he recoiled. He placed his hat on and pulled down the brim as he surveyed those sitting nearby. Wasting no time, he reached up and yanked the cord above his window. He stepped off the bus and walked away without turning, disappearing around the corner. He opened the newspaper again.

HAVE YOU SEEN THIS MAN? the headline asked in large bold letters. Corbett saw his photograph. He hadn't changed his appearance at all. Same haircut. Same glasses. No facial hair.

"Sometimes uses the name Walter Osborne, William Chiffins, and James Barron." Corbett was still using the name Walter Osborne in

Toronto. He'd signed the application for his apartment under that name, and he used that name at his warehouse job. (He'd lost his lab technician job when his references didn't check out.) He wouldn't be going to work today. He had to leave Toronto immediately.

Within minutes, Corbett headed for Winnipeg, carrying only the money in his wallet, where he kept most of his cash. He couldn't chance retrieving his things. Perhaps his landlord had called the police.

Later, he told the FBI he'd taken a plane from Toronto to Winnipeg, but that seems unlikely. It was expensive, and he could easily be identified on a plane or at an airport where it would be difficult to escape. Most likely, he stole a car. Whatever means he used, it is clear the intelligent suspect in the Coors disappearance had run out of a plan. Now he was simply on the run.

CHAPTER 16

On Wednesday, September 14, the FBI delivered all bones recovered from the dump (nine ribs, the sternum, two clavicles, the left humerus and radius, a fibula, six thoracic and three cervical vertebrae, and two scapulae or shoulder blades) to the Douglas County Coroner's Office around 3:30 p.m. The first thing the surprised coroner Doug Andrews did was telephone Douglas County sheriff John Hammond to inform him what had been going on in his backyard for the last three days.

Sheriff Hammond rushed to the coroner's office and watched as the coroner assembled the bones into a human skeleton. Deputy Ardell Arfsten photographed the skeleton atop a white cloth stretched over a table. Some bones were darkened. Others were bleached by the sun. Many were missing, and those the coroner did have were badly damaged by gnawing of wild animals feeding on the dead and putrefying body. "No doubt animals have torn the body apart," the coroner told reporters that Wednesday. More than 140 bones picked up by law enforcement were determined by the coroner to be from animals and discarded.

The partial stature and maturity of the bones suggested they were of a human male, around six feet tall, in his forties. This coincided with Dr. Ogura's secret determination in Denver a day earlier. From the bones' condition, the coroner believed the person had been dead six to twelve months, depending on the temperature and insect infestation.

None of Sheriff Hammond's men had been involved in the sweep concealed by the FBI for three days, and that bothered him greatly. Like Sheriff Wermuth, Sheriff Hammond wore Western shirts and string ties with a Western hat and boots. Both were stocky, weighing in at more than two hundred pounds, with Hammond being about three inches taller at five foot nine. Unlike his Jefferson County counterpart, the Douglas Country sheriff dodged reporters. He was a low-key, thoughtful sheriff who rarely wore a gun. He was sincerely altruistic, not trying simply to be authoritarian or grab an occasional headline. Though he didn't have Wermuth's war record, the ordinarily easygoing Sheriff Hammond could become pugnacious—someone not to be tangled with in his own backyard, which the FBI would soon understand.

"John was a mild-mannered, caring person, with strong character. A straight shooter. If John told you something, you could take it to the bank as accurate as he knew," recalled Deputy Arfsten.

Full of information, but out of patience, Sheriff Hammond grabbed Deputy Arfsten and headed to the Shamballah Ashrama dump. They arrived as darkness was falling. They were met by FBI agents Scott Werner and Doug Williams in what best could be described as a lively jurisdictional conference. After a heated discussion, Sheriff Hammond made clear his belief that since Ad Coors had not been carried across state lines, only into his county, the FBI didn't have jurisdiction any longer. It was his county. He demanded that once the FBI Lab finished analyzing all the evidence they found from the dump, the evidence must be delivered to his office.

And so, after the FBI Laboratory completed its analysis, all clothing and effects discovered at the dump were turned over to the Douglas County Sheriff's Office. The FBI and local law enforcement agreed that discolored holes in the navy jacket were caused by two muzzle blasts either in contact with a gun barrel or within an inch of the barrel. The two holes matched those in the shirt and undershirt. The bullets entered the back and were two and a quarter inches apart. There were no exit holes.

When the time came, the coroner would explain his findings to a Jefferson County jury:

> As for the right scapula, there were two defects or holes in this scapula which in my opinion were made by objects passing through it at high velocity. The location of these defects was such that the resultant wounds of the chest would be of themselves sufficient to cause death. In all medical probability, Mr. Coors died of severe bleeding and shock from receiving two gunshot wounds to his right shoulder that penetrated his chest and right lung.

One strap of the undershirt had been cut, as had the necktie, seemingly indicating the killer had loosened his victim's clothing for a better look at the wound, probably while Ad was bleeding to death on the bridge or in the back seat of Corbett's car, assuming they were the bones of Ad Coors. Because despite the clothing and all the bones, and the coroner's determinations of size, gender, race, and age, and his conclusion that two gunshots through the right shoulder blade at close range brought about death, the bones could not be positively identified as belonging to Ad Coors. For that, the coroner needed the skull.

At five o'clock Thursday morning, Tom Berry and Ardell Arfsten joined other Douglas County deputies and FBI agents as they continued the search. Even the county coroner showed up with his son-in-law John W. Abbott to lend their assistance in locating the skull. The sheriff called in the Douglas County front-end loader at 9:30 a.m. to begin shoving, digging, and lifting garbage from the perimeter of the woods. The loader's efforts revealed nothing. Though the lawmen uncovered a few more scattered bones along the steep hillside, none had discovered the skull. Their spirits began to fall. That changed at 12:30.

"Get the sheriff!" yelled the coroner's son-in-law, walking up the hillside. "And the camera!"

Coroner Doug Andrews, standing in his suit and bow tie at the edge of the shallow Garber Creek, 1,300 feet down a ravine and more than 200 feet from the other bones, had located the skull. It lay on its side in a clearing with the lower jawbone a few inches away. They were photographed in the midday sun before being placed in a cardboard box. A staked flag bearing the handwritten number thirteen was shoved into the ground at the spot of the discovery.

Word quickly spread of the coroner's find. Several searchers abandoned their positions and made their way down the steep terrain. They were met by Andrews puffing a cigar and Sheriff Hammond carrying the box containing the skull and jaw up the rugged hill.

When the skull was presented to the other searchers, there were no backslaps, handshakes, or whoops of success. There was only reverence and solemnity. In Hammond's hands was the skull of what once had been a good husband, a good father, and a good son and brother, who'd done nothing to deserve such an unconsecrated and cruel committal at a dump visited by wild animals.

"I was there when the skull was discovered," Deputy Arfsten later recollected. "There was a sinking feeling throughout the group that was searching the area. There was a mixture of sadness and a little anger that someone would do such a thing to another person. The kind that takes the wind out of your sails."

The cardboard box containing the skull was properly marked and immediately taken to the Douglas County Coroner's Office. Coroner Andrews determined the skull and jawbone showed no signs of violence—in other words, the victim had not been hit or shot in the head.

Dr. Arthur G. Kelly, a dentist since 1904 who'd cared for Ad's teeth for two decades, was called to meet Sheriff Hammond and the agents at the coroner's office. All stood quietly as Dr. Kelly made his examination. He switched on an overhead light and positioned it above the skull. He commenced the one-hour examination by probing the jawbone and upper teeth before placing them behind an x-ray machine. He clicked a button a few times. The elder dentist removed the film from the machine and placed the developed slides on a lighted panel beside film from Ad's mouth taken a year earlier. "It's an out-and-out match," he declared.

"Are you sure?" asked Sheriff Hammond.

"A hundred percent sure. This is the skull of Adolph Coors III."

The death certificate was typed up and signed by Coroner Andrews. It stated that Ad Coors died on February 9, 1960, "shot two times or more from the back by an unknown" and that he died from "excessive bleeding from two or more gunshot wounds in the right shoulder."

Rocky Mountain News printed what everyone had suspected, including Mary:

COORS' BODY IDENTIFIED!
Adolph Coors III, long-missing business executive, is dead.

Three days later, Ad's son Spike "celebrated" his fifteenth birthday.

After the positive identification of Ad's remains was made public, Steve Hart's young associate Bruce Buell entered the Jefferson County Court clerk's office and filed a petition to probate Ad's last will and testament. The court clerk set the hearing for October 31—Halloween.

Every last bit of hope, no matter how illogical, that Mary had clutched to so tenuously was now completely spent like her husband's last breath on that fateful blustery morning seven months earlier. The discovery of Ad's bones strewn about a garbage dump high in the mountains, some bearing teeth marks from hungry animals, his head carried hundreds of yards away in the jaws of a wild beast, hardly eased her pain or her nightmares. The find had been an exclamation point to an already horrible experience.

Following the find, Mary waited for her children to arrive home from school. When the kids did arrive, she gave them a few minutes to change clothes, snack, and mill about before—

"I need to talk to you," said Mary. "Let's go into the living room."

Those words made the kids tired, full of dread. They'd been called into family meetings far too many times that year, and it was almost always bad news. It had to be about their father.

The children sat near Mary, some on the couch, some on the floor. Brooke wasn't there. She'd left a few weeks earlier to join her college freshman class. She wanted to be a teacher.

"Okay, you know how we thought your father may have died because it's been so long since we've heard from him," Mary likely began. "And how we've held out hope that your father was somehow alive despite the odds against it. Well, I learned the FBI found his body yesterday afternoon."

Mary hesitated as tears began filling her children's eyes. It was really no surprise to them, but it still hurt. Seven months had passed with no word from their father. Seven months of sadness. Seven months of unanswered prayers. Their mother had told them months earlier he was likely dead. But it wasn't until now that all hope was gone, like their father, forever.

As the children huddled around their mother, crying, one of them surely asked, "How did Daddy die, Mama? Was he in pain?"

"No, he died almost instantly." Mary was being kind.

"But how?"

"He was shot in the back." Mary had seen the holes in Ad's jacket and shirt. Agent Fox had confirmed they were from two gunshots.

The room was quiet.

"Did they catch the man who did it?"

"Not yet, but they will."

There was brief silence.

"I hate him," said one of the kids.

"Me, too," said Mary.

Again, there was silence.

"Know that your father will always be with us," Mary may have lamented. "He's in our memories, and he's in your blood. He was very proud of all of you, and the one thing he desired most was for you to grow up into honest, responsible adults and be happy. He's in heaven now looking down, so let's continue to make him proud of us, okay?"

Heads nodded back and forth. Mary stared out the living room window as her children continued sobbing and rubbing their eyes. She began to pray for Ad's killer to be captured and sent to the gas chamber for what he'd done to her family. If there was a hell, she wanted him to burn in it for all eternity.

"Seven months [after his disappearance] my dad's remains were found in a garbage dump near Denver," Spike recalled years later. "In the meantime, my family had fallen into a deep hole of hate. Mother, especially, allowed hatred for Joseph Corbett to consume her life. In that hatred she turned to the only crutch she knew, alcohol."

Sheriff Wermuth pushed his chair away from his desk, dissatisfied. Life at the Jefferson County Sheriff's Office had returned to the mundane.

There was the occasional excitement of a local sighting of Joe Corbett, but all of the reports had proved bogus. The FBI handled interstate reports of Corbett sightings, so there was little else to do in Jefferson County regarding the Coors case. Wermuth couldn't fall back on his old reliable tactic of conducting a search for Coors to gain the media's spotlight. Ad's body had been discovered and worse, in Douglas County, where Sheriff Hammond and the county coroner were in possession of Ad's remains. There was nothing Sheriff Wermuth could do but stand by and watch as the media pendulum had swung Sheriff Hammond's way.

Wermuth considered his situation. Ad's body may have been dumped in Douglas County, but the fatal crime occurred in Jefferson County, so he continued to clutch the jurisdictional trump card.

He believed his only hope to return to the public eye was to be in on Corbett's arrest or, more likely, participate in his extradition to Denver should the FBI ever catch up with him.

But there was something brewing, an insignificant matter that was beginning to snowball into something big, as many things do, and it would thrust Sheriff Wermuth back into headlines. An investigation would soon be opened that would have nothing to do with Ad Coors's murder, but would focus on certain irregularities within the sheriff's office.

"I do say there is absolutely nothing illegal now or in the past," Sheriff Wermuth soon would be saying to reporters.

Corbett pulled open the door to Hertz Rent a Car on the west side of the city of Winnipeg.

"Can I help you?"

Corbett walked to the counter, behind which stretched a banner on the wall that read, "Let HERTZ put you in the driver's seat."

"I'd like to rent a car."

A young woman opened a portfolio of colorful photos of automobiles available for lease and laid the binder on the counter.

"This Impala is a popular car. It has air-conditioning and an automatic transmission."

Corbett ignored her suggestion and flipped the page. "How much for this Pontiac Bonneville convertible?"

"Oh, that's a fine car. Excellent choice. And we have one in red just like the picture. Let me look that up."

Corbett removed his checkbook. He scribbled out a check for the amount of the rental, signed it "Walter Osborne," and accepted the rental agreement.

"Do you have a road map I can use to get to Vancouver?" he asked.

"Of course. It's mostly Highway 1 all the way. Takes you to Calgary and then Vancouver."

Corbett drove the shiny red car to his boardinghouse. He'd only lived in Winnipeg a few weeks, but could sense the FBI was on his trail, and he needed to keep moving. He was right. The deposit he gave to his Winnipeg landlady was by check, written on his old Toronto checking account. Worse, it was a bad check, and still worse, it wasn't the only bad check he'd passed. He'd also just given one to the Hertz rental agency. Now agents knew the type of automobile Corbett was driving and where he might be staying in Winnipeg. They weren't far behind. So Corbett drove on, heading west.

III

THE
CAPTURE
AND TRIAL

CHAPTER 17

I'm calling about the American fugitive Joseph Corbett who's wanted by the FBI," said a man to a Toronto police officer. It was October 25, 1960. "I know him. I worked with him this summer at McPherson's Warehouse, here in Toronto . . . but he didn't call himself Corbett. Said he was Walter Osborne."

The day before, the man had read the November edition of *Reader's Digest* that included a large photo of Corbett and a headline that read, THE FBI WANTS THIS MAN. The opening paragraph of the article began:

> High on the list of the Most Wanted Fugitives is tall, brown-haired, intelligent and scrupulously neat, 32-year-old Joseph Corbett Jr. Agents in all 54 field offices of the FBI are hunting for him. A convicted killer, Corbett escaped from prison five years ago. Now the finger of suspicion is pointing at him again . . . an intensive investigation is under way to locate him.

The article continued with a description of Ad Coors's murder and Corbett's early life and prison record. The article described Corbett exactly, his teeth, clothing, and habits, but it was the photograph that was critical to gaining the readers' attention.

The FBI headed to Toronto and learned that when filling out a new employee card, Corbett used the alias he'd used most often in Denver, Walter Osborne, and incredibly used his actual boarding-house address. Realizing his stupidity, Corbett marked through the actual address and added a fake one, but the real address was still visible underneath. The FBI and the Royal Canadian Mounted Police spoke with Corbett's Toronto landlord.

"Yes, I had a roomer, but he left several weeks ago," Antanas Laurinaitis recounted. "He didn't take his things with him. He left everything he had, his clothing, books, screwdrivers, whatever he had. He left everything. I have them stored in the basement."

On that August day when Corbett quickly exited a Toronto bus and fled to Winnipeg, he had abandoned more than he had at the Perlmor Apartments in Denver. A wallet with his Colorado driver's license, California union card, Colorado hunting license, Denver library card, Social Security card, and pass to enter the Benjamin Moore factory; a four-foot length of chain similar to that found at his Denver apartment; several magazines that included the American crime pulp, *True Detective*, and a large stack of paperback books, such as *Teach Yourself Flying*, *Teach Yourself Spanish*, and, ironically, the bestseller *Anatomy of a Murder*. The FBI realized that by leaving behind so many personal effects, Corbett had been in a hurry and was becoming careless.

Before the FBI could write a report on the evidence left at the Toronto rooming house, the Royal Canadian Mounted Police relayed a call they'd received from the manager of Corbett's rooming house in Winnipeg.

"I read *Reader's Digest* about that man Joseph Corbett Jr. I'm sure he roomed here last month. But he said his name was Ian McIntosh."

It seemed *Reader's Digest* was very popular in Canada.

Eight months after the kidnapping, the FBI finished gathering all the evidence it needed. As field agents followed a warm trail left by bungling Joe Corbett, FBI special agents, fingerprint experts, lab specialists, and forensic scientists solidified the case against Ad's suspected murderer. They had assembled so much evidence that it filled a five-inch-thick investigation report that included guns, hand and ankle restraints, typewriters, paper, camping supplies, chain, fingerprints, cars, hats, and witnesses. The only thing the report lacked was the arrest and conviction of their suspect. But that chapter was very close to being written; but to write it, they needed to find Corbett.

Mary had not waited for Ad's remains to be discovered before leaving his dream home behind. Four months after his kidnapping, Mary moved her children to exclusive Cherry Hills Village, composed of only a few hundred wealthy residents just outside the Denver city limits. Mary's new home in the Polo Club subdivision sat near the thirteenth hole of Cherry Hills Country Club, where Arnold Palmer had famously defeated Jack Nicklaus that summer in the 1960 US Open golf tournament. Bill and Geraldine Coors had lived there since the early '50s.

The change of scenery had not helped Mary, and the discovery of Ad's remains provided no finality to her grief. She couldn't even have a memorial service. Ad's bones were amassed in a refrigerated cabinet in the Douglas County Coroner's Office. When she asked for them, she was told they couldn't be released until after the trial. Like everything in her life, a memorial service would remain in limbo.

Mary found comfort in alcohol more often. Though she was still graceful, friends and family could see the effects that alcohol was having on her appearance and demeanor. Her children had been stung by the loss of a father. They were beginning to lose their mother, too.

On Friday, October 28, Mary awakened and pulled open the bedroom curtains of her beautiful Cherry Hills home. It was almost noon. She'd sent the kids off to school and returned to bed. Her daily routine now. She ambled into the den and clicked on the television set. The smell of lukewarm coffee in the percolator coming from the kitchen filled the air. She poured a cup and added a little gin and sugar. Before she could make it to her chair in front of the television, the phone rang.

It was Holly, asking to have Spike and Jim stay over that night. Mary agreed and then hung up the phone and picked up her cup. It may have been *As the World Turns* or *The Guiding Light* she sat down to watch. She may not have even noticed. The soap operas all seemed the same. Exaggerated story lines clouded by gin and despondency.

Before she knew where the hours had gone, the door from the garage flung open, and in ran Jim, followed by Spike and Cecily. Mary stood and met her children in the kitchen and gave them hugs. She was still in her robe. She asked about their day, made them a snack, and then walked out of the kitchen and down the hallway. Her bedroom door closed.

Mary had shut out the world once again. But on the following day, her solitude would be unexpectedly interrupted.

Corbett entered a café in the West End neighborhood of Vancouver, British Columbia. Ordinarily, he ordered a hamburger and a Coke, but today was not ordinary. It was October 25, his thirty-second birthday.

"Ever been to Seattle?" Corbett asked the bartender. "I grew up in Seattle. My father still lives there," said the typically quiet Corbett.

No one could accuse him of looking over his shoulder that day. He was affable and carefree. He was using a different alias at last, but he had not changed his appearance.

Out came a cherry pie topped with a burning candle carried by a waitress singing, "Happy Birthday." Corbett blew out the candle, and despite being warned not to, he divulged his wish.

Corbett was having the best time he'd had in months. The normally closemouthed fugitive was talking to everyone, telling them everything, except that he was a fugitive. And not just any fugitive. One of the FBI's Ten Most Wanted. Did he have a plan? After all, he was in Vancouver, the busiest port city in Canada and one of the busiest in all of North America. In fact, he had been hanging around the docks and asking about jobs aboard liners leaving port soon.

"I'm expecting the delivery of a typewriter. I rented one to type some résumés. Would you let the deliveryman up when he arrives?" Corbett asked his new landlady, Mary Bell. Not since he'd typed the Coors ransom note had he used a typewriter.

He left his Vancouver landlady at her desk and walked out the front door onto Bidwell Street. His flashy 1960 fire-engine-red Pontiac chromed convertible he'd rented in Winnipeg but failed to return was parked out front. He drove down the street a few blocks and abandoned the car in a parking garage. From there, Corbett walked to a nearby park and sat on a bench on the Vancouver shore, gazing out over the largest body of water on the planet. Before him stretched more than sixty million square miles of international and territorial waters, where ships from every major sovereign nation can freely sail on a seemingly infinite blue surface under the protection of their flags, providing asylum to all those aboard from US interference and capture. Corbett understood this, and so did the FBI. It was a race against time for both, and time was running out.

"Men, we're searching for an American driving a 1960 red Pontiac convertible with Manitoba plate U9. He's wanted for attempted kidnapping and murder in the United States. Here's a description with a photo," visiting special agent Don Hostetter announced to a team of Vancouver police constables on the morning of October 29.

After the briefing, one of the constables hurried to his patrol car and drove to the rear of an old Mission Revival style apartment called the Maxine Hotel. He was sure he'd seen a red Pontiac exactly like the one described in the briefing parked in front of the Maxine two weeks earlier, but didn't want to alert his superiors until he was sure. He entered the apartment building.

"Hello. I'm Jack Marshall, constable for the Vancouver police. I'm looking for a man. His name is Joe Corbett."

"I don't have anyone here by that name," said the sixty-one-year-old proprietress, Mary Bell, standing behind a counter. "I know everyone, and he's not a resident."

"Maybe he's here under another name. He sometimes uses Walter Osborne or Ian McIntosh."

The landlady shook her head.

"How about William Chiffins or Michael McLean?"

"No, I don't know anyone by those names."

The Vancouver constable reached into his uniform pocket and withdrew the FBI circular distributed by Hostetter at the morning briefing. "Have you seen this man? An American. Tall. Over six feet. Drives a brand-new red Pontiac convertible."

The landlady looked at the photo. "Oh, you mean Mr. Wainwright. Is he in some kind of trouble?"

"Wainwright? What's his first name?"

"Thomas. It's right here in the register. See? 'Thomas C. Wainwright. Room 15.' I can't believe he's done something wrong. He impressed me as a very nice person. Always keeps to himself. Paid sixty dollars in advance."

"Is he here now?"

"Yes, I believe he is. He came to the lobby for a newspaper about an hour ago. Would you like me to ring him for you?"

"No. Absolutely not."

Marshall directed the landlady to go to the basement. "Now don't say a thing. Not a word. This man is dangerous. Don't do a thing until I come back," Marshall instructed. He then hurried out the rear of the Maxine to his patrol car. He drove to the nearest call box and telephoned the Vancouver detective bureau. Minutes later, Canadian detectives Sam Fowlow, Harry Gammie, and William Simmons met Marshall at the Sylvia Hotel, where Special Agents Hostetter and Al Gunn were staying. By sheer coincidence, in a metropolitan area of more than 750,000 people, the FBI agents' hotel was only three blocks from the Maxine.

Several unmarked cars swarmed the hotel as seven FBI agents and a handful of Vancouver detectives in plain clothes sneaked into the building and took their positions. Some covered the exterior entrances and exits, two others covered the stairs on the first floor, and the remaining men met Mrs. Bell in the basement. She was nervous and a bit afraid, but was assured by the lawmen that she and her tenants would be safe.

"What did he say when you spoke with him?" asked Detective Fowlow, a middle-aged man, over six feet tall and stocky.

"Only that he'd come from Winnipeg and needed a place to stay," the landlady replied.

"Anything else?"

"The usual, you know, what everybody asks—how much for the room, is there a deposit, is it refundable, is it quiet here, that kind of thing. Oh, he did ask me to help him rent a typewriter. It's coming this afternoon."

"There's our hook," said Special Agent Gunn, looking at the others. "Let's go."

Agent Hostetter and Detective Simmons stayed with the landlady while Detectives Fowlow and Gammie and Agent Gunn slipped up the stairs to the first floor. They drew their revolvers as they neared Corbett's room. Each gave one another the signal they were positioned and ready. Agent Gunn knocked on the apartment door. He was the only one visible. Detectives Fowlow and Gammie hid along the wall to one side of the door, waiting for it to open.

There was no answer. Gunn knocked again.

The men heard a faint "Who's there?" from behind the shut door. It was 9:45 a.m., October 29, 1960.

Before Gunn could reply, "I'm here with your typewriter," as he'd planned, he heard the door lock click as it unbolted. The detectives braced, gripping the handles of their revolvers. The door opened wide. There stood Joe Corbett without a gun, wearing matching green gabardine shirt and trousers with the same haircut and horned-rim eyeglasses he'd worn in Denver. Gunn couldn't believe it. Corbett appeared as if he'd posed for the FBI Most Wanted poster earlier that morning.

The lawmen pushed the door and rushed in, shoving Corbett backward into the one-room apartment and against a wall.

"Joe Corbett?" shouted Gunn as he pulled Corbett's wrists behind him and squeezed handcuffs on.

"Yes," said Corbett calmly. "I'm your man. I'm not armed. I give up."

"Where are your guns?" an agent shouted. Before Corbett had a chance to answer, someone yelled again, "Where are your guns?"

"It's over there, in the bag," said Corbett, jerking his head in that direction.

Detective Gammie grabbed a brown zippered travel bag that was open. He withdrew a Llama 9 mm pistol fully loaded with six rounds of .38-caliber ammunition in the clip and one in the chamber.

"What about the others?" yelled Gunn.

"That's it. That's all I got," said Corbett.

"Check under the bed, in the closet . . . and check the washroom," Fowlow told Gammie.

"Where's the car?"

"Car?"

"The red Pontiac. Where is it?"

"I don't know what you're talking about. I don't own a car."

"Cut the act. We know you rented a red Pontiac convertible in Winnipeg. Where is it?"

"In a garage on West Fourteenth Street. The street number's in the bag. I parked it there a few days ago."

The man responsible for Corbett's capture, Constable Marshall, had not been allowed to participate in the arrest because he was still in uniform and at six feet, three inches tall, he could have been spotted by Corbett. He arrived at the Maxine soon afterward and joined detectives and FBI agents canvassing Corbett's room. Among Corbett's few possessions, the lawmen discovered a new brown felt hat, size 7⅜.

Corbett's captors escorted him out, jerking and tugging him along a hallway and out the back of the hotel into an awaiting Vancouver police car. Inside the patrol car, Fowlow began questioning Corbett.

"How long have you been in Vancouver?"

"You know the answer to that," replied Corbett.

"I think we should wait to question him further till we get to the station," interrupted Agent Gunn.

Fowlow agreed. He knew the FBI had its procedures, and after all, the man was not wanted for anything in Canada other than possessing an unregistered firearm and passing bad checks.

When the men arrived at Vancouver police headquarters, Corbett was taken into an interrogation room and seated across from FBI agents Hostetter and Gunn and Vancouver detectives Fowlow and Gammie. The FBI wanted a confession. The desire was partially personal. Corbett had eluded the FBI for eight months, and a Canadian constable had tracked him down.

"Before we start with the questions, anything you need?" asked Agent Gunn.

A glass of water already sat on the table. Corbett shook his head.

"I want you to understand, Mr. Corbett, you are not required to make a statement, and any statement you do make may be used against you in court. You may obtain the services of an attorney of your own choice if you wish, and can have free counsel if you are unable to pay." The landmark case of *Miranda v. Arizona*, which made the reading of certain constitutional rights mandatory, wouldn't be decided for another six years, but the FBI was already advising individuals of their right against self-incrimination.

Corbett acknowledged his rights, and the questioning continued.

"Are you Joe Corbett?"

"Yes."

"When and where were you born?"

"Seattle. October 25, 1928."

"Happy birthday," said Fowlow.

Special Agent Hostetter shook his head at Fowlow.

The FBI agents asked more questions. Corbett said very little, but did tell them, "I realized the futility of being a fugitive while living in Toronto. I couldn't make a lot of money and was away from my family without a real life, so I decided to go back and give myself up in California, but I ran out of money, so I sold my car. You caught up with me before I made it."

The agents weren't completely sold on that story, since their investigation had uncovered that Corbett had attempted to locate a ship to board that would take him to Australia.

"Oh yeah?" asked Gunn. "What kind of car was it?"

There was a long pause. He didn't answer.

"Did you live in Denver earlier this year? Did you ever live in Denver?"

"Yes," he answered.

"While you were in Denver, did you order a .32-caliber revolver from the state of Maine?"

"Yes, I did."

"Why did you burn your 1951 Mercury near Atlantic City, New Jersey, on February 17, 1960?"

Corbett simply stared at the agents.

"Where is the brown hat you wore while you were in Denver?"

Again, Corbett didn't answer. He crossed his legs and twisted to one side away from the agents.

"What information are you willing to furnish about the old automobile you used to move some of your personal property from your apartment at 1435 Pearl on the morning of February 10, 1960?"

Corbett didn't turn around.

"Where were you at about 8:00 a.m. on February 9, 1960?"

Again there was silence before Corbett said, "This is the end of the questions. I want a lawyer."

"You sure about that?" asked Gunn.

"Yes. You know all the answers anyway. Lock me up. You're just trying to build a case."

"It will go easier on you if you cooperate."

"Easier for you. I got nothing more to say. Take me to my cell."

CHAPTER 18

CORBETT CAUGHT! Large letters jubilantly proclaimed across the front page of *Rocky Mountain News*—COORS SUSPECT SEIZED IN CANADA.

It was over. A long 263 days had passed since Ad Coors drew his last breath. A long 263 days of sadness and worry for Mary and the Coors family. Far too many days for a family wanting answers to the disappearance of a husband, father, son, and brother.

The loud clang of iron doors echoed throughout the block as visitors entered the fifth floor of the Vancouver jail.

"Hello, son," said Corbett's father as he entered with his fourth wife, Helen, who was fifteen years his junior. They'd flown from Seattle the day after his arrest.

Corbett stood and hugged his father. "Hello, Dad."

The three talked for almost an hour. Only they knew what was said.

When Mr. Corbett and his wife stepped off the elevator that had taken them from the fifth-floor cell to the main floor, Mr. Corbett told reporters he had not discussed the case. "We only talked as father and son."

When asked how his son was, the forlorn-looking father replied, "He appears happy and relieved that it's all over. You must remember this is the first time he's seen me in more than five years . . . since I visited him in Chino the day before his escape."

"Thank God, he didn't resist," added Corbett's stepmother.

Corbett's father, a linotype operator for *The Seattle Post-Intelligencer*, said, "I'm a newspaperman myself, and I know what you're up against. He—"

Mr. Corbett's wife tugged on his coat sleeve, shaking her head.

"We have nothing more to say," said Mr. Corbett, "only that my son is thirty-two, not thirty-five like he sometimes says."

The news of Corbett's capture hit Colorado like a blizzard in October. Folks snatched up every newspaper and tuned their radios and televisions to catch the breaking bulletins as news agencies exploded with a barrage of reports of the arrest, drowning out coverage of the 1960 presidential election, only a week away.

Reporters interviewed anyone who had anything to say about the case—the Coors family, Corbett's neighbors, landladies, coworkers, gas station attendants, store owners, laundry operators, used car dealers, and even passersby. However, no one's opinion mattered more than that of the victim's widow. Mary's quote in the newspaper summed up her pain and hatred: "I think he should get the gas chamber. There is no excuse for anyone like that going around alive."

Mary wasn't simply being macabre out of her hatred for her husband's killer. Colorado had executed an inmate in the gas chamber two weeks before Ad's disappearance, and four more were scheduled for execution, three of which would be carried out within the upcoming eighteen months.

Readers understood Mary's hardness. Many felt the same, and Ad had not been their husband or the father of their children. Others would have been more than happy to execute Corbett themselves.

Mary despised Corbett. To her, he was filth. As she stood with three of her children in the living room of her Denver home, informing them of the capture of their father's murderer, she may have gotten some satisfaction out of dropping the cyanide pellets herself. No one would blame her. She and her children had grown weary of such family meetings about the disappearance. All they wanted was their husband and father back home, alive and well, the way it used to be. They'd have to settle for the hope of legal justice.

A tired Corbett stood before Vancouver police magistrate Oscar Orr inside the wire-fenced dock, wearing the same green gabardine shirt and trousers he'd been arrested in Saturday. It was ten o'clock, Monday morning, October 31. He was charged with possession of an unregistered firearm, punishable by a two-year prison term in Canada. Bail had been denied. All of this was mere legal maneuvering to hold Corbett for extradition to the United States.

"This man is wanted in the United States on more serious charges, including a Jefferson County, Colorado, District Court warrant charging murder," said the Vancouver city prosecutor to the magistrate in a sparsely attended courtroom.

The judge, wearing black robes like judges in the United States, though with a starched white collar, peered down on Corbett standing with hands folded in front of him.

"I have a police arrest warrant for murder," said the magistrate. "I do not want you to feel bound to accept this warrant without reservation. Do you understand what you are doing?"

Corbett nodded without speaking.

"You have the right to a formal extradition hearing. Are you willing to return to the United States and waive the extradition hearing, knowing the charges you face?"

Corbett's lips twisted, like a faint smile. He didn't have a lawyer, but he was no dummy. He had told the FBI he was familiar with the Canadian Citizenship Act of 1947 and intended to resist extradition at the hearing. If Corbett stuck to his position, he would be entitled to an extradition hearing for which counsel would be appointed and time given to prepare, and even then, Canada might not extradite if there was a chance of the death penalty in the States. FBI agents listened, anxiously awaiting Corbett's answer.

"Yes, sir. I want them to take me right away." Corbett had either been bluffing or simply believed any further delay would be pointless.

"I will continue this matter until next Monday," said the magistrate. "If there is no action taken by Canadian and American officials on the matter of extradition by then, we will rearraign the prisoner."

That was the end of the first hearing. Corbett was removed from the dock and taken directly to another courtroom down the hall. "I understand you are here before me to formally waive your right to an extradition hearing," said Judge Stanley Remnant.

"Yes, sir," replied Corbett, once again standing in a Canadian dock near the center of the courtroom.

"You are entitled to a further hearing on this matter if you so desire," instructed the judge, giving Corbett another opportunity to object.

"No, sir. I wish to return to the United States."

"Do you understand your rights and waive them freely without threat or coercion?" continued the judge, realizing that Corbett could be executed if returned to the United States.

"Yes, sir."

The judge directed Corbett to lean across the dock's wooden rail to sign extradition papers placed on a table. He did as instructed and shortly thereafter was driven by Canadian officials forty miles to Blaine, Washington. Corbett said nothing during the hour-long ride, and his Canadian escorts asked him nothing about the Coors case.

Corbett was removed from the Canadian police car and handed over to FBI and US Immigration officials at Peace Arch Park on the US-Canadian border, a lovely two-park point of entry that allows visitors to stroll between countries amid flowers, ponds, and various works of art. The beauty was lost on Corbett, who was exhausted from the questioning and hearings and being shuffled about in heavy, uncomfortable shackles. He'd been on the run for eight months, eluding authorities on his trail in an effort to abscond to another country. Yet now he calmly waited as though for a bus back to Denver, where he could rest on a comfortable cot in a quiet cell.

Mounted Police removed Corbett from Canadian handcuffs and leg irons as FBI agents immediately placed Corbett in federal hand-cuffs and shackles. The hand-off process between countries, with the sound of the metal restraints clacking and clicking as Corbett was twisted and turned by agents, annoyed the prodigal fugitive. Agents then placed Corbett in their sedan and whisked him away to the nearest federal court for a hearing before US commissioner Richard Fleeson in Seattle. Now physically in the state of Washington, Cor-bett waived a preliminary hearing and signed a waiver for extradi-tion to Colorado. He was taken before US district court judge William Lindberg, who set Corbett's bail at $100,000. It was almost five o'clock. From there, a US marshal escorted Corbett to the King County jail in Tacoma, thirty miles south of Seattle, where he would wait until transported to Denver by Sheriff Wermuth, Captain Bray, and Dis-trict Attorney O'Kane, who held the Colorado warrant for his arrest.

"Mr. Coors! What do you think about the arrest of your son's sus-pected killer?" asked one of a gaggle of reporters assembled in the hallway of the brewery.

"It's a wonderful thing," said Mr. Coors in his dark suit and bow tie. "There's a person who shouldn't be on the streets for the general good."

No photographs were allowed. That was one of the elder Coors's stipulations for permitting reporters access inside the brewery.

"Are you relieved now that your son's killer has been jailed? Were you afraid—"

"I'm happy about it. I can say that."

"Did you think he might get away?"

"I never had any doubt he'd be apprehended. The FBI gets their man. The percentages were against him."

"Do you think a jury will find him guilty of murder?"

"Yes. There's no question in the world this man is guilty of kidnap-ping and murdering my son."

Mr. Coors rarely was generous with words.

"You think he should be executed?"

The father hesitated. He was not a religious man; however, he believed strongly in good morals and that every person's life is sacred, given by God.

"This is one of the instances when capital punishment, an eye for an eye and a tooth for a tooth, should apply."

"Do you plan to attend the trial?"

Mr. Coors placed a hand on Bill's shoulder to move him forward, signifying to reporters he was finished answering questions.

Rather than a visit from reporters, Mary received a telephone call from a reporter with *The Denver Post*. She'd stopped speaking to the press months earlier, refusing their calls in an attempt to reclaim some of the family's privacy. This time she spoke.

"Have you heard the FBI captured Joe Corbett?"

"Yes, I have."

"Were you notified by the FBI?"

"No. Actually, a friend called who'd heard it on the radio."

"How do you feel, Mrs. Coors, with word of Joe Corbett's capture?"

"I am naturally very glad and relieved. I was sure he would be caught. The FBI is infallible at this."

"Do you think he did it? Killed your husband?"

"I'm sure he did it."

Mary could not share law enforcement's exultation over the arrest. Corbett had beaten her husband and then cowardly shot him in the back, twice. Ad had suffered in the cold. Then he died, and his body was dumped like a piece of garbage in a scrap heap for animals to devour. She wanted to say the gas chamber was too humane for that cold-blooded killer. He deserved to die slowly and painfully—not only for Ad's terrible death but for what he'd done to her and her children.

Just before leaving for Vancouver to serve an arrest warrant on Corbett, Sheriff Wermuth had posed for a newspaper photograph snapped in front of the sheriff's bulletin board that displayed a large red *X* across Corbett's FBI Ten Most Wanted poster, even though he'd had nothing to do with Corbett's capture. Wermuth always craved the publicity, but it also was an election year for Barney O'Kane. O'Kane was running for reelection as the district attorney for the First Judicial District, which included Jefferson County. The election was in ten days, and his Republican opponent, Ronald Hardesty, had made it a close race. Wermuth had been elected in '58, and his bid for reelection wouldn't be for another four years. The Republican Wermuth had crossed party lines to support the Democrat O'Kane rather than his own party's challenger, Ron Hardesty, a decision that made him few friends in the local GOP.

On Monday afternoon, having chartered a plane after missing their scheduled flight, Wermuth, accompanied by his new wife, Julia, along with Captain Bray and O'Kane, landed in Vancouver. They talked to Corbett briefly before he was transported to the nearest FBI office, which was in Seattle. Once Corbett was in Seattle, the Coloradans wasted little time meeting with FBI Special Agent in Charge Earl Milnes and the city prosecutor.

"We'll take it from here," Wermuth told the FBI chief. "This is a local matter now."

"We're in the state of Washington, and you are a county sheriff in Colorado with a local arrest warrant," Milnes pointed out.

"But extradition has been waived," said O'Kane, sporting a white cowboy hat similar to that of Wermuth's. "We have the authority to take him."

"Tell you what. Stop by my office first thing in the morning, and I'll have all the paperwork ready to release him from the Tacoma jail to your custody."

It seemed things couldn't have worked out better for Wermuth. He knew there'd be a crowd of newspaper and television reporters at Stapleton Airfield the following day when they stepped off the plane in Denver with Corbett in shackles. With that kind of press, Wermuth could be sheriff as long as he wanted, he thought.

Wermuth, O'Kane, and Bray arrived at Seattle's art deco federal office building just before eight o'clock the next morning as planned, ready for the publicity parade to commence. A reporter saw the Coloradan entourage walking down the hallway. Curious, he asked why they were there.

"We're here to escort the Coors murder suspect back to Colorado," the sheriff said proudly with O'Kane nodding, both in full regalia, complete with brushed white Stetsons.

The reporter smiled. "I hate to be the one to tell you, but your prisoner left with the FBI on a plane to Denver last night."

"What?"

"He was booked in the Denver City jail early this morning."

The sheriff turned and said to O'Kane, "Those goddamn bastards," and walked away.

As part of a federal and local jurisdictional rivalry that's frequently stereotyped, the FBI had intentionally flown Corbett out of Seattle in the middle of the night for publicity purposes and hoodwinked the Colorado delegation.

"My father was violently opposed to the draft," said Corbett, handcuffed to Special Agent Hostetter on the midnight flight. "He's Canadian. That's how they feel. Canadians weren't drafted during World War I. Dad kept me from being drafted into Korea."

"Is that right?" muttered Agent Hostetter, who hoped Corbett would slip and say something that would send him to the gas chamber.

"Yeah, but who knows. If my father hadn't kept me out of the service, I'd probably be a colonel by now. So I guess you could say it's all my father's fault for the trouble I'm in." Corbett was content to babble on. "You know why you caught up with me so easy?"

" 'Cause you got sloppy?"

" 'Cause I'd decided I was done running," Corbett said arrogantly. "I just wanted to eat a few steaks before turning myself in."

"Is that why you were hunting for a ship to board in Vancouver? To turn yourself in to the ship's captain?"

Corbett scowled and gazed out the airplane's window into the darkness.

Flashbulbs popped as throngs of newsmen snapped photographs of Corbett stepping off a plane wearing a gray-and-black-checkered fingertip overcoat, clutching a fedora to cover his manacles. Special Agents Hostetter and Gunn escorted Corbett down the concourse ramp and into Werner's awaiting Plymouth, whisking Corbett not to the Jefferson County jail but to the Denver City jail.

While Wermuth and O'Kane were asleep in Seattle, newspapers developed photographs of the FBI's airport transfer for print later that morning. The two Coloradans forfeited a front-page photo with their infamous prisoner; instead, a small photo of them retrieving Corbett from the Denver City jail appeared on page five. Wermuth and O'Kane, who'd traveled 1,500 miles to Vancouver and then to Seattle and back, caught up with Corbett a mere fifteen miles from the sheriff's office. Yet Wermuth made the most of the occasion.

"Joseph Corbett, you are charged with the murder of Adolph Coors III, and you are being turned over to my custody to stand trial in Jefferson County," Wermuth decreed before reporters. "Here is a copy of the murder charge." Wermuth attempted to hand the official document to Corbett, whose hands were manacled and linked to a large leather restraining belt around his waist.

Corbett smiled. "I'll accept it without reading it."

Wermuth also used the occasion to accuse the FBI of what he called "glory grabbing."

"They deliberately lied. . . . They're trying to grab credit for cracking the case by attempting to get a statement from Corbett," said Wermuth. "The FBI can expect little welcome cooperation from my county or officers, and I intend to write J. Edgar Hoover advising him of the lack of cooperation and goodwill between local and federal officers."

What Wermuth didn't realize was that in all likelihood Hoover had authorized the secret flight. If anyone relished favorable press more than Wermuth, it was the FBI director.

The fiasco provided the opposition candidate for district attorney, Ron Hardesty, plenty of fodder during the final days of the campaign.

He described O'Kane's "ridiculous" failed trip to Canada as a "wild-goose chase at taxpayer expense" that accomplished nothing and was only taken to receive free publicity during an election. Thereafter, the junket was labeled the "Canadian Wild Goose Caper" by the press.

Wermuth received no better treatment. Besides being part of the Canadian Wild Goose Caper, a local newspaper carried a cartoon headed, "Gee Whiz, Marshal Dillon," lampooning Wermuth and O'Kane as gangly, Old West–style lawmen unwittingly shackled together walking up to a Colorado locksmith with a bag labeled, "Corbett or Bust."

On Halloween 1960, the same day Joseph Corbett was standing in a Canadian court, Mary was seated in a Jefferson County court beside Bruce Buell, an estate attorney, and Thomas R. Walker, a banker.

Most mothers were preparing for trick-or-treating, a scary night for the very young and a few older superstitious ones. A night of knocks on doors, candy, and plastic masks and costumes of monsters—Frankenstein, Dracula, Werewolf, and the Creature from the Black Lagoon—while *Psycho* and *The Fall of the House of Usher* played at movie theaters. But these were only fictitious monsters created to sell tickets and popcorn. They were fantasy, "just pretend," Mary had always told her children. Mary would make certain Jim had a fun Halloween, but first she had to experience a veritable horror of her own—walking through the courthouse hallway before the probate hearing commenced.

Mary didn't want to be in court that day, but she was a co-executor of Ad's estate, and the judge always required executors to affirmatively acknowledge in his presence the solemn undertaking for which they'd been named in the last will and testament. Yet it was a public place, and Mary, who once enjoyed any opportunity to go out and socialize, now wished to avoid it.

Several people recognized her. Others had gotten word of the probate proceedings in the newspapers and came solely to catch a glimpse of her. Whether by chance or design, those who knew she was Ad Coors's widow greeted her as she passed. A courthouse employee asked if she needed water. Another asked if there was anything she could get her. Mary was accustomed to being treated nicely, being a Grant and a Coors in Colorado. People had smiled, nodded, and held doors open for her all her life, but this was different. The awkward smiles, sad faces, and courteous gestures emanated not from respect but pity. For perhaps the first time, many were glad they weren't Mary Grant Coors.

The side door of the courtroom opened, and the judge, dressed in a black robe, stepped up to sit at the bench as the bailiff barked out the traditional introduction to open the court. The Honorable Roscoe Pile took his seat behind the elevated bench and below the Great Seal of the State of Colorado. The clerk handed the judge a file.

"In the Matter of the Estate of Adolph Coors III, Deceased, Case No. 6971," called the court clerk, W. W. Churchill.

"Hello, Mrs. Coors," said the bespectacled Judge Pile, straying from his typical courtroom demeanor to pay respect to the prominent petitioner. "This will only take a moment." Her deceased husband's probate matter had been placed at the top of the docket.

Mary sat on a wooden pew at the front of the courtroom. The courthouse in Golden was not a modern facility. The Victorian-style, three-story building had seen better days. Built in the previous century, its wood-paneled walls and creaky floors smelled musty. (It would be razed three years later.)

Standing before the judge, Buell requested permission to speak. "The decedent, Adolph Herman Joseph Coors III, died on or about February 9, 1960, and his remains were discovered on September 11 through 15, 1960. At the time of his death, Mr. Coors was a resident of Jefferson County. As Mr. Coors is deceased, I would like to offer his last will and testament into probate with the court. It was signed by Mr. Coors on February 19, 1959, in the presence of two witnesses, Stephen H. Hart, esquire, and Mr. W. D. Embree Jr., esquire. I have two affidavits signed by Messrs. Hart and Embree stating . . ."

The estate attorney continued with the many procedural details required by courts, particularly in probate matters, carried over from old English common law when matters of death were handled by the ecclesiastical courts under the control of the Church of England.

Buell handed the sixteen-page last will and testament and affidavits to the court clerk. The clerk in turn handed the documents to the judge for his review. The judge scanned the documents and announced, "I hereby admit this as the last will and testament of Adolph Coors III and open his estate for administration. And I grant Letters Testamentary to the co-executors of the estate, Mrs. Mary Grant Coors and the First National Bank of Denver, represented here today by Mr. Thomas R. Walker, evidencing their authority to act on behalf of the deceased's estate."

Most in the courtroom didn't appreciate the true meaning of the judge's words. Perhaps only two did—the estate attorney and Mary. Even the judge, who said basically the same thing at every probate hearing, only changing the names, probably didn't realize the true import of what he'd just said. A Colorado court had ruled that Ad Coors was dead.

Attorney Buell held open the swing gate leading into the gallery as Mary walked through first. Down the center aisle Mary walked, not making eye contact with all the sympathetic onlookers. Halfway to the doors, she caught herself and raised her chin, poised, showing all that she still was a Grant and a Coors. Though only a few seconds, it seemed to Mary like one of the longest walks she had taken. She stepped into the hallway, which was thankfully free of people.

Twelve weeks later, Buell filed an inventory of Ad's estate with the court. The value of the estate for death tax purposes was $618,657.17. A large estate for anyone in 1960 (worth $5 million today), though not commensurate with that of a chairman of a huge company like Adolph Coors Company and the heir of a multimillionaire father, in part because he was only forty-four and had not lived to inherit his share of his father's wealth.

The filing of a detailed inventory of Ad's assets and their values was now a matter of public record for reporters to publish in their newspapers for all to read. Just another indignity Mary had to suffer. They seemed to be never ending—caused not by a Halloween character but by a real-life fiend who'd ruthlessly murdered her husband and dumped his body in the snow-covered mountains. And that was only the beginning. There was no plastic mask for this monster, but Corbett's depraved face and his evildoing were no less frightening. For regardless of what judicially lay ahead of him, he would torment Mary for the rest of her life with nightmares, hatred, alcoholism, and ultimately a premature death.

For a person convicted of murder to be sentenced to death in Colorado in 1960, one of two conditions was required. There must be an eyewitness to the killing. No eyewitness had yet stepped forward in the Coors case, so that left the other condition, a confession to the murder. So far, Corbett wasn't talking. Sheriff Wermuth said he would see to it that Corbett not only confessed but confessed to him, providing the sheriff with a chance to regain some respect after appearing foolish in the press.

Wermuth's quest to browbeat a confession out of the suspect started the minute Corbett stepped foot in the Jefferson County jail. The sheriff chatted with Corbett through the entire booking process and even while Corbett changed into his prison uniform, but Corbett was defiant, saying nothing more than what was necessary to complete his processing into the county jail.

After Golden physician and Jefferson County deputy coroner, Dr. John Hunt, examined Joe Corbett, Wermuth led his new prisoner to a cell and sat to question him while his first meal was served on a metal tray.

"Do any fishing while you were in Canada?" Wermuth asked, trying to break the ice with his "celebrity" prisoner.

Corbett gave Wermuth a look as if to say, "You're kidding, right?" Corbett wasn't a typical prisoner. He wasn't going to be tricked into some best-pal discourse with his jailer, especially about fugitive fishing. Not only was Corbett intelligent, he'd been a guest in several correctional facilities—Beverly Hills, Marin County, San Quentin, Soledad, Terminal Island, and Chino, not to mention his brief stay in Vancouver and Tacoma.

Wermuth continued with his questions.

"You writing a book?" replied Corbett.

The sheriff chuckled, though Corbett's remark angered him.

After four and a half hours of questions, Captain George Drazich (called "the man with the keys") unlocked the cell door from the outside and Wermuth stepped out to give his prisoner some time to reflect on how it would be wise to spill the details of the crime. The sound of Wermuth's boot heels clicking the concrete floor told Corbett his captor was finally gone. He stretched out on his cot and closed his eyes.

A lobby filled with reporters greeted Wermuth as he exited the cell block. He pulled a comb from his pocket and raked it through his hair. Dispatcher Madeline Pearce handed him his Stetson.

The journalists began asking questions all at the same time, each attempting to have their question answered first. "You drag a confession out of him yet, Sheriff?" could be heard more clearly than the others.

"Not yet, but I will. You have to go about this kind of thing scientifically, boys. Corbett's a smart cookie. He just won't blurt out that he did it. That's why I've been softening him up, you know, making friends with him, making small talk."

Wermuth didn't mention that Corbett truculently told him, "You're only interested in your political future."

Photos were snapped of Wermuth standing at his office door. Later, he led newsmen into an empty cell as Corbett was showering for more photos of Wermuth holding the cell bars and pointing out Corbett's meal on a prison tray.

"How much longer you plan on softening 'im up?" asked a reporter.

"Maybe he and I will have a little powwow in the morning, and it'll get a might hostile in that cell if he doesn't cooperate because we're not spending months more pussyfootin' around," the sheriff boasted.

Two days later, things were indeed getting hostile. Wermuth was frustrated. Corbett wasn't saying a word, not even looking at his interrogators. The interrogation would begin at nine o'clock each day, stop for lunch at noon, and then resume until 3:30 with spot interrogations conducted at any moment thereafter, even if they had to rouse Corbett at two or three o'clock in the morning.

"We're starting the interview in teams for only straight interrogation, no manhandling or abuse," said Wermuth. "We're trying to draw him out of his shell and put him in a receptive frame of mine. Captain Bray and Lieutenant Kechter are our first team."

"Has he told you anything you can use in court?"

"Well, the prisoner talks in generalities mostly. When we ask him anything skirting on the Coors case, he merely stares at us."

"Is it frustrating waiting for him to break?"

"You're damn right it's frustrating, but we got plenty of time. He's not going anywhere," continued Wermuth. "It seems to me to be a question of finding the right moment of feeling and the right personality he will respond to. But he will, and before he knows it, he'll be strapped in the chamber waiting for ol' Harry to pull the lever." (Harry Tinsley was the warden at Colorado State Penitentiary in Cañon City charged with carrying out all state executions.)

Wermuth would soon learn Corbett wasn't stupid enough to confess and send himself to the gas chamber. Until then, Wermuth played up his interrogation in front of reporters as if to portray that Colorado justice rested entirely on his broad shoulders. His chats with reporters would continue up to and throughout Corbett's trial.

If that publicity seeking wasn't bad enough, Wermuth and his collaborator District Attorney O'Kane had their photographs taken by newspapers reading the FBI investigation report (O'Kane was photographed holding the full report), which was supplied to *The Denver Post* and touted as an "exclusive," even though Special Agent Werner had supplied the FBI report to the district attorney "confidentially for your official use at the time it is determined that prosecution is to be had by your office." *The Post* printed its exclusive on September 22, detailing key points in the report.

Six years later, long after Wermuth and O'Kane were ousted from office, a Colorado Supreme Court justice would have an opportunity in a legal opinion to address Wermuth and O'Kane's propensity for leaking information during the Coors investigation:

> We do not sanction improper publicity, nor the activities of those who caused it in the present case. . . . Certainly not all the blame for the harmful publicity can be laid at the feet of the press. Most of the information which they published would never have been available had it not been for the overzealous release of material by the law enforcement and prosecution officials. These officials have the very important responsibility of protecting the rights of the accused.

The Colorado Supreme Court justice was gracious enough not to name the two foremost offenders.

CHAPTER 19

On Election Day, November 8, 1960, John F. Kennedy narrowly defeated his Republican opponent, Richard M. Nixon. The race was so close that Nixon did not concede until the following afternoon. The election of the district attorney for the First Judicial District that included Jefferson County wasn't as close. Incumbent Barney O'Kane, who had been part of the Canadian Wild Goose Caper, was out. The baby-faced thirty-six-year-old Ronald J. Hardesty would be the new district attorney beginning January 10. His first big case would be the Coors murder trial.

Hardesty had worked as an FBI agent, a former position that would serve him well working with the tight-lipped FBI on the Coors case. He'd also practiced law for the previous eight years while serving as assistant Colorado attorney general and as Jefferson County attorney after losing the election for the district attorney's office to O'Kane in '56. He was easygoing and amiable, but effective.

The young prosecutor also had an impressive war record, though he didn't tout his like the county sheriff. He had been a Hellcat fighter pilot in the Pacific during World War II, assigned to the carrier USS *Yorktown*. He flew numerous missions and several times returned in a plane ripped by enemy bullets. Once, his plane was so riddled that sailors shoved the assemblage of holes and dangling metal parts off the deck into the ocean.

Hardesty would be aided by Assistant District Attorney Edward

Juhan and a well-respected friend of Hardesty's, Richard Hite, as well as a friend of Juhan's, Tony Zarlengo. Sitting with the prosecution to assist with the FBI's evidence (over the objection of defense counsel) would be FBI special agent Jesse Orr.

H. Malcolm Mackay, a thirty-six-year-old nondescript Denver attorney, was appointed by the court to defend Corbett. One of his first acts was to stand in court beside his infamous client on November 15 when the official charge was read.

"Mr. Corbett, that's a charge of murder," said the judge. "How do you plead?"

Corbett was dressed in a new brown suit, white shirt, and olive-gold tie mailed by his father. Without hesitation and in a loud, clear voice, he answered, "I plead not guilty."

A few days later, Mackay realized he couldn't handle the case alone. After talking it over with his client, Mackay requested, and the court appointed, an intelligent and meticulous attorney, William H. Erickson, to serve as cocounsel. Like Hardesty and Mackay, Erickson was also thirty-six-years-old. He was a well-respected trial lawyer in Denver who graduated from the Colorado School of Mines in Golden with a degree in petroleum engineering and received his law degree from the University of Virginia. He was more than capable of handling the case alone; however, since Mackay had already been appointed, Erickson would technically serve as Mackay's assistant without pay from the county. Mackay would have to split his county fee with Erickson, a fee much lower than Erickson was accustomed to receiving. Despite the low pay, Erickson believed Corbett was entitled to receive the best representation possible and, of course, understood what the publicity and prominence of the case could bring to his career. (Erickson would become a Colorado Supreme Court justice in 1971, and would chair the Columbine Review Commission in 2000.) He brought with him the services of a smart, young legal associate, Charles Brega.

As their first order of business, Erickson and Mackay addressed the constant barrage of interrogation hurled at their client in the county jail by the overzealous sheriff and his deputies.

Corbett couldn't even talk with his lawyers without the sheriff or his deputies interrupting or strolling past. Wermuth had hoped to cajole a confession out of him, but now with Mackay and Erickson on board, that wasn't going to happen. The best Wermuth could hope for was to "overhear" something of importance or uncover it in Corbett's mail.

The sheriff also paraded Corbett in front of newsmen—cell transfers, bed checks, searches, and seemingly choreographed shackled marches to and from the county jail and courthouse.

Incensed, Erickson filed a motion requesting Corbett be moved to another jail because Sheriff Wermuth, his deputies, and agents were "assaulting, battering, beating, cursing, or otherwise mistreating Joe Corbett. . . . They question him for long periods and the interrogation has been accompanied by threats of great bodily harm and treatment designed to destroy the mind of Corbett and compel a confession." The motion also accused the sheriff of brainwashing in an attempt to force a confession of murder in violation of Corbett's rights under the Fifth and Fourteenth Amendments.

Wermuth took the stand to answer the charges in Erickson's motion. The sheriff swore, under oath, he had never abused or mistreated a prisoner in his four years as sheriff. "I don't interrogate them. I simply talk to them. . . . Any accusation that Joe Corbett is being mistreated in my jail is completely untrue," said the sheriff. "He has been treated properly, the same as any other prisoner. . . . As for interrogations, he has never been subjected to harsh questioning. It's always more of a discussion. We have never made any flat accusations. And the discussions are not prolonged."

But the lawyers, like many in town, knew the sheriff had the propensity to stretch the truth, and a statement that Corbett was being treated the same as any other prisoner wasn't saying a whole lot. But in this case, Brega, years later, confirmed part of the sheriff's denials, saying, "There was no physical abuse I was aware of, just interfering with defense lawyers speaking with Corbett and giving them privacy, and interrogating for long hours."

In response to Erickson's motion, Judge Stoner issued a protective order precluding Wermuth and his deputies from mistreating or questioning Corbett. The judge found nothing to substantiate charges of physical abuse.

Despite the protective order, the sheriff's star was on the rise. Hosting the alleged murderer of the former Coors brewery chairman in his jail garnered nationwide news coverage. Wermuth was asked to endorse products as if he were Mickey Mantle or Arnold Palmer. Even as far away as Garland, Texas, the Resistol Hat Company promoted its new "County Sheriff" hat in the newspapers and magazines, with an inset photo of Wermuth wearing the hat: "Designed for the Western Man-of-Influence . . . the County Sheriff combines dignified good looks and top quality with comfortable fit."

But every rising star must fall . . . and Wermuth's star was about to do just that.

The Denver Club Gala Ball was the first in years not attended by Mr. and Mrs. Adolph Coors III. Like all socials at the Denver Club, the night of Friday, December 16, 1960, brought out the wealth and pageantry to open Denver's winter social season atop the newly constructed Denver Club Building that replaced the old red-stone clubhouse on the same site. Red carnations spelled out the year 1880 in honor of the eightieth anniversary of the founding of the Denver Club, one of the country's oldest and most prestigious. Photos of the grand party would gild the Sunday edition's society sections of *The Denver Post* and *Rocky Mountain News* the following day.

Everyone regaled that evening wore fine tuxedos and luxurious gowns, except Mary. She was home in her nightgown. She believed if she attended the gala, she'd be sitting at a table like the latest exhibit at Denver Zoo, on display for all the curious.

No, that's the last place on earth I want to be tonight, thought Mary. *I'm right where I want to be. Home with my family.*

Brooke was home from college for winter break, and Cecily was on the phone with her latest boyfriend. Jim was asleep. Spike was in the living room with Mary, watching television. The Christmas tree was up. The girls decorated it with help from Jim. Bing Crosby, Nat King Cole, Perry Como, and Brenda Lee still sang in their home, but their music no longer brought Mary joy. She could only think of the years of Christmas with Ad in the living room, listening to Christmas music, and looking at the lights of the Christmas tree beside the fire. Ad had driven the family around their previous Denver neighborhood at night, looking at the multicolored Christmas lights on houses and the wreaths hanging on lampposts along the city streets.

But Ad's death had tarnished Christmas for everyone. The kids lamented their father, and Mary's state of mind made it even worse. The loss of the love of her life had left a chasm in her heart and mind that even her children couldn't fill.

On the night of the ball, Mary was drinking gin, her defense against the pain. She was drinking, missing Ad, and hating his killer.

Corbett wasn't having a ball either. His defense attorneys had filed a variety of motions addressed during a ninety-minute hearing on Monday after the weekend's gala ball. Some observers called it throwing motions against the wall to see if anything stuck.

- A motion for a copy of the voluminous FBI investigation report in the district attorney's possession—DENIED.

- A motion for a list of FBI agents the prosecution intended to call as witnesses during the trial—DENIED.

- A motion to set bail for Corbett predicated on the dearth of evidence—DENIED.

- A motion to move Corbett from the Jefferson County jail in Golden to another place of incarceration—DENIED.

- A motion to dismiss the case charging Corbett with murder because his constitutional rights had been violated and he had been denied due process of law—DENIED.

- A motion for a delay of trial to interview newly named prosecution witnesses and court approval of expenses for travel—DENIED.

- A motion for a continuance—DENIED.

- A motion for discovery—DENIED.

- A motion for the appointment of an expert—DENIED.

- A motion for a change in venue. Defense counsel argued that it would be impossible to have a trial by an impartial jury based on the local prominence of the name *Coors* and the almost daily news coverage since Ad Coors's disappearance. Counsel offered affidavits of twenty-nine persons from various walks of life in the county to support the motion—DENIED.

Not all of the legal maneuvering had negative results. A motion to have a court-appointed psychiatrist, Dr. John P. Hilton, was approved, and a motion was granted that prohibited photographers, television cameras, and live radio from the courtroom and from the second-floor hallway outside it. However, ten newspapermen, with their tablets, pens, and pencils, were permitted to sit at a single table inside the bar of the court where typically only lawyers and witnesses are allowed. The judge also ruled that the sheriff's office could no longer place Corbett in handcuffs while escorting him to and from the courthouse in order to avoid potentially prejudicing jurors.

As the legal lines of battle were being drawn, Corbett rested in his county-provided cell, isolated from the other prisoners, and waited. The sheriff and a deputy would take him out to attend a hearing about this or that legal point, when he would dress in a suit for the trip across the snowy, blustery street to the courthouse, escorted tightly by each arm. Reporters waiting in the jail lobby were notified before each march from confinement to judicial wrangling. County police officials also provided reporters with the particulars of what Corbett ate, how he slept, and what he read.

Corbett, an avid reader, accepted whatever magazines or books lay in the jail's waiting area and offices—*Field & Stream, Sports*

Illustrated, *TV Week*, and a bawdy magazine like *Plush*. Wermuth also offered Corbett his personal influx of magazines. Despite his recent business reversal, Corbett's favorite magazine turned out to be *Fortune*.

Corbett received three meals a day. Breakfast at 7:30, lunch at noon, and then an early dinner at 3:30 so the cook and dishwashers could leave for home by five o'clock. The county menu included oatmeal, fresh eggs, biscuits, fried potatoes, fruit preserves with butter for breakfast, and pork chops, meat loaf, mashed potatoes, gravy, spinach, buttered bread, tea, coffee, cake, and Jell-O for lunch or dinner.

The murder trial was set for March 13, giving Corbett a respite of three months in the county jail to relax, eat good meals, and read the sheriff's magazines. Aside from Sheriff Wermuth's initial barrage of questioning, the sheriff had been forthright when he took the stand in defense of his interrogation protocol. There was no longer any mistreatment of Corbett in his jail.

District Attorney Ron Hardesty wasn't pleased he'd been summoned to leave his Golden office and drive to Denver to meet with a corporate attorney. In one of Denver's finest buildings, with marble floors and brass elevator, the office boasted a pair of heavy wooden doors and a brass plate carrying the law firm's prestigious title.

The corporate lawyer had requested the list of questions Hardesty sought to ask Mary before he'd permit her to take the stand. A district attorney always has the option of issuing a subpoena to force a witness to appear in court, and continued refusal could be met with fine and imprisonment in the county jail, but Hardesty couldn't jail the widow of Ad Coors. If he did, he would be the shortest-serving district attorney in history.

On the other side of a large, ornate mahogany door, Mary was reading the district attorney's intended questions. Other than her name and address, each question seemed to ask more than she felt she could give.

Why do they need me at all? she thought. She didn't know anything about the crime. She was at home when it happened. They had all the evidence: the bloody clothes, the pictures of bones, the FBI's massive investigation report.

She blanched at the question: "Can you tell us about the morning of your husband's disappearance?"

"I can't answer this question. I really can't. It's too painful," Mary told the attorney.

"I understand, Mrs. Coors, truly I do, but we've been through this. Keep your answers short like they're written and follow them like a script—without taking the papers into court, of course."

"How did you feel when you didn't hear back from the kidnapper?" was another question.

"How do they think I felt?" Mary shot up from her seat and paced across the room. "How would they feel if it had been their husband or wife?" she asked, raising the papers and pointing them at the lawyer. "How would they explain it to their children who were crying themselves to sleep every night?"

"I know," said the attorney softly, his tone emanating from genuine sympathy or perhaps from fatigue dealing with the grieving widow. Not the typical corporate transaction to which he was accustomed. "But the DA has to show the jury the cruelty not only of the act itself but its effects on you, his widow, and your children. It makes a case that otherwise may seem like just another story out of a newspaper come alive, become something real, affecting real people, even—"

"Even me? Someone it's not supposed to happen to? Is that what you mean? After all, no one thinks anything bad ever happens to people of wealth."

"These people are your friends, Mrs. Coors. They feel badly. Who wouldn't? They want to help send the man who did this terrible thing to prison."

"Most of them just want to come and watch the circus," said Mary, glaring at the attorney. "Get a seat up front. The grislier, the better. They should sell tickets. People crowding into the courtroom, pushing and shoving for a chance to see some bloody clothes and Ad's bones, all hoping to see me cry on the witness stand."

The attorney stood and walked around his desk to hand Mary a handkerchief. She accepted it and wiped her eyes. A minute passed before she finally said, "Okay, I'm ready."

"You sure?"

"Yes."

The attorney returned to his desk and pushed a button on the intercom.

"Tell Mr. Hardesty to come in."

"Hey, what is this?" asked Corbett. A Jefferson County deputy cuffed Corbett and led him from his cell down a corridor and out a side door, where three men waited near a dark sedan on the night of February 28.

"Just shut up and come along," said James Buckley, a former sheriff's deputy, now an investigator for the district attorney's office. Bray and Kechter were with Buckley as they shoved Corbett into the back seat of Buckley's sedan and sped off into the darkness.

"Where you taking me?"

"You'll find out soon enough. Relax."

Corbett couldn't relax. He'd heard about these kinds of things. Being stuffed into a car by vigilantes and taken to a remote spot to be beaten and hanged like the days of the Old West. That or tossed into a river wearing cinder blocks for shoes. It was happening all over the South. Beatings, lynchings, shootings, with the law turning their heads or, worse, participating. And here he was stuffed in an unmarked car heading to God knows where late at night.

"I want to call my lawyer," said Corbett.

"Get a load of this guy. Hey, Ray, you got a dime for our passenger?" Buckley laughed. "Says he needs to make a call."

Corbett sank into his seat.

Twenty minutes passed, and Corbett could see the lights of Denver. Were they going to put him on a plane? This didn't make sense, but at least they were heading into the city.

Buckley turned off the highway, and soon Corbett saw *Denver Police Station* on a brick building.

"What are we doing here? I'm supposed to be in the county jail, not the city," protested Corbett, knowing the judge had not approved the switch.

The sedan pulled into the garage, and the men exited the car. One pulled Corbett out of the back seat. "Come on."

Half an hour later, Corbett was standing alongside four other men of similar height, weight, and features facing a mirrored wall.

"Number one, step forward," called the Denver police officer. "What is your age? . . . What is your occupation? . . . How long have you been in Denver? . . . That's all. Step back."

The man did as he was told.

"Turn to the right. Turn back facing forward. Step back. Number three. Step forward."

The first three men did as they were told.

"Number four. Step forward. . . . Number four step forward." A petulant Corbett didn't move. State your name and age." Corbett said nothing. "Number five. . . ."

Corbett knew a policeman stood with a witness behind the mirrored wall. That was the whole point of a lineup. He didn't know fifteen potential witnesses were watching him: Denver store clerks, gas attendants, and Turkey Creek Canyon residents.

Buckley instructed the men to march off the elevated platform and assemble in the hallway. All were told they could go, except Corbett.

"Come with me," said Buckley.

Corbett was taken into an interview room in handcuffs, where Buckley questioned him for forty-five minutes.

"I don't have to answer any questions. You're not even supposed to have me here," Corbett protested. "The judge signed a protective order. Keeps you fellows from asking me questions."

"That only applies to the sheriff's office, not the district attorney's office," said Buckley, who'd resigned as a deputy only a few weeks earlier.

"Same thing," said Corbett.

"No, I'd have to disagree with you there, Mr. High IQ. We're all detectives for the DA's office. Nobody here is from the sheriff's office. Not anymore. So here, answer these questions," instructed Buckley, who slid a sheet of paper with fifteen questions toward Corbett, all asking for an incriminating answer, a go-straight-to-the-gas-chamber type of answer. "You should give a full and complete confession. It's the right thing to do. It would help the family. Wouldn't you like to make them feel better after what you did to a husband with four kids? Just withdraw your denial and confess. I'm giving you good advice. The judge will give you a fair shake if you do."

Corbett didn't touch the paper. Instead, he leaned back in his chair and folded his arms in defiance. There'd be no mea culpa. He hadn't bowed to the FBI in Vancouver or to Wermuth's pressure to confess in Golden, and he wasn't going to confess to the DA's office in Denver or anywhere else for that matter. He knew it meant the death penalty. He'd have to sit out whatever was going on and call his lawyers when he had a chance. The following day, that's exactly what he did.

Corbett's defense lawyers were furious and immediately filed a motion for contempt against Wermuth, Buckley, and all others who were involved in the late-night questioning. Erickson demanded jail for the conspirators.

Instead, the judge scolded the district attorney and broadened the original protective order against the sheriff's office to include the district attorney's office.

"I don't want this man interrogated by you or anyone else," Judge Stoner angrily instructed the district attorney.

"But one witness positively identified him, Your Honor. I'd like to request another lineup," asked an obstinate District Attorney Hardesty.

"You'll not get it from this court," the judge replied.

For Judge Stoner, two kidnappings were enough.

CHAPTER 20

I will recommend that a special grand jury be called to investigate the office of Sheriff Art Wermuth," the district attorney told reporters. "It's necessary because some folks in the sheriff's office won't come forward without being brought before a grand jury."

The newly installed district attorney, Ron Hardesty, had other cases to work besides the headline-grabbing Coors murder trial, but none was of great interest, except one: the Sheriff Wermuth expense probe.

For the first time in seven years, a Jefferson County grand jury was convened by the district attorney's office. "You will be expected to probe the financial affairs of the Jefferson County Sheriff's Office," Hardesty instructed the grand jury.

Sheriff Wermuth countered by doing some probing of his own. According to Assistant District Attorney Edward Juhan, the married sheriff intimately discovered at least one female ally on the grand jury who might assist in thwarting the indictment. Yet as Wermuth drove his county vehicle to work, his days of savoring the limelight were swiftly coming to an end.

"No one has approached me," Wermuth told a reporter accosting him in a parking lot. "I have no intention now or in the future of resigning." The newsman was following a story that many members in the local Republican Party had asked Wermuth to resign over his inventive bookkeeping methods. "If there is anything illegal about mileage vouchers, expense accounts, or anything else, I have no knowledge of it."

Shortly after Wermuth submitted an expense voucher to the county commission for his humiliating boondoggle to Vancouver in an attempt to retrieve Corbett, outgoing county commissioners George Osborne and Bob Schoech refused to reimburse the sheriff. Commissioner Osborne told reporters he requested more information that had not been forthcoming. When asked if the sheriff would cooperate soon, the commissioner said, "I'm not worried. The sheriff will be in when he doesn't get paid."

Expenses included a stay at the Hotel Vancouver and the Olympic Hotel in Seattle, not only for him but his third wife. When asked why he'd taken his new wife along on official business and sought reimbursement from taxpayer dollars, Wermuth first explained, "She took the original call on the dispatcher's board about the missing Adolph Coors and continued the chain of evidence." When commissioners said that didn't make sense, the sheriff changed his story. "She is a stenographer who would be needed to take a statement from Corbett should he make one."

When reporters relayed Wermuth's story, Commissioner Osborne replied, "Unless she's taken some schooling in the last year or so, I doubt very seriously if she would qualify as a stenographer."

In addition to the Seattle hotel, meals, and other expenses, the sheriff had chartered a plane and had deemed much of his trip as overtime pay. Commissioners also learned that Wermuth gave deputies overtime pay to paint his wife's house with county paint, and he'd tapped into the courthouse water pipes and furnace to divert water and heat to the sheriff's residence next door.

As the story heated up, the sheriff told the press, "I don't say there couldn't be a mechanical error in these vouchers, but I do say there is absolutely nothing illegal now or in the past in the manner in which this office submits expense accounts for payment. I hope this whole thing is cleared up as quickly as possible."

The first newspaper article about the expense probe appeared on

Thanksgiving Day. Other newspaper articles followed, keeping the investigation in the news all the way up to the Coors murder trial. Like the Coors disappearance, this was a story that wouldn't go away. Only this time, Wermuth wasn't posing for photographers.

District Attorney Ron Hardesty and his assistants Dick Hite and Ed Juhan continued their discussion in Hardesty's office about the most likely scenario of Ad Coors's murder in preparation for the upcoming trial. Hardesty had just described the struggle on Turkey Creek Bridge and the shots fired as Ad tried to escape to his Travelall. Now Hardesty turned to the more gruesome part of the case.

"I'm sure Mr. Coors let out a groan when the bullets tore into his back, penetrating his right shoulder blade and piercing his right lung, which likely collapsed. Blood sprayed everywhere: on the railing, on his car, even on the rocks along the creek bank with help from the gusting wind. He reached for the railing as he fell and twisted on the way down, landing on his back, groaning and gurgling as blood drained from his body seeping into the gravel. A stunned Corbett looked around and didn't see anyone. He knelt beside the ashen-faced Coors, breathing fast and coughing, blood exiting his mouth as one lung filled with blood. Corbett felt for a pulse and removed his pocketknife and cut the defenseless Coors's tie, opened his shirt, and cut the shoulder strap of his undershirt to look at the wound. There were no exit wounds on his chest. By this time Coors was falling unconscious from blood loss."

"That plays well for juries, but I don't think we can get in the moans and all the bleeding, too speculative and prejudicial," said Hite. "I like the theater of it, however."

"We'll try to get some of it in," replied Hardesty. "Okay, I'm almost finished. Corbett didn't freeze. He had to have acted quickly because the veterinarian drove by at 8:04 exactly, and he said he saw no sign of anyone. The way I see it, Corbett sprinted to his car, grabbed the green blanket out of the trunk, placed it on the ground, and rolled Coors on it. He carried or dragged Coors to the rear car door and slid him onto the back seat or floorboard. Corbett shut the door, slammed the hood, and with one last look around for eyewitnesses, climbed into the car and sped away, digging gravel as he left. That accounts for the tire marks at the north end of the bridge. By this time, Coors was either dead or had only minutes left before he bled to death."

"Makes sense to me," said Juhan.

"I've got a bit more here about dumping the body," Hardesty said, looking down at his notes.

"Go on," said Hite.

"All right. As Corbett drove, he had to decide on a location to dump Coors's body, because I'm sure he hadn't planned to kill him, at least not at the bridge. So he chose some place he'd been before, target shooting. The Shamballah Ashrama dump. We have the FBI's sighting of the three-pawed bear at the dump that Brynaert told us Corbett had described to him, and we have the statement from the lodge proprietor that put Corbett near the dump. He drove twenty miles south into Douglas County, taking Jackson Creek Road up the mountain to the dump. Mud from the melting snow mixed with pink feldspar stuck under the Mercury's carriage and fenders. He reached the dump and dragged Coors's body from the back seat, still wrapped in the blanket, a hundred feet or so into the thick woods, away from the area where folks dumped garbage. Wild animals did the rest."

"Too bad we can't get the death penalty," said Juhan.

"Mrs. Coors's testimony hopefully will make the jurors feel as you do, Ed," said Hite. "What do you have, Ron, about what he did with the car and how he cleaned up afterward? I'm not clear on that."

"Neither am I," said Hardesty. "But we don't have to know for certain. I'll tell you what I think happened, though. I think he drove to Denver. The smell of warm blood and urine filled his car's interior, so he went to some location to clean up the Mercury and himself. Probably parked the Mercury in a garage. Then maybe he switched vehicles, taking an already mud-covered Dodge to mail the ransom note around 2:15 p.m. He parked the Dodge at a secret location and walked to his apartment, where he showered and listened for news about the crime."

"That whole Dodge/Mercury thing bothers me," said Juhan. "The FBI couldn't find the Dodge."

"He just had two cars is my guess," said Hardesty. "The gas station attendant said he saw Corbett in a '46 or '47 Dodge. He probably dumped the Dodge somewhere. We'll be ready for this. Okay, I'm almost done."

"Yep. Go ahead and finish," said Juhan.

"Around 5:30 that evening, Corbett heard a news report about the kidnapping and began losing his nerve. According to what he told Agent Hostetter on the plane from Seattle, he kept watch out his apartment window for anything suspicious. It's then he spotted a man in a car he mistakenly believed was the FBI already staking out his apartment. He panicked, packed up that night, and the next morning loaded the Dodge, drove it to an undisclosed location, transferred his belongings to the Mercury stained with blood, and left Denver. He drove all the way to Atlantic City and burned the Mercury to get rid of the blood-soaked upholstery and carpet. He then crossed the Canadian border to live in Toronto. The rest we know."

The men contemplated Hardesty's conclusions and Corbett's greed and senseless murder of Ad Coors.

"That's a fine job, Ron," said Hite. "Very close to my thoughts."

"Yeah, I think that's the way it happened, too," said Juhan. "Now we just need to lock up that son of a bitch for life."

"Five hundred, five hundred, five hundred–dollar bid, now five-fifty, I got five-fifty, who'll give me six?" sang out an auctioneer's chant at the Denver Union Stockyards. Ad's prize Angus steer, which had been the 1960 Grand Champion of the Denver Bellringer Sales, was being sold along with the rest of Ad's prize Angus feeder cattle and his commercial stock. It was an auction Ad intended to have at some point, moving away from raising cattle to breeding quarter horses—with one big difference. He'd planned on selling them himself, not through his executors.

Ad's pride and joy as a rancher, his prize quarter horses, were also sold. He, Mary, and the kids had ridden them about the ranch and had given them names. Now Brooke was in college and had no interest in keeping any, nor did Cecily, who was leaving for college in the fall. The boys would have liked to keep a couple, but they were now living in the exclusive Polo Club subdivision, and despite its name, the Polo Club only permitted the boarding of expensive automobiles, not horses, in the mansions' garages.

The ranch equipment also was auctioned: an old Ford pickup, a homemade trailer, a grain truck, a Chevy, some horse tack and troughs, fencing, tools, and so on. Just the typical ranch or farm equipment that auction-goers hope to pick up at a bargain, and in this case, pick up a little piece of history—something owned by a murdered Coors.

The house and the ranch sold in April and May 1961. Mary had moved to Denver the previous summer, but held on to the ranch until Ad's remains were discovered. Sadly, Ad's dream house and his plan to ultimately leave the beer business and work full-time on his Jefferson County ranch had lasted only eighteen months.

COORS FIGHT WITNESSED: DA SAYS WOMAN SAW CORBETT professed the headlines of *The Denver Post* on March 16 as jury selection for the murder trial was nearing an end. An eyewitness to the crime could send Corbett to the gas chamber.

"We were about here when I saw two men fighting over there," Beulah Neve Lewis told District Attorney Hardesty. Both of them were standing on Turkey Creek Bridge in overcoats on that cold March day. "I was driving my husband, Walter Linn, to Idaho Springs. I picked him up at the veterans' hospital in Denver. He's a World War I veteran. Anyways, I took the back roads to miss all the traffic and wandered around out here confused and worried because

I couldn't remember the exact road I had taken before. When I got to the top of the hill there, we come down around that curve and I saw that Corbett man wave down Mr. Coors with his hands. He stopped and got out."

"Then what'd you see?" asked Hardesty as DA investigators Buckley and Hawley (the former undersheriff) took notes.

"Well, the men were fighting, struggling on the bridge. And I drove very slow. When I pulled up behind them, behind the two cars, why, I saw him hitting him on the back of the head like that and throw him in the back scat of his car. One of the men turned toward us, and his shirt was covered in blood. I recognized him as Adolph Coors III."

"How'd you know it was him?" asked Hardesty.

"Me and Walter Linn went through the Coors brewery once. Mr. Coors took us on a tour and treated us to beer. I knew him very personally."

Hardesty and Hawley looked at each other. Ad Coors wasn't in the habit of giving brewery tours or being around to be seen by tours, but still, he could've done what Lewis claimed. But "knew him very personally"?

"What happened next?"

"Like I said, the other man hit Mr. Coors over the head with somethin', maybe a gun, then he pitched forward like that, and Corbett grabbed him like that, took him, dragged him back, and loaded 'im in the back seat of his car. Yes, sir, I was there. I was an eyewitness."

"How close were you?"

"About fifteen to twenty feet. I was parked in back of their car."

"You parked?"

"I had to drive up and stop. I couldn't cross the bridge."

"Did you see him shoot Mr. Coors?"

"No. I only saw him clobber 'im and put 'im in his car."

Hardesty turned to look at the others. Buckley shook his head.

"Then what?" continued Hardesty, realizing that her story conflicted with the evidence.

"The killer saw me and Walter Linn sittin' in the car. He looked at me eye-to-eye. He had the coldest eyes. I remember I yelled to poor Walter, who couldn't 'ave done nothing no ways. Thank goodness, the man climbed in his car and drove off."

"Just so I understand correctly, Mrs. Lewis, you say you saw them fighting and Corbett hit Ad Coors in the head and loaded him into Corbett's car. You didn't see or hear anything else?"

"No, that's about all there was."

"All right, Mrs. Lewis. That'll be all," said Hardesty, leading her to Hawley's car. "Mr. Hawley will drive you home. I have to get back to the office. We're still in jury selection."

Members of the district attorney's office continued investigating Lewis's statements throughout the afternoon and evening. A neighbor told one investigator he'd always driven Lewis's husband to the veterans' hospital, not her. She didn't drive. Another investigator heard her speaking about someone as if he were alive, but the man had been dead for years. She also thought her phone was tapped.

Back at his office that evening, Hardesty spoke to Assistant District Attorney Ed Juhan, who also had talked briefly with Beulah Lewis. Juhan, a short, wiry fellow who said what was on his mind in a colorful fashion, had received his law degree from the University of Denver. He served as assistant state attorney general and practiced law until joining Hardesty in January 1960.

"What did you think, Ed?"

"I think she's got a screw loose is what I think," said Juhan. "What she saw isn't the way it happened. And even if she looked away for a few seconds, how could she not hear two gunshots? Witnesses a quarter mile away or more heard the shots. And there's the blood spray over twenty feet."

Earlier that afternoon, Hardesty had asked prospective jurors during voir dire how they felt about the death penalty, thinking he had an eyewitness. (Voir dire is basically the questioning of prospective jurors by prosecution and defense attorneys prior to trial to determine potential bias or other cause why a juror should not serve.) The change in questioning to include inquiries about potential jurors' feelings about the death penalty had alarmed Corbett's attorneys. The judge called a break to the questioning and asked the lawyers to join him in chambers, and that's when Hardesty explained he believed he had an eyewitness.

"Judge Stoner wants us in his chambers with Mrs. Lewis at ten o'clock tomorrow morning to explain what she knows," added Juhan.

"I know," Hardesty said, "but it's almost worth getting a horse-whipping from Stoner to have seen Corbett shaking in his boots today when he thought we had an eyewitness. Looked like he'd seen a ghost."

Indeed, Corbett knew all about Colorado's death penalty law. He had told Special Agent Hostetter about it on the plane during his extradition flight from Seattle to Denver. "I know the conditions under Colorado law that have to be satisfied to sentence someone to the death penalty," he said. "Oh, yeah? What are they?" asked Special Agent Hostetter.

Corbett said nothing for a moment. "Anyway, surveys reveal the death penalty is not a deterrent to murder."

Hostetter had grown tired of his fugitive's grandiose chatter for the last hour. He wasn't saying anything about the Coors case. "Maybe, maybe not. I know one thing for sure, though," said Hostetter.

"What's that?"

"It deters the guy who gets executed."

Corbett did know the conditions required to send him to the gas chamber. He wasn't going to confess, but perhaps he'd made a mistake and this woman did see him. That's why he was feeling so sick to his stomach after Lewis came forward. He no doubt spent a restless night in his cell running the bungled kidnapping through his mind, over and over, wondering if Beulah Lewis had stopped her car nearby. Prison for life was one thing; he had done time at San Quentin and Terminal Island. That he could handle, but death by cyanide gas? He was only thirty-two years old.

The next morning, a pipe-smoking Buckley along with Hawley flanked Beulah Lewis as they entered the courthouse. A heavyset woman of seventy-three, she wore a purple dress and white coat with a white bonnet. She covered her face from cameras like she was under arrest.

"Why did you wait until now to come forward?" asked a reporter as she walked by him. A full thirteen months had passed since Ad's disappearance and the trial was about to begin.

"Because I feared for my life. I still am," she replied. "But when I read that man might have an alibi, I felt it my duty to come forward and see that justice is done."

The "alibi" Mrs. Lewis referred to appeared in a newspaper article that stated a man and his son were willing to testify that Corbett was at a gas station having his car repaired on the day Coors disappeared. But the two wouldn't be called as defense witnesses because Corbett bewilderingly told his lawyers, "That's just not true. Someone may have been at that gas station, but it wasn't me."

The meeting about Mrs. Lewis's claims among the lawyers in Judge Stoner's chambers went badly for the prosecution. The district attorney explained to the judge, who was upset about this late revelation, that he'd never heard of her until she'd called his office at lunch the day before; that he immediately took Lewis to Turkey Creek Bridge to hear her account of what she saw; and that after hearing her account, admitted she was "just short of an eyewitness."

Judge Stoner questioned her at length, and so did defense attorneys. Her answers to questions were inconsistent, and she couldn't provide answers to questions about obvious events she should have known if they happened only a few feet away from her, as she claimed. The judge permitted the prosecution to endorse her as a potential witness, but investigators on both sides reported that statements by Mrs. Lewis were not only ridiculous but journeyed into the bizarre. She wouldn't be taking the witness stand for the prosecution. The prosecution and defense attorneys had disagreed about almost every facet of the case, except one. As Hardesty later stated it, "Beulah Lewis was a nut."

Corbett would sleep easier that night.

CHAPTER 21

The first day of the trial had come at last: *The People of the State of Colorado, Plaintiff, v. Joseph Corbett Jr., alias Walter Osborne, Defendant. Criminal Action No. 2815.* The charge was murder in the first degree. Kidnapping wasn't included, showing the prosecutors' confidence in their case. It was only the second jury trial in Golden in thirteen years, and the verdict of the last jury was guilty—of a traffic violation, a twenty-five-dollar fine.

The case would be heard before sixty-one-year-old Christian D. Stoner, a judge's judge of twenty years on the bench, rumored to have carried a pistol strapped to his side concealed beneath his black judicial robe. The judge expected lawyers to be prepared and professional and tolerated absolutely no nonsense in his courtroom from the lawyers or the gallery.

He had come to Colorado during World War I when he was stationed at Fort Logan. The fifth of ten children, the judge and his wife, Minnie, had no children of their own. Locals said you could set your watch by his early morning routine. He always rose at 5:00 and arrived at the courthouse by 7:00. His trials started promptly at 9:00 and recessed at 4:30, with a one-hour lunch and a brief recess in the morning and another in the afternoon. He also held court till noon on Saturdays.

The jury was composed of eight men, ages twenty-six to fifty-nine, and four women, ages twenty-three to thirty-seven, with educations ranging from the fourth grade to a master's degree. All lived nearby, at Golden, Arvada, Wheat Ridge, and Lakewood, but would be sequestered for the duration of the trial because of the unceasing news coverage.

"We have done everything we can to get a fair and impartial jury," said Bill Erickson, who exhausted the defense's preemptory challenges. "Unfortunately, all seventy-nine jurors quizzed in the long selection process indicated they have read something about the case."

That wasn't surprising. The newspaper, radio, and television coverage would have saturated anyone within a hundred miles with a guilty bias toward Corbett. It was only natural. The coverage had run for a year—from the disappearance, the FBI's naming Corbett as one of its Ten Most Wanted, the discovery of Ad's remains, Corbett's capture, and now the trial, with plenty of damning filler throughout. Most of the coverage was accurate. On occasion, however, front-page articles and special news bulletins had unintentionally misled readers and listeners, such as Beulah Lewis's claim to have seen Corbett attack Ad on the bridge or the conclusion that Corbett's typewriter matched the one that typed the ransom note. The fact that these news bulletins turned out to be untrue was not explained until after the trial, when the damage had already been done, much as when a judge strikes a statement made in open court from the record and then instructs the jurors to disregard the stricken statement. It can't be done.

Adding to the problems of the defense, one juror's cousin was married to Sheriff Wermuth. Another had been a Hardesty supporter in his recent campaign for district attorney. Another knew Hardesty from church. Another knew the assistant district attorney through his work in the Boy Scouts. And another sold machinery and equipment to Bill and Joe Coors. All innocent associations, yet ties just the same.

After the sequestered jurors ate their first breakfast together at the Holland House Hotel on Saturday morning, March 18, they were transported by school bus to the courthouse for the start of the trial. Each would be earning six dollars a day, twice what they'd been paid during jury selection, plus free meals and lodging until the verdict was read. Some were a bit nervous while others felt a sense of importance as they stepped off the bus at the courthouse steps. Each was one of twelve (and one alternate) selected out of more than three hundred individuals screened for the jury and seventy-nine who'd undergone voir dire. Only *they* would be sitting for the Coors murder trial.

Four sheriff deputies stood guard at each of the doors to the courtroom. Not a typical procedure, but with an infamous defendant, Sheriff Wermuth insisted on the precaution.

The bailiff took a roll call of the jury, and then Ron Hardesty presented a brief opening statement.

"If the court pleases, ladies and gentlemen of the jury, at this time on behalf of the People, I will make to you an opening statement, which will explain the prosecution's case and state what we will prove as the trial progresses.

"The People's case will be divided into generally three phases. First, we will establish the death of Adolph Coors III and that it was caused by excessive bleeding and shock due to two bullet holes in the back. Second, we will establish the scene of the crime as Turkey Creek Bridge in the vicinity of Soda Lakes in Jefferson County. We will show this is where Ad Coors was shot. And third, the large amount of circumstantial evidence will show that Adolph Coors III was killed by this defendant.

"As to the first phase, the testimony of Edward Greene will indicate . . ."

Hardesty proceeded to summarize the facts his office intended to prove during the trial. A dentist would identify the teeth of a skull as those belonging to Adolph Coors III. Ad Coors's widow and his brothers would identify the clothing and personal effects discovered with the bones. Photos and the actual right shoulder blade would show two irregular shaped holes caused by projectiles at high velocity. Gunpowder residue would show the gun was held against or within an inch of Ad Coors's body when fired. The milkman would testify to discovering the abandoned Travelall with its radio playing and engine running. Various witnesses would testify about a hat, type-writer and paper, cars seen, and soil samples. Finally, the prosecution would show Corbett and Osborne were one and the same man.

Immediately following Hardesty's opening statement, rather than launching into his own opening statement, defense attorney Bill Erickson requested to make a motion out of the presence of the jury. The judge asked the jurors to retire to the jury room. Erickson then made a motion before the judge to direct a verdict of not guilty (a request that the judge, not the jury, determine that the prosecution failed to present legally sufficient evidence for a reasonable jury to reach a verdict of guilty).

"If the matters set forth by Mr. Hardesty are true and established beyond a reasonable doubt," asserted Erickson, "the prosecution has fallen short of establishing that a crime of first-degree murder has been committed . . . Assuming the evidence to be just as it was out-lined by Mr. Hardesty, they have failed to show that the allegations and charges they have made are true."

Erickson presented citations to court cases procedurally favoring his motion and then continued. "Favoring it in every way and giving them the benefit of every reasonable doubt . . . all that . . . they have said is that Adolph Coors III is dead, and that there are circumstances which might cause some people to wonder . . . It is a clear case where there is no evidence . . . that would in anywise connect Joseph Corbett Jr. with the crime charged by the district attorney."

After hearing arguments by the prosecution that the sufficiency of the evidence should be determined by the jury, Judge Stoner agreed with the prosecution and promptly ruled, "The motion will be denied. Let's call the jury back in."

Corbett's murder trial would continue.

"Then, Your Honor, the defense will reserve its opening statement to the close of the trial," said Erickson, preferring to wait until the end of the murder trial to directly assert before the jury the defense counsel's belief that the prosecution failed to prove Corbett murdered Ad Coors.

With no defense opening statement, the prosecution commenced presenting its case to the jury.

"If it pleases the court, the prosecution calls Edward Greene," said Mr. Hardesty, as the court reporter tapped out the prosecutor's words on a stenotype machine and then paused while a bailiff escorted the witness into the courtroom.

A young man in a starched white shirt and gray slacks with a meticulously groomed, lustrous pompadour entered the witness-box. He was awkwardly sworn in by the bailiff, since both were nervous standing in front of a courtroom packed with spectators. Not one space on the courtroom benches lay bare, and if one did become vacant, a line of folks in the corridor stood ready to snatch it up.

"State your name, please."

"Edward Greene."

"Where do you presently reside, Mr. Greene?"

"5595 West Twenty-eighth Avenue . . ."

"Now directing your attention to September 11, 1960, . . . what did you do when you arrived at the dump?"

"I got out and walked around, hunting for a place where I could shoot a gun. . . ."

Greene told of finding Ad's pants with loose change and a pocket-knife with Ad's initials *AC III*. Following Greene, FBI agent Robert Nelson took the witness stand and testified of traveling to the dump site with Greene and Riddle and Special Agents Doug Williams, Jesse Orr, and Bill Malone to comb the area. Next, Special Agent Scott Werner testified to directing a five-day sweep for more bones and personal items. Sheriff Hammond wasn't called, since his testimony wasn't essential. The items of jewelry and blood-soiled and ripped clothing were introduced as evidence and passed among the jurors over fierce objection by the defense. Some jurors studied them carefully while others only glanced with revulsion.

The testimony and exhibits may have opened the trial with solemnity and horror, but the courtroom would not always be so somber. There were moments when Corbett actually smiled. One of those moments occurred that first morning when Judge Stoner gave the bailiffs a blistering lecture in court. During the morning recess, Bailiff Smith took hot coffee to the jury room. That was a nice gesture by the court, except the bailiff served the coffee from a discarded box that carried the bright red letters COORS, an act viewed by the judge as having the potential to signal court partiality for the Coors family. Such an act could prejudice or sway the opinions of jurors outside the courtroom where defense attorneys could not object. Judge Stoner was furious. "I have warned and warned and warned you about matters like this. It is inexcusable. Here I have four bailiffs; none of them knows what they're doing."

Corbett's smiles were welcomed by journalists who wrote about the defendant's every gesture in their next editions.

"He was courteous, but his eyes were cold and emotionless. There was nothing there when he spoke about the case," said Charles Brega years later, the young legal associate assisting Corbett's defense attorneys, Erickson and Mackay. District Attorney Hardesty agreed, having observed Corbett during the trial smiling and nodding, yielding to others who walked near, and being respectful to everyone in court. He was "friendly and quiet," said Hardesty. "He carried himself like he was anybody else. You wouldn't know he was the defendant in the biggest murder trial in the state."

Hardesty especially had reason to commend Corbett's courtroom demeanor. Once, when Corbett and his attorneys were standing near the judge's chambers, Hardesty asked, "Is the restroom occupied?" Corbett spoke up and replied yes, but after a few moments realized he may have been mistaken and checked. Seeing it was empty, Corbett held the door for the prosecutor to enter and politely said to the man who was doing his best to send Corbett to prison for life, "I must have been mistaken, Mr. Hardesty, sorry, there's nobody in there."

So affable had Corbett been during jury selection earlier in the week that Assistant District Attorney Richard Hite angrily complained to the judge. "Your Honor, during recesses, the defendant is being treated by the bailiffs and reporters like he is an A-1 citizen, acting all buddy-buddy in full view of potential jurors."

Defense counsel objected. "How is he supposed to act? After all," said Malcolm Mackay to the judge, "he is innocent until proven guilty."

With the burden of proof and having only circumstantial evidence in their arsenal, the prosecution would have its hands full convincing the jury of Corbett's guilt. The prosecution needed all twelve jurors to agree on Corbett's guilt to obtain a conviction. Corbett needed only one.

Workers at the brewery didn't notice Ad's absence anymore. There was no statue of Ad out front, no bronze plaque inside, no speeches made, and no epitaphs given. It was the Coors way. Still, the news reports of the trial echoed throughout the brewery. Workers read newspaper accounts and spoke to coworkers about the case during breaks.

Yet management was determined to operate their business as usual. As Bill later said, "To me nostalgia is a waste of time. It doesn't do you any good. You have to look ahead."

Bill and Joe absorbed or delegated Ad's duties, and the company didn't miss a beat. After a respectful amount of time passed, Bill packed up Ad's personal effects from his desk and returned them to Mary: a family photo, a Denver Bears paperweight, a photo of an Arlberg Ski Club group from years earlier, and sundry items that become a fixture on a person's desk through the years. The desk itself remained for a long time, acting as an appendage to the desks of Bill and Joe and a reminder of their brother's absence until they eventually moved to new offices a few years later.

Even the electricians' strike was unaffected by the murder of the Coors company chairman. Though Ad was considered by most union management as the best of the bunch, they finally struck about the time Ad's remains were discovered.

Ad's kidnapping and murder, coupled with more union interference, pulled a scab off an old wound for Bill and Joe, causing the brothers to be more suspicious of their employees than ever before. Joe believed he would be kidnapped at any moment. He even recorded the serial numbers of bills he carried in his wallet. Joe's fear may have emanated partly from his conservative beliefs, which could be as passionate as Holly's had become about Christianity. Besides firm conservative views about the world, its races, and other social subjects, Joe was distrustful of those less fortunate, though he firmly believed there should be the less fortunate. A worker class who were to remain workers unless they, like his grandfather Adolph Coors, became entrepreneurs and pulled themselves up into the ownership class by hard work and determination (even though Joe had not done so himself).

Bill was more practical, and his opinions on issues were either black or white, leaving the ideological philosophy to his brother Joe. Bill's biggest concerns were not social but business. Yet Bill's views about workers coincided with Joe's, regardless of political labels. When it came to running the brewery and handling the union, Bill stated bluntly, "I don't remember Grandfather telling me any of these people's ancestors were his partners." At the end of the day, it was his family's business. Period. They could do what they wanted to do with it. No one, including the workers or their union, could tell the Coors family how to run the company. To Bill, the main issue was the foundation of capitalism and basic freedom, not politics. The freedom to do with one's own property the way he wishes. Coors would pay what the market required. An honest day's pay for an honest day's work. They would do whatever was necessary to retain skilled, honest, and loyal workers. As Bill later recalled, "I asked [a staunch union employee] why he stayed at Coors, then, if everything was so bad. He replied, 'If I could find a job half as good as this one, I'd quit.'" Thus, if a worker didn't like the pay or working conditions, he was free to go work somewhere else. It was that simple.

Yet in truth, their labor relations had become complex, if not paranoid. The brothers began requiring applicants and existing employees to take a lie detector test to weed out "undesirables." The tests were said to include questions such as:

1. What is your sexual preference?

2. Do you get along with your wife?

3. Are you a subversive, revolutionary, or communist?

4. Do you have money in the bank?

5. Have you ever smoked marijuana?

6. Are you applying for a job with this company so you can do it or any of its employees harm?

7. Are you presently wanted by the authorities for a felony?

They asked these questions even though Corbett had not been an employee. Yet they feared that an employee could become another Corbett. The fear of the unknown troubled them now. Fear of physical or financial harm.

"We decided that in the future, obscurity would be our best security," Bill later said. "We retreated as best we could from public view."

Corbett had done more than kill one Coors brother. He'd frightened two more into suspecting everyone.

The case against Corbett was circumstantial but extensive. FBI agents had located his yellow Mercury, sighted numerous times near the Coors ranch and Turkey Creek Bridge with him in it or standing near. The same car he burned in Atlantic City. They had testimony that he purchased guns, handcuffs, leg irons, and camping equipment. Chain had been found in a pail at the rear of his apartment with his fingerprint. They also had a hat from Turkey Creek Bridge that was his size and according to some witnesses matched the general type and color of the one he wore. Clerks testified Corbett purchased a typewriter and paper of the kind that matched the ransom note. The FBI said it collected soil from underneath the yellow Mercury that matched soil near the bridge and the site where Ad's body had been dumped. Corbett also was a fugitive who'd told two coworkers he was planning something big. In addition, he'd told coworkers he'd

changed his plan several months before, which happened to coincide with the time Ad Coors and his family moved from Denver to
their ranch. Moreover, Corbett had hastily left Denver the morning
after Ad's disappearance, telling his landlady only the night before
he was leaving. He'd run all the way to and across Canada, where
he came close to a confession when he blurted out during his arrest,
"I'm your man."

Hardesty's opening statement at the start of the trial might have
made the prosecution's case sound solid, perhaps even irrefutable.
But it wasn't. Corbett still had a chance at acquittal. The prosecution
had absolutely no direct evidence. There was no eyewitness. In fact,
no one had seen Corbett or the yellow Mercury or the dark-colored
Dodge anywhere near the bridge or the dumpsite on the day of the
disappearance. The prosecution didn't have the typewriter that
typed the ransom note, or paper matching the note from Corbett's
apartment, or bullets from Ad Coors's body that matched a gun belonging to Corbett. Even the hat found at the scene of the disappearance wasn't without doubt.

During the trial, Hardesty called Harry Merys, the husband of
Corbett's landlady, to the stand. The district attorney asked several
questions about Corbett, his car, the bucket with chain that Mr. Merys
found out back, and received several incriminating answers. He
should not have asked Merys about the hat.

"Mr. Merys, calling your attention to People's Exhibit C2 [the brown
fedora], will you state whether or not you have seen that before?"

"I saw a hat that he wore that was similar to that, but I wouldn't say
that I saw this hat before," Mr. Merys replied from the witness box.

"About how many times did you observe the defendant wearing
a hat?"

"A number of times."

Hardesty moved on quickly without drawing attention to Merys's
answer, which aided the defense. He called to the stand Corbett's
coworker Arthur Brynaert, and once again he shouldn't have asked
about the hat.

"Do you recall his hat at all?"

"Yes, I recall his hat," replied Brynaert.

"What color was it?"

"It was brown—a light tan."

"I call your attention to People's Exhibit C2 and ask you if the hat you saw him wearing is similar to that one?"

"No, sir. It wasn't."

Hardesty must have been surprised. Apparently, he had not spoken with Brynaert about what his testimony would be before calling him as a witness, or perhaps Brynaert had not been completely forthcoming. Whatever the case, Hardesty had to hope it wasn't too damaging to his case.

Another exonerating factor was the mysterious fingerprint found inside Ad Coors's Travelall by the FBI.

After Hardesty had called several FBI agents to the stand to bring out the evidence of the pail found at Corbett's apartment containing chain, which agents dusted for fingerprints and took eighteen photos of, FBI fingerprint expert Sebastian Latona from Washington, D.C., testified, "On the basis of comparing the fingerprint on the paint bucket with the fingerprints that appear on the fingerprint card taken by Deputy John Phillips, it is my opinion that this latent print was made by the left middle finger of Joseph Corbett and only his left middle finger could have made that. No one else's finger could have made that contact print which appears in People's Exhibit T3 [the paint bucket]."

While Hardesty was pleased with the FBI agent's testimony regarding the fingerprint on the pail, defense attorneys decided to attempt to flip the testimony in their favor. Malcolm Mackay handled the cross-examination of Agent Latona.

"Now, you received a packet of film in the mail from Agent Orr in the early part of February 1960, didn't you?"

"Yes," replied Latona.

"That was identified to you as coming from a Travelall automobile belonging to Adolph Coors III?"

"That is correct."

"How many films did you receive at that time?"

"Actually, only one latent fingerprint of value in those negatives."

"There was one latent fingerprint of value. Did you make positive identification of that one latent fingerprint?"

"That print has not been identified."

"That has not been identified by anyone?"

"That is correct."

"Thank you very much."

Even before the defense attorneys put on their evidence, their cross-examination of state witnesses had revealed conflicting testimony regarding the hat and the existence of an unidentified fingerprint in Ad Coors's Travelall to the jury. The defense would hammer those facts later on during their closing argument, ardently pointing out the discrepancy concerning the identification of the hat and how the prosecution had failed to mention the unidentified print in the Travelall even though they'd painstakingly taken eighteen photographs of the solitary print on a paint bucket from Corbett's apartment that contained a few feet of chain. Defense attorneys hoped this evidence, taken with the fact that the prosecution's case was entirely circumstantial, would create reasonable doubt in the mind of at least one juror.

Mary read the newspaper, but when she turned to the coverage of the trial, she only read the headlines. She wanted no part of it. She only wanted Corbett convicted. She'd prefer that he go to the gas chamber, but she understood that there'd be no execution.

Mary had not attended any of the murder trial, nor had any other Coors. But on Tuesday, March 21, Mary and her brothers-in-law, Bill and Joe Coors, would be asked to testify. Mary arrived wearing a tailored camel hair coat with a brown scarf and white gloves. She entered the courthouse with Holly Coors and Cecily Kendrick. Mary was soon joined by Bill and Joe as they sat in the hallway on the second floor outside the courtroom door, waiting to be called to testify.

Mary's nerves should have been popping, but she'd taken something earlier to settle them.

"Just stay calm, Mary. Don't let him scare you. He can't do anything to anybody now. You don't even have to look at him," said Holly.

"That's right," said Cecily. "If anybody should be nervous or feel bad, it should be him. He'll get his comeuppance, rest assured."

Mary had grown comfortable with the district attorney's questions during the meeting with the Coors corporate attorney and Hardesty. Her biggest worry, the one keeping her up nights recently, was being in the same room with the man who killed her husband and her children's father. He'd be sitting at the defense table not far from the witness-box. She hated him, and now she had to remain composed as she spoke about the consequences his horrible acts had caused her family. She didn't want to give him the satisfaction of seeing her break down.

Bill was called to testify first. He was handed a red crayon and asked to trace the route Ad had taken on the morning of his disappearance and to identify articles of clothing recovered from the dump site as those belonging to his deceased brother. After the lunch break, he and Joe would be called to the witness stand to testify about their arrival at Turkey Creek Bridge. But first the DA wanted to hear from Mary.

"The People call Mary Grant Coors," announced Assistant District Attorney Richard Hite.

All heads in the gallery turned as Mary entered the courtroom. It felt like a march to the guillotine for her. She raised her right hand and swore "to tell the truth, the whole truth, and nothing but the truth, so help me God."

Mary saw Hite approaching, glanced at friends in the gallery, and then . . . she saw her husband's murderer. He was no longer merely a photograph in the newspaper, but a well-groomed man wearing a suit and tie, trying to mask that he was the monster who'd stolen the life of her husband.

"Would you give us your name, please?" asked Hite, who would tone down his customary flamboyant courtroom demeanor out of respect for the victim's widow.

"Mary Grant Coors," she said in a low, hardly audible voice.

"What is your address?"

"C/o Adolph Coors Company, Golden."

"Where did you live until July 1958?"

"Until July 1958, at 840 South Steele Street," she said, her voice growing stronger as she spoke firmly with deep breaths.

"After July 1958, did you move?"

"Yes."

"Where?"

"To Morrison, Colorado."

"Are you familiar with Jefferson County?"

"Yes."

Mary was shown a black-and-white aerial photo of the area that included their ranch and Turkey Creek Bridge and was asked to point out her home and then the bridge. Those in the courtroom were hushed, hanging on her every word.

"When was the last time you saw your husband, Adolph Coors III?"

"About eight o'clock the morning of February 9, 1960."

"Have you seen him since that time?"

"No."

"What was your husband's condition of health?"

"Very good, indeed, excellent."

"What was his mental health?"

"Cheerful, good, as it always was."

"Objection, Your Honor," said Erickson as he stood. "This line of questioning is incompetent, irrelevant, and immaterial."

"Overruled. Please proceed."

"Do you recall, Mrs. Coors, how he was attired when you last saw him that morning of February 9, 1960?"

"I certainly do."

Mary was then asked if she had spoken to FBI agent Raymond Fox on September 11, 1960, about the personal effects and clothes that had been discovered near the dump.

Hite continued with his questioning. "Are you married?"

"Yes, I am," Mary replied in the present tense.

"What is your husband's name?"

"It *was* Adolph Coors III," she said, emphasizing the past tense with a sarcastic tone.

"Do you have any children?"

"Four."

"What are their names and ages?" The prosecution wanted the jurors to hear who the youngest victims of Corbett's crime were.

"Mary Brooke, nineteen; Cecily Grant, seventeen; Adolph Coors IV, fifteen; and James Grant, eleven."

Richard Hite walked to a table at which sat deputy clerk Mrs. JoAn Ardourel to retrieve another exhibit. He rejoined his witness.

"Do you know who owned this?" asked Hite, showing Mary a key ring tagged *Exhibit A*.

"Yes."

"Who?"

"My husband."

Hite picked up each of Ad's articles of clothing and jewelry he was wearing the day of his disappearance and, for consideration by the jury, asked Mary to identify each one—the bloody jacket, the blood-soiled and torn shirt, the pants ripped apart by wild animals, shoes that were chewed, a soiled monogrammed handkerchief, his wrist-watch, his tie clip, and his gloves, all recovered from the mountain-side dump. Each time, Mary answered that it was owned by her husband or it looked like his or the item he wore.

"Thank you. You're excused, Mrs. Coors," said Judge Stoner, gently smiling, after the defense attorneys indicated no interest in cross-examining her.

Mary walked past Corbett without taking another glimpse.

Corbett simply looked down at his hands, making steeples with his fingers like a child. She had done as she intended. She had remained calm and unemotional.

Everyone watched Mary as she walked gracefully down the courtroom aisle toward the door, as she'd done almost five months earlier after her husband's estate hearing. Some in the gallery bent or rose slightly in their seats to get a better view.

As *Rocky Mountain News* reported, "Her appearance was brief. But her presence will be felt for the duration of the trial."

CHAPTER 22

Corbett was confined to his cell that Tuesday evening, having changed out of his suit to prison clothes. He stretched out on the narrow cot as he read Sheriff Wermuth's March copy of *Fortune*. A smile flashed across his face as he recalled how that morning his attorney had wrangled over legal jargon with the judge, who scolded counsel for it in an old-school, Western manner.

The trial actually was a welcome distraction for Corbett from the tedium of being locked in a six-by-eight-foot cell for the last five months. Besides the change of surroundings, it provided intellectual stimulation. Corbett analyzed each day's evidence, the testimony, the judge's rulings, and most important, the countenances of the jurors. Some days seemed to go in his favor. Other days were even funny, like the day plaster from the ceiling fell on a juror during a rainstorm, or when his former coworker Arthur Brynaert said on the witness stand, "I don't believe the three-pawed bear treed him, but if there'd been a tree, I bet Walt would've climbed it."

Yet he'd also had bad days, like the day Beulah Lewis showed up during jury selection saying she'd seen the whole thing, scaring the daylights out of Corbett until it was revealed she was just short of a full deck. Then a few weeks earlier, the prosecution had revealed that its witness list included white-haired, bespectacled Irene Jones, who said she saw Corbett at the Shamballah Ashrama dump at 9:45 a.m. on February 9, only ninety minutes after Ad's disappearance. She remembered it distinctly, she claimed to the DA and the newspapers, because she was test-driving a car and wanted to try it out along Jackson Creek Road toward the dump.

"I followed this track of another car. It was snowing when I come up on this dark car. The hood was up, and this man was standing by it. He was wearing a coat and walked to my car and said he was sorry for blocking the road, saying he had car trouble, but his clothes and hands were clean. I didn't see any grease or dirt on them. That is why it stuck in my mind. I remember him speaking in a soft voice and in an apologetic manner. Something like a school professor."

Once again, the witness proved to be bogus. After FBI agents interviewed Jones, they easily concluded she was mistaken. She hadn't been at the Shamballah Ashrama dump. It wasn't the day of the disappearance. It wasn't snowing. He wasn't driving a 1951 Mercury but a Chevrolet. And the man she saw wasn't Corbett. Like Beulah Lewis, newspapers had splashed her false claims across their pages, but she wouldn't be called to testify.

He'd not been so lucky when, despite a fierce objection by defense counsel that it violated Corbett's right against self-incrimination, Judge Stoner, for identification purposes, required Corbett to open his mouth to reveal his front teeth to Hilton Pace, who'd spoken to Corbett about target shooting around his mine. Also, at the prosecutor's request, the judge instructed Captain Bray to step down from the witness stand and place Exhibit C-2, the brown felt hat found floating in Turkey Creek, on Corbett's head. It fit. (Captain Bray's wife later claimed that Corbett had whispered to Bray, "I'll get even with you.")

"I was taking a big risk with the hat near the end of my case because if it hadn't fit, it could have fouled the jury," Hardesty would later admit. "But I looked him over for a while before putting it on him," he added with a smile.

And then he'd had really bad days like when photographs of Ad's skull and other bones were passed around the jury. And like earlier that very Tuesday when Mary, the murdered man's widow with four

children, took the stand. Corbett saw the faces of the jurors struggling to absorb her words, words that caused each of them pain and
sympathy, some telegraphing their resultant anger in his direction.

Corbett tried to relax in his cell and put Mary's court appearance
out of his mind. He stretched out, folded his arms behind his head,
and stared at the ceiling, an occupation he'd grown quite experienced
at the last five months. The smooth gray surface reinforced by steel
bars hidden beneath the heavy cement stared back at Corbett every
day and night. Sometimes he envisioned a movie screen and would
permit his imagination to run his favorite film across it. Once reality
crowded in again, the ceiling transformed into simply the other side
of the floor above him. That's when Corbett would grab a magazine
and hold it between his face and the ceiling, no longer wishing to
view the concrete lid on his cage.

Waiting for the end of the trial weighed heavily on the accused.
He wished the trial could last for weeks or months, giving him as
much time possible as a big fish in a small county jail rather than an
educated minnow in an overcrowded state prison full of sharks. At
times, the thought of where he was going made him nauseated.
Surely at other times, he kicked himself for flubbing up the kidnapping. He could have knocked Coors out with the pistol or shot up in
the air and ordered him to stop. He couldn't stop thinking about the
half-million-dollar ransom he'd forsaken. He could've been living
the high life in South America by now.

Corbett had had months to second-guess his mistakes. To him, it
was a good plan. It should have worked. It just didn't. If anything,
he probably blamed Ad Coors for his plan's failure. Corbett never
appeared the least bit contrite.

"Naturally, there's some tension," said Sheriff Wermuth to reporters asking how Corbett was coping with the wait. "But as far as
not being able to sleep or sit, no. The man seems to have no feeling
at all."

Corbett wasn't going to give them the satisfaction of seeing him
squirm. Something, ironically, he and his victim's wife held in

common, though unlike Mary, most believed Corbett was impervious to emotion, particularly kindness and compassion.

"He was calm and cooperative, didn't seem to have a care in the world," said Captain James Shumate.

"Would you state your name, please?" asked District Attorney Hardesty on March 24, the twelfth and penultimate day of the trial. Handheld fans and hats waved back and forth as the courtroom grew stuffy from an overactive boiler.

"Mary Grant Coors."

"And you are the same Mrs. Coors who previously testified?"

"Yes."

"Mrs. Coors, I hand you People's Exhibits B-5 [the ransom envelope] and A-5 [the ransom note]. I ask if you can identify the exhibits."

"Yes, I can. This is the letter I received on February 10 of 1960."

The courtroom was perfectly quiet as Hardesty began to read the ransom letter and then asked the judge if the ransom letter and envelope could be passed among the jurors. A bailiff handed them to the jury.

"Who was present when you first observed those exhibits?"

"My brothers-in-law, Bill and Joe Coors, and certain members of the FBI. I cannot remember who."

"What did you do when you first observed the letter?"

"I felt a little bit relieved, because it gave us hope that Ad could still be alive. And the family met together, and we decided to go ahead and comply with the request in this note."

"What did you do in an effort to comply with the note?"

"Well, it took a little while obviously to fulfill the requests that were put into this note. The unmarked, used money was prepared and transported to us from a bank in Boston. I stayed at home. I sent my children to be with their grandparents, because the household was very upset. I didn't want the children upset any more than I could help. And we went ahead and got the money and waited."

"How often did you see your children after that?"

"Objection, Your Honor. Irrelevant."

"Overruled. Let's find out. You may answer, Mrs. Coors."

"I talked to them every day. They didn't go to school. They were upset. They didn't go to school for two weeks. They did their work at their grandparents' home. I talked to them every evening, and I went over and saw them every other day."

"Do you recall whether or not the other items of the note with relation to the newspaper ad were complied with?"

"They were as soon as possible."

"When did you first observe the ad in the paper?"

"Saturday evening, the thirteenth of February."

"How long did the ad run, do you recall?"

"It was close to three weeks."

"During this three-week period that the newspaper ad was in the paper, what did you do?"

Mary hesitated and cleared her throat. "I waited for the telephone to ring. That's all I waited for," she said softly.

"How many phone calls did you receive during this period?"

"Well, we told all of our friends not to call because we wanted to keep the line open. I would say during the three-week period that we had a few calls that were not . . ." Mary's memory flashed to all the crank calls, the extortionists, and the nosy people. "Just people interfering. I would say probably three or four a day. But we never got the one we were waiting for."

At this point, Mary believed she could no longer hold back the tears. She'd read the questions and talked to the corporate lawyer about the answers, and she'd testified three days earlier, but something about saying the answers out loud before people in the court this day caused her stomach and head to ache. She thought she'd break into tears any moment or, worse, vomit. Just as quickly, she remembered her promise to herself: *Don't give them the satisfaction. They won't get their money's worth today.*

Mary heard the assistant district attorney's voice again.

"Mrs. Coors? Do you need a break?"

"No. Sorry. I'm fine. Please continue."

"Okay. On what times of the day would these calls come in?"

"Any time, at night sometimes, in the middle of the night."

"Did you always answer the phone?"

"I answered the phone every time that I was awake, and if I was asleep and anybody asked for me, I was brought to the telephone."

"During this three-week waiting period, did any other events occur?"

"Well, I can remember the snow very well. It began to snow hard and steadily, and that again gave us a little hope that possibly whoever had taken Ad was not able to contact us. And it gave us hope, and yet again, it was bad because we knew that he had been hurt and possibly he was somewhere where he could not get medical attention. I just remember snow and wind and very bad roads. There were days when we couldn't get out of the house at all."

"You couldn't see your children on these days you couldn't get out of the house?"

"No, we lived on a hill. The road is very difficult to go down. And without a snowplow, we couldn't."

"Did you observe anyone in the vicinity of your home during this waiting period?"

"No, I didn't."

"During this three-week waiting period, did you receive any indications of any nature that your husband was still alive?"

"No."

"Is your phone number listed in the phone book?"

"Yes."

"The same number that appears in the ransom note?"

"Yes."

"Why did you conclude that three weeks of waiting was a sufficient period of time?"

"Objection, Your Honor," Erickson said as he stood.

"The objection is good."

"Mrs. Coors, when was the last time you saw your husband alive?"

"The morning of February 9, 1960."

Some people in the courtroom shook their heads. "We all felt sorry for her," said one juror after the trial.

There may have been some who also felt sorry for Corbett's father, though no one saw him in the courtroom. Before and during the trial, Joe Corbett Sr. and his wife, Helen, stayed away, at the request of their defendant son. He'd written them occasional letters after his arrest and during the trial, such as when he wrote, "The trial is going well as can be expected . . . Messrs. Mackay and Erickson, both keen-minded and experienced, are handling things very capably. . . . I wouldn't become unduly optimistic, since the odds against us are tremendous."

Still, his father never visited. It was difficult for Mr. Corbett. The sins of the son aren't necessarily visited upon the father, but in this case, many considered the father must have borne some blame. Perhaps his son's waywardness was due to the father's drinking, his selfishness, or his four wives.

The Seattle Times and the newspaper for which Mr. Corbett worked, *The Seattle Post-Intelligencer*, printed articles about his son continually for a year—the FBI search, the capture, and now the trial. Mr. Corbett's boss, coworkers, neighbors, and friends read all about his son as the suspected killer of Adolph Coors III and his murder conviction in California a decade earlier almost to the day, on March 16, 1951.

The last time Mr. Corbett saw his son was at the Vancouver jail, and it appears that it may have been the last time he'd ever see him. Mr. Corbett wouldn't attend the trial and wouldn't be present for the verdict. He'd never visit his son at another jail or prison or, in all likelihood, at his home or workplace. It's not clear if that was by instruction from his son or if he'd simply had enough.

Mr. Corbett's obituary in *The Seattle Times* on February 3, 1980 (six days shy of the twentieth anniversary of Ad Coors's murder), may have stated it best:

Joseph CORBETT 84. Beloved husband to Helen M. Corbett. Father of Walter Corbett, of Downers Grove, Ill. Two cousins: Maurice Corbett, Victoria, B.C. and Gwen Moors, of Transcoma, Manitoba, Canada. Prior to his retirement in 1963, he served as the Wire News Editor of the Seattle Post-Intelligencer. At his request, there will be no services.

Mr. Corbett's son, the first Joseph R. Corbett Jr., died at the age of six in 1927 when he was hit in the street by a passing car. Based on the obituary, it seems the second Joseph R. Corbett Jr., his only living biological son (Walter was a stepson), died at the Coors murder trial in Jefferson County in 1960 at the age of thirty-two.

On the last day of the trial, the final prosecution witnesses called by District Attorney Hardesty were FBI agents who recounted Joe Corbett's surrender and arrest in Vancouver. Hardesty concluded the prosecution's presentation of evidence after five weekdays and two half Saturdays, plus an hour and twenty-five minutes on that Monday. It was 9:55 a.m., March 27, 1961.

More than 150 spectators crowded the courtroom pews dressed in their best Sunday clothes, expecting to hear Joe Corbett's side of the story. Another forty stood in the hallway, hoping to grab a seat abandoned by a tired onlooker.

The defense lawyers' backs were against the wall. They were embroiled in a legal battle with terribly damning facts. Their client had been convicted and imprisoned in California for murder, escaped from prison and lived in Denver using an alias, and behaved suspiciously before and after Ad Coors's disappearance, including fleeing Denver the morning after, burning his car, and hiding out in Canada for months. He offered, "I'm your man," upon arrest.

He had said very little to defense attorneys other than deny his guilt without any facts to support his innocence. That's why defense attorneys had relied principally on procedural attacks before and during the trial. Most of their motions had been denied. They also had not been granted access to most of the state's witnesses or evidence, including the copious FBI report that assembled and analyzed the evidence gathered by the agency. The defense was left with attacking only the evidence presented by the prosecution. Evidence mentioned in the newspapers and read by jurors before the trial, but not presented by the prosecution, could not be addressed by defense attorneys, regardless of biases the news reports may have created in the jurors' minds.

Burdened with these handicaps, Bill Erickson stood to present the defense's case and asked the judge permission to make a motion outside the presence of the jury. The judge dismissed the jurors to the jury room.

"Your Honor, the prosecution has not presented any evidence that the defendant murdered Adolph Coors III. The State has failed to show that a death even occurred in Jefferson County, and therefore this court is without jurisdiction. No evidence was presented to show the blood retrieved on Turkey Creek Bridge belonged to Adolph Coors III. And there is no evidence to show the defendant was connected with the cause of death or the murder of Adolph Coors III. . . . Therefore, I move that the defendant is entitled to a directed verdict of acquittal." Erickson had unsuccessfully made the same motion following the prosecution's opening statement at the beginning of the trial. This time, the defense hoped for a different outcome. It would be Erickson's last procedural attack before closing arguments.

"The prosecution's evidence establishes that Adolph Coors III met his death either by accidental means or by criminal agency not connected with the defendant," explained Erickson, trying to support his motion with his version of the prosecution's evidence. "There is only some evidence circumstantial in character relating to the crime of kidnapping, which is not a crime before the court. There has been some evidence which might show that Adolph Coors III at some time suffered some type of a wound in the shoulder. It has not been established that these holes were caused by any type of missile. There is no evidence whatsoever that the defendant was at the scene of the crime.

There's nothing that would even establish Mr. Coors's death at Turkey Creek Bridge. The prosecution has blood spots on the bridge, but it hasn't been shown to be the blood of Adolph Coors III.

"But even if the prosecution has proven the corpus delicti by circumstantial evidence, they must show that the defendant was the criminal agency that caused the death. Now, what evidence do we have that would connect Joseph Corbett Jr. with the crime charged? There is evidence that he was seen in the vicinity of Turkey Creek Bridge on December 9, 1959, by the Paces. . . . There was a 1951 Mercury seen by Massey and Cable prior to February 9, 1960. There was the departure of Corbett from Denver on February 10, and the discovery of his automobile on the dump at Atlantic City on February 17. There was a purchase of a K-32 in 1957 and apparently the purchase of a 9 mm Llama from Stoger's Sporting Goods some two years before this. Neither gun has been shown to be connected with the crime charged.

"The soil samples showed the defendant's car to have been at the town of Louviers, Colorado, which is at least fifteen miles from the dump and probably an equal distance from Turkey Creek Bridge. And there are unidentified tire tracks.

"We feel, Your Honor, that the evidence is indeed thin. Therefore, it is the duty of this court to direct a verdict in favor of the defendant."

The judge wasted no time in responding. "Let's hear from the people. The motion is denied."

"Then, if the court pleases, the defendant stands on his motion and rests."

Noises rose from the gallery as though Erickson had just committed a crime himself. Sounds of surprise, disappointment, and annoyance resonated throughout the courtroom. How dare the defense lawyer rob those in the gallery of their judicial floor show? They'd expected another week of testimony, at least.

"We believe the State has failed to establish any element upon which to obtain a conviction," Erickson explained later to *Denver Post* reporters. "We decided to rely entirely on closing arguments to try to convince jurors that District Attorney Ronald Hardesty failed to connect Joe Corbett in any way with Mr. Coors's kidnapping and murder on February 9, 1960."

Hardesty viewed it differently. When asked why the defense rested without presenting any evidence to rebut the prosecution's case, the district attorney replied, "Because they didn't have any evidence."

CHAPTER 23

All that remained were closing arguments, mere biased summations of the weeklong court battle. The commotion in the courtroom quieted as the judge instructed the prosecution to begin. Suffering from a cold, Hardesty asked the assistant prosecutor to make the closing argument.

Assistant District Attorney Richard Hite, known to friends and the legal community as Dick, a prominent horse owner who'd been appointed by the governor to the Colorado Racing Commission and who would be killed six years later in a car crash, was a tall, thin, distinguished-looking statesman in his fifties, with graying sideburns and a pencil mustache. His presentation sometimes resembled that of a Shakespearean actor, with an excessive touch of melodrama.

"Ladies and gentlemen," began Hite, nodding to the jurors. "You have listened to the evidence. You are about to embark upon the second part of your important duty—namely, to deliberate on that evidence. But first, Mr. Hardesty and I are very appreciative of the fine manner in which you have served as jurors. And now it is our privilege to draw inferences from the evidence and urge upon you that those inferences are logical and correct."

Hite walked around the lectern to stand directly in front of the jury. The jurors sat more erect and looked directly at Mr. Hite.

"Let me set the scene, if I may," he said as if he were about to tell a chilling tale around a campfire. "We see an apartment house at 1435

Pearl Street in Denver and in apartment 305 lives a man known as Walter Osborne. We see later that this man worked at Benjamin Moore & Co. and made the acquaintance of two coworkers, David Reigel and Arthur Brynaert. Both coworkers testified that by 1957, this man commenced designing something big; I believe they described it as a 'big score of a few hundred thousand to a million.' They also revealed that the man known to them as Walter Osborne was forced to revise his hedonistic plan in the summer of 1958, which just so happens to coincide with when Adolph and Mary Coors relocated from Denver to their ranch in Morrison. . . .

"But this man was determined. He continued making preparations for that big score. Mr. Smith of Daking Sporting Goods in Maine testified that on June 8, 1957, Corbett ordered a K-32 Smith & Wesson Combat Masterpiece under the name Walter Osborne and arranged for its delivery to him at #305, Perlmor Apartments. . . .

"Then on February 24, 1959, this man purchased four pairs of leg irons from a US Navy surplus mail order company, according to the testimony of Daniel Beisher, the proprietor of Kline's Prince Enterprises. Two months later"—Hite paused to study his notes before continuing—"on April 25, 1959, he purchased four pairs of handcuffs from Big Three Enterprises Inc. in New York and sinisterly signed the mail order receipt, 'Walter Osborne.' Byron Rowland testified to that."

The assistant DA walked across the room and stopped in front of the defense table. "Now, the defense wants you to believe the defendant is just a hunter. I ask you, what does he do, take his game prisoner?"

Laughs scattered about the room, including a chuckle from one of the jurors. Judge Stoner banged his gavel. Hite continued.

"To carry out his insidious plan for that all-important big score, this man needed an instrument of extortion, a typewriter. But he's an intelligent man. He already possessed a typewriter but knew his old correspondence could be compared with the ransom note and then the jig would be up, wouldn't it?" Hite asked as he looked at Corbett and then the jury. "So what did he do? He skulked out on October 8, 1959, and purchased a new one, a Royalite portable typewriter from the May-D&F store. Jerry Davis accurately testified that this man bought the typewriter from the store in Denver for cash rather than on a change account like other buyers. He recognized him despite this man giving him one of his many aliases, the name—excuse me for a moment while I check the exact name, he used so many—"

"Objection, Your Honor. Inflammatory, prejudicial."

"The objection is good," said the judge, who rarely used the courtroom terminology *sustained* or *overruled*.

"Here's the alias he gave: William Chiffins."

The assistant district attorney walked toward the jury again, raising his hands chest high. "Now, this is important, ladies and gentleman. This typewriter is like a fingerprint because it was a new-model typewriter. According to FBI agent Elvin Barton, in all probability the ransom note was typed on that Royalite typewriter. Other buyers were investigated. They cooperated with the FBI and agreed to hand over their typewriters to the FBI for comparison tests and were cleared. But the man known as William Chiffins, or should I say Walter Osborne, well, he didn't have his Royalite typewriter when arrested, and he's still not telling where it is. We did find his old Underwood about fifty feet off Rampart Range Road in the woods near Castle Rock, which so happens to be only a few short miles from where Ad Coors's body was discovered. I'm sure the Royalite met a similar fate, though clearly he did a much better job disposing of it."

Hite stepped to the lectern and sifted through his notes. "Ah, yes," he said aloud. "And the typewriter paper. Every kidnapper needs paper for his ransom letter. In this case, Kenneth Haynes, an executive of Eaton Paper Company, identified the ransom note as paper similar to that purchased by the man known as Walter Osborne from the Denver Dry Goods Company on December 9, 1959. Miss Ann Thompson, a young clerk, testified to that."

Hite paused as the sound of coughing rose from the prosecution table. District Attorney Hardesty had been coughing throughout the proceedings, frequently raising a handkerchief to cover his mouth. The district attorney drank some water and nodded for Hite to continue.

"Now, the automobile. Several witnesses testified they saw a yellow 1951 Mercury parked suspiciously near the Coors house and Turkey Creek Bridge again and again for weeks. James Cable, a former constable with an eagle's eye and an elephant's memory, did one better. He memorized the yellow Mercury's license plate, AT-62, he recited to the FBI, perhaps AT-6205, he thought. Turns out the plates of only four Mercurys in all Denver County started with AT-62 and only one of those four Mercurys was yellow and could not be found."

Hite took a sip from a glass of water sitting on the lectern. "Moving on. Southwest of Denver, there is another man with a wife and four young children. Adolph Coors III and his wife just returned home from a trip to Florida. . . . That brings us to the morning of February 9, 1960," Hite announced with a countenance and tone of impending doom.

"Adolph Coors III left home that morning, according to his widow, happy and cheerful. He waved goodbye to his ranch manager. Little did he know the sands of time were running out on him because two short miles later he met his death at Turkey Creek Bridge." Hite paused for a moment as if the thought upset him.

"Two men were on that bridge at approximately 8:00 a.m. One is dead. He can't tell us what happened. We know because we found his car and cap there and a large pool of blood. His lips are sealed in death. Bone by bone and tattered item by tattered item, we have reconstructed the identity of the deceased man. Dr. Kelly testified from his dental examination that the skull was positively that of Adolph Coors III.

"And there was . . . ah, excuse me for a moment, Your Honor, if I may confer with cocounsel." With a nod from the judge, Hite walked to the prosecution table and leaned over Hardesty and spoke. Hite returned to the podium with a notepad.

"Ladies and gentlemen, you saw the jacket that Adolph Coors III was wearing on that morning. Mrs. Coors told you it was her husband's. You saw the two holes in the back of the jacket. You saw the shirt he had on and the undershirt. You saw where those two holes were in juxtaposition when you put the three items of clothing together. And you have the medical testimony that a bone found on a desolate hill, a scapula bone, had two holes in it.

"You also heard Dr. Toll testify that Mr. Coors had been fatally wounded in the back, the most cowardly of all murders. FBI agents testified he'd been shot with a firearm bearing a caliber less than .45, perhaps a .32 or a .38 caliber. You also heard testimony that in addition to the K-32, the defendant owned two .38-caliber pistols and a 9 mm pistol (that's roughly a .35 caliber) and that the 9 mm, a powerful and deadly weapon under a .45 caliber, was confiscated when he was so heroically captured in Canada."

While Hite spoke, the defense attorneys took notes and conferred with each other. Rarely did they speak to Corbett. The jurors listened attentively to Hite, scarcely removing their eyes from the assistant prosecutor.

"We also found another hat on Turkey Creek Bridge. Who was the other man at the bridge under that hat? For that, we have to review the immutable circumstantial facts.

"Ladies and gentlemen, it's thirty-seven miles from the bridge to the Shamballah Ashrama dump. That would take about an hour and fifteen minutes to drive. How long would it take to remove a corpse from the back seat and cast it into the mountain mausoleum, the guardians of which are nature's man-eating beasts? Another ten minutes? Fifteen? And how long would it take to drive into the heart of the city of Denver to drop off dry-cleaning? An hour? An hour and fifteen minutes? You can see that the man under the hat could be in Denver by 11:30 or noon at the latest.

"Then we see a very interesting thing. Denver's postal inspector, Joe Murphy, testified that a ransom note bearing a 3:00 p.m. postmark was mailed between 1:45 and 2:15 p.m. that same day. There were no news releases of Mr. Coors's disappearance until after five o'clock. Who knew what happened on the bridge? The man under the hat."

Hite approached the evidence table and asked for Exhibit A-5. It was the ransom note. He read it to the jury.

"Ladies and gentlemen, the moment this note was mailed, its writer knew that Adolph Coors III was dead, yet the note informs Mrs. Coors that Adolph's life is in her hands. 'We have no desire to commit murder. All we want is that money.' The lust and cupidity of the note's writer."

Hite paused and returned to the podium. He flipped his notes.

"The next morning, the man known as Walter Osborne hurriedly loaded his car with boxes. The man whose car was always immaculate was splattered with mud, neighbors testified, even the windows were splattered, they said, just as if driven along the back roads of Jefferson County and Douglas County in the winter months."

Corbett sat stoically, listening with a strained expression at times as if he were the defense counsel and Erickson and Mackay were the defendants.

"Remember, ladies and gentlemen, that fourth car, the yellow one with the license plate number beginning with AT-62 that James Cable's eagle eyes spotted? Do you know where it was? Parked at an apartment in Denver? No. Burned in faraway Atlantic City, New Jersey, an act of arson so intense that it couldn't be put out by ordinary means. It took a high-powered fog to douse those flames of concealment. And whom did it belong to? The man called Walter Osborne.

"And how many times did we hear from witnesses that the man calling himself Walter Osborne told them he was going back to school, maybe to the University of Colorado at Boulder? Well, I'll agree he was going back to school, but not to Boulder. Instead, he enrolled in the University of Flatrock because he was trying to crawl under it."

A few laughs burbled about the courtroom.

"Objection," barked Erickson.

"The objection is good," ruled the judge.

"He had something to conceal. Otherwise, why did he flee? I hear news bulletins every day, and I don't hightail it out of town. Why did he want to burn the inside of his car? Could there have been something on the cushions? A spot perhaps like the one found at Turkey Creek Bridge? Circumstantial evidence, ladies and gentlemen, does not lie.

"And where is the man known as Walter Osborne? Living in Canada, where he buys a new brown felt hat, size 7⅜. Why did he buy that new hat in Canada as winter approached, size 7⅜? Because he'd lost his old one in a creek back in Colorado.

"So who is the man under the hat?" Hite asked and then paused, before turning and pointing at Corbett with an extended index finger. "I submit the defendant supplied the answer on October 29, 1960, in Vancouver, British Columbia, when he stated to FBI Agent Alfred Gunn while being arrested, 'I'm your man.' Walter Osborne is the man under the hat, ladies and gentlemen, and Walter Osborne is Joe Corbett Jr., the defendant."

Hite sipped some water and gently rubbed his hands across the sides of his head, brushing his hair back neatly.

"All the evidence points to the defendant. It builds a collar of circumstantial evidence that fits around his neck, this man who wears a size 7⅜ brown felt hat. The one who said, 'I'm your man.'"

Hite paused a few seconds before closing. He lifted a piece of paper from the podium and walked over to the jury.

"The official charge against the defendant reads in part that Joseph Corbett Jr., alias Walter Osborne, did on or about the ninth of February 1960, feloniously, willfully, and of his premeditated malice aforethought kill and murder one Adolph Coors III against the peace and dignity of the People of the State of Colorado.

"We submit, ladies and gentlemen, the language of the charge couldn't be any truer, for I ask you, what dignity attended the burial of Adolph Coors III when his body was cast to the wolves and to the bears and to the other predators of the forest? What dignity attended the long vigil suffered by Mrs. Coors waiting by the telephone, hoping for word of her husband's release? What a cruel instrument of torture. He never called. And she waited. Dutifully. Tearfully, as it snowed, just like it's snowing today. Little did Mary Coors know that the same snow that gave her hope was the burial blanket of her beloved husband lying up there on that mountainside," Hite said, his voice crescendoing as he pointed toward Pikes Peak while keeping his eyes on the jurors.

"The defense would like you to believe there is little evidence or that the evidence doesn't add up. I tell you that the People's case is unrebutted, uncontradicted, and undenied. There is a mountain of circumstantial evidence as high as that mountain the multinamed defendant dumped Adolph Coors's body on. And I will tell you what that evidence indubitably adds up to, one five-letter word, G-U-I-L-T. Guilt beyond a reasonable doubt.

"Ladies and gentlemen, search the evidence for the truth. If you will analyze it, you will find the truth, the truth of the charge, the truth that this man deliberately and premeditatedly murdered Adolph Coors III, and I hope that will be your verdict. Thank you."

Richard Hite had spoken for thirty minutes. Now it was the defense's turn. Defense attorney Malcolm Mackay waited for Hite to return to the prosecution table before standing and approaching the jury box.

"Defense counsel may proceed," announced Judge Stoner.

"Ladies and gentlemen of the jury, first on behalf of Joseph Corbett Jr., we want to thank you for sitting as a jury in this case. You have listened attentively. Your verdict, no matter what it may be, you can be proud of. You can look anybody in the eye who should comment adversely upon your verdict and ask them if they heard the evidence.

"Now, ladies and gentlemen, the thing that brings us together is the tragedy that happened in this community, and nobody more than myself has sympathy for the Coors family. But that is not the contest here.

"The prosecution has alleged that Joseph Corbett Jr. murdered Adolph Coors III. I submit they have not proven their case beyond a reasonable doubt," Mackay said in a firm but convivial voice as he faced the jury. "It's that simple. . . . They tried their best, there's no doubt, what with the unlimited resources of the district attorney's office and the Federal Bureau of Investigation, and believe me, they used every one of those resources, but still haven't proved the defendant's guilt.

"Let's consider for a moment all the questions that have not been answered. Questions that if answered would clearly prove Joe Corbett Jr. did not commit this crime and because they aren't answered create reasonable doubt. But before we do that, I would like to take a moment to comment upon the credibility of some of the prosecution's witnesses." Mackay proceeded to point out the testimony of witnesses like James Cable, Al Gunn, Virginia Massey, and others who sounded confused or changed their stories or were hostile to defense questions. He then shook his head with a grimace. "You have got to analyze this evidence, ladies and gentlemen, and scrutinize it for the truth. Now let's look at the holes in the prosecution's case," Mackay said as he flipped the page of his legal notepad and stuffed a hand in his pants pocket.

"Let me ask you, why would a person who is going to kidnap one man need four pair of handcuffs and leg irons? It doesn't make sense. . . . They rely on circumstantial evidence. Well, they are bound by that circumstantial evidence.

"Much has been made about the defendant's car being seen in the area surrounding Turkey Canyon. Ask yourself this: How many other makes and colors of cars were seen by witnesses in the area in addition to Joe Corbett's yellow Mercury? It's hard to keep count, isn't it? One witness saw a yellow Ford pickup, another a green Ford sedan, there was a green Dodge, a maroon Dodge, a green-and-blue Ford, a gray-and-white Ford, and a Ford station wagon. One car resembling the defendant's was even seen in that area's lovers' lane. James Cable read a partial license plate number. Maybe he saw it correctly, and maybe he didn't. It doesn't matter, because the defendant doesn't dispute the fact he drove about the countryside just like all these other folks in their cars, to target shoot, camp, or simply to get out of the big city and get some fresh air. But Mr. Cable took down license numbers of the other cars, too, and handed them over to the FBI. But where's the testimony about those cars?

"And how many were in the cars? No one knows. Some said one, some two, even a few said it could have been more than two."

Mackay flipped through some notes, took a sip of water from a glass on the defense table, and continued to speak.

"Much has been made about an Underwood typewriter and a Royalite typewriter and this kind of paper and that, but there was absolutely no testimony, zero, that a typewriter owned by Joe Corbett, like hundreds of others owned in this country, just not in Denver, typed the ransom note demanding $500,000. And there was absolutely no testimony that the paper on which the ransom note was typed was identical to paper taken from the defendant's apartment. But there was testimony during our cross-examination of the FBI that comparisons of correspondence and income tax returns obtained from the defendant's apartment with the ransom note showed no similarities in the style of typing or paper. Now that is absolute."

Erickson motioned for Mackay to join him at the defense table. "Excuse me a moment, Your Honor." Mackay leaned across the front of the table as Erickson whispered. Mackay nodded and turned to face the jury as he tucked his tie back neatly behind his vest.

"Much has been made of the rifle and pistol belonging to Mr. Corbett and the dirt under his car," Mackay said, bending down and making a motion with his hand as if sticking dirt under the car. "They say this dirt was from this mountain, and this dirt was from that road and from this dump." Mackay paused. "Lord knows I've driven a lot of places, and so has Joe Corbett. Several of the prosecution's own witnesses attested that he's an avid target shooter and hunter. Sure, he drove along the back roads and mountains with his pistol and rifle. Last I checked, a man can't target practice on Main Street."

Chuckles scattered about the gallery.

"FBI agents testified they collected 457 soil samples. You can be sure they got plenty from Turkey Creek Bridge and the Shamballah Ashrama dump. But out of those 457 samples from fourteen counties in the area, only two were introduced as evidence against the defendant, and neither of those conclusively matched the soil at the bridge or the dump. I think the odds are good you could find two out of those 457 under any of our cars."

Erickson tapped the top of his head. Mackey nodded.

"And what about the hat? The star piece of evidence that the prosecution has picked up, passed around, shown pictures of, and shoved down to Mr. Corbett's eyebrows? What a ridiculous display of theatrics of no substantive value. It didn't even fit. Do you know how many folks in the area wear brown hats? In the country? In the world? I bet I've got a couple in my closet at home. And I bet you gentlemen do, too. Dave Reigel, who worked with Joe Corbett Jr., testified he believed the defendant's hat band was darker than the prosecution's hat. Arthur Brynaert, another coworker, testified that the defendant's hat was light tan and didn't match the color of the prosecution's hat. And where is the testimony that Joseph Corbett Jr. bought this hat? The label was in the hat, May-D&F, but there was no such testimony.

"But as egregious as that is, it's not the most disturbing piece of evidence, or should I say, lack of evidence. That would be the mysterious fingerprint discovered in Mr. Coors's Travelall. No matter how hard the FBI tried, with all their millions of fingerprints on file in Washington, and all their agents and all those man-hours, they couldn't find a match. It certainly didn't match Joe Corbett Jr. It didn't match any Coors family member, friend, or coworker. Believe me, the FBI checked. So to whom did it belong? I say to the real killer, the one whose brown hat was found at Turkey Creek, not to Joe

Corbett Jr. . . . Reasonable doubt, ladies and gentlemen, reasonable doubt.

"And what about the so-called eyewitnesses? They were really 'earwitnesses,' and none heard or saw Joe Corbett Jr. anywhere near the area at all that entire day, much less shoot Mr. Coors and dump his body. The prosecution hasn't produced a murder weapon, a typewriter that wrote the ransom note, paper that matched the notepaper, nor any fingerprints on Mr. Coors's vehicle, or anything else that belongs to Joe Corbett Jr., except on a paint bucket in the basement of his apartment. The prosecution said plenty about that bucket, and the FBI was so interested that agents took eighteen photographs of that solitary fingerprint, but did you hear them talk about the fingerprint in the Travelall? Absolutely not, only a paint bucket at the defendant's apartment. So what does that make the defendant? Guilty of painting? He worked at Benjamin Moore & Co., for god's sake. The true assailant has his fingerprint on that Travelall. More reasonable doubt.

"Ladies and gentlemen, in conclusion, let me ask that the good Lord grant you wisdom to analyze the evidence and the law in this case in the spirit of fairness, and give you wisdom to apply the laws to the facts in the spirit of justice."

Malcolm Mackay slapped his hand against the side of the lectern and walked to the defense table. As he approached, defense cocounsel Bill Erickson stood. He would be delivering the final words of the defense's closing argument.

"Hello, ladies and gentlemen," began Erickson, who spent his time, as he had during the trial, focusing on legal procedures and technicalities while dissecting the judge's jury instructions and complaining about the newspapers, TV, and radio. An impassioned Erickson gazed at Corbett and reached out an open hand as he invoked vague expressions like, "We all know that a mathematical equation has to fall and cannot be solved if the unknowns go beyond the limits of the equation," and quoting an "ancient proverb" that "a thousand probabilities do not make one truth," and even quoting from Oscar Wilde's poem, "The Ballad of Reading Gaol."

"We have conjecture, surmise, passion, prejudice, and every other whim of the human mind brought into this case to try to sway you in your duty of determining what this man will do for the rest of his natural life. But, ladies and gentlemen, as a wise scholar of the law once said, 'A defendant cannot be convicted on conjecture, however shrewd; on suspicion, however justified; on probabilities, however strong; but only on evidence which establishes guilt beyond a reasonable doubt.' Erickson then approached the lectern to face the jury a final time.

"The loss suffered by the Coorses is great. Anything that you do or I do or that anyone does in this court today . . . will not replace Adolph Coors. But that is no excuse to punish an innocent man. . . . You are determining what this man will do for the rest of his natural life. . . . Possibilities do not make the law. . . . The district attorney must establish his case by proof beyond a reasonable doubt.

"Thank you very much."

After a brief rebuttal by Richard Hite in which he poked fun at Erickson's flamboyant use of the extraneous, he closed with, "The defense has indicated that you should consider each piece of evidence individually, one by one. That is wrong. The court has instructed you to consider all the evidence in context as one relates to the other in determining the defendant's guilt. And when you have gone down the evidentiary path and have found the truth, this evidence will lead you to concur with what this defendant said in Vancouver: 'I'm your man.'

"Ladies and gentlemen, the case is yours."

The trial, which included jury selection, had lasted thirteen full days and two half days on Saturdays. The prosecution had examined ninety-two witnesses and presented one hundred and four exhibits during the trial. The defense had not called a single witness.

CHAPTER 24

At 10:45 on the snowy morning of Tuesday, March 28, the jury began its deliberations. Joe Corbett was out of his suit and back in prison clothes at the county jail. The man who tried his best to keep Corbett in a cell, District Attorney Ron Hardesty, was home sick in bed with a stubborn cold. Defense attorneys were in their offices, trying to catch up on other work. All they and everyone in Golden and Denver could do was wait.

That first morning, Leroy Sweet, an employee of the US Bureau of Land Management, was selected as the jury foreman. His first order of business was to take a ballot of the jurors to see where everyone stood before deliberations. He was surprised by the results. The vote was four guilty, three not guilty, and five undecided.

"All right, it's almost a tie. Let's roll up our sleeves. We've got some work to do," said the foreman.

They deliberated more than three hours before taking a break at noon. They returned after lunch and deliberated all afternoon and into the night with only a break for dinner. More ballots were taken. Progress was slow. Jurors were unsure, sought answers to questions, and reviewed the evidence more. They kept going until they retired, frustrated, at 11:30. No one wanted to be a part of a hung jury.

The entire day, Corbett rested in his cell. Perhaps *resting* is not the right term. He was dreading the verdict. While he hoped he would be acquitted, he knew that a guilty verdict would be the death knell for anything he'd wanted to do in the future. He would be sent to a maximum-security prison for the remainder of his life.

The following day, the jury reconvened its deliberations. When a bailiff exited the jury room after delivering lunch, he was questioned by a reporter.

"Anything?"

The bailiff shook his head.

"How did they look? Mad? Crying? You think they're almost ready?"

Bailiffs were instructed not to discuss the case with anyone.

Foreman Sweet directed another ballot: ten guilty, two not guilty. Quite a bit of movement toward guilt, yet their job was unfinished. The two could stand pat or convince others to join or rejoin them. Even if they did decide not guilty, or the jury ended up hung, it didn't mean Corbett would go free. California officials had placed a hold on Corbett and were prepared to fly to Colorado to escort him back to complete his second-degree murder sentence, probably in Folsom Prison, should the jury fail to find him guilty of Ad Coors's murder.

"What is taking them so long?" Mary asked a friend. "It's clear to me he did it. There's plenty of evidence. The FBI doesn't make mistakes. Don't they know that?"

She was not the only one worried about the delay.

"What in blue blazes is going on over there?" Hardesty asked Juhan on the telephone. Juhan's choice of expletives indicated his shared displeasure.

Wermuth was just as agitated about the delay. He'd hoped for the gas chamber and had tried his best to obtain a confession to send his infamous guest there. Corbett had to get life, thought Wermuth, otherwise the entire state would be a laughingstock and him with it.

But not everyone was upset. Defense attorneys Erickson and Mackay were encouraged by the continued deliberations. Perhaps the defendant would receive an acquittal or a hung jury. Their client had professed his innocence despite their doubts, but it was their job to see he got the best defense they could give, and that meant an acquittal.

"Everything Joe Corbett told me was accurate, that I was able to investigate," Erickson told a reporter of *The Denver Post* years later.

A few hours afterward, another ballot was taken. It was close—eleven guilty, one not guilty. A single holdout stood between Joe Corbett and a first-degree murder conviction. But only those in the jury room knew the count. Those on the outside could only speculate and hope.

The continued wait had become agonizing. Corbett read. Mary tried to keep busy. The lawyers worked on other cases. They believed they knew what the outcome should be, but they also knew it was impossible to predict what happens in a jury room. The dynamics inside that room take on a life of their own during deliberations. Ordinary citizens can reason with extraordinary clarity, sometimes with more insight than the lawyers.

At last, after several hours of deliberation and an astounding twelve ballots, the foreman stepped out of the jury room at 4:17 on Wednesday and motioned to one of the bailiffs, A. W. Buell. "We've reached a verdict."

The bailiff entered the judge's chambers to notify Judge Stoner.

"Call Wermuth and the lawyers. Round 'em all up. Tell 'em to hurry. This jury wants to go home," said Stoner.

Wermuth delivered his message with a laugh. "Get your suit on, Joe. The jury has a one-way ticket to give you."

Without expression, Corbett sat up from his bunk and began dressing. Minutes later, with Wermuth on one side and Captain Bray on the other, as they'd done several times before, Corbett and his armed escorts walked across the street and into a courthouse already filled with people, many of whom had spent all day there awaiting a verdict.

Assistant District Attorneys Hite and Juhan arrived quickly, but a sick Hardesty would be the last to show.

Corbett sat quietly as he waited for his lawyers. The only emotion he displayed was an occasional smile as Sheriff Wermuth stood near and needled him with wisecracks. But Corbett didn't break his silence. He simply ignored the sheriff. Secretly, he may have wanted to say, "You may be joining me soon, Mr. Sneak Thief." But Corbett's defense attorneys joined their client at the defense table. Nothing more was said.

A single "sound camera" was set up to record the verdict and share its film with other radio and television stations. The judge had forbidden television cameras and live radio during the trial.

The gallery grew quieter with each passing minute until the courtroom was completely still.

"All rise!" shouted the bailiff as Judge Stoner entered. "The First District Court of Colorado, the Honorable Judge Stoner presiding—" The judge banged the gavel before the bailiff could finish.

"Has the jury reached a unanimous verdict?" he asked as soon as he was seated.

"We have, Your Honor," replied the jury foreman. It was 4:45 on March 29, 1961, one year, one month, and twenty days since Ad's disappearance.

"The bailiff will pick up the verdict of the jury, if you please," instructed Stoner. The bailiff handed it to the judge. "Ladies and gentlemen of the jury, you will listen to your verdict, if you will, please. 'We, the jury, duly empaneled and sworn in the above entitled cause, find the defendant Joseph Corbett Jr. guilty of murder in the first degree as charged in the information herein, and fix the penalty at imprisonment for life, at hard labor, in the penitentiary.'"

The room rustled with commentary, but most were not surprised. Corbett actually smiled and laughed, in all likelihood from nervousness or defiance. However, the jury's sentence of life in state prison could not be imposed immediately. Corbett's defense counsel had six weeks in which to prepare and present an argument for the judge to consider granting a new trial—a procedural long shot.

"At last," was Mary's only comment after receiving a call from a friend. She hung up the phone and returned to her bedroom. Ad Coors's remains would be cremated and spread on Aspen Mountain three months later as part of a small family ceremony. Corbett's conviction changed nothing in Mary's life.

"No comment," were Corbett's words as he was led back to jail by Sheriff Wermuth. He'd said nothing to his jailer or lawyers or the judge. He'd been self-contained for five months. He wasn't about to change now. (But in a brief 1964 interview, Corbett uncharacteristically changed his tune. "No man should be incarcerated for a crime he did not commit. I am innocent." He did so again three decades later in 1996. "I can see why so many people think I'm guilty, that it's an open-and-shut case. But it wasn't. The jury was out three days," Corbett told *Denver Post* reporters through a cracked door. "It would be futile to retry the case in the newspapers now. What's the point?")

Defense counsel's motion for a new trial, which included a list of legal errors that supposedly occurred during the trial and pretrial proceedings, was denied by Judge Stoner on May 12, 1961. That same day, the judge signed the order committing Corbett to prison:

> THAT THE SAID defendant Joseph Corbett Jr. alias Walter Osborne be . . . conveyed by the Sheriff of the County of Jefferson with all convenient speed to the Penitentiary of the State of Colorado, there to be delivered to the Warden or Keeper thereof, to be by him kept and confined therein for life at hard labor, to be clothed and fed as the law directs.

On the morning of May 23, 1961, a shackled Corbett, accompanied by his armed escort Sheriff Wermuth and Wermuth's wife, Julia, made the 125-mile trip by automobile to the Colorado State Penitentiary in Cañon City, where Corbett would begin his life sentence at hard labor. The prison, called "Old Max," had been built in 1871 and enlarged in the 1930s, including the addition of a gas chamber. It was not a pleasant place to spend a single day, much less one's life. It was built of sandstone and rough concrete, hot in the summer and cold in the winter, a prison of the Old West, built to lock up stagecoach bandits, cattle rustlers, and gunslingers.

"So long, Joe," said Sheriff Wermuth, after receiving a "body receipt" signed on behalf of the warden, Harry Tinsley. A few minutes later, Corbett was clothed in prison garb and led to his cell. Gone was his old Chino prisoner number, A-17293. Now he would simply be known as Joe, Prisoner No. 33322. Unlike the minimum-security prison at Chino, Corbett wouldn't be escaping from Old Max.

But Joe Corbett would get out. Colorado changed state law to require a parole hearing after ten years for those serving life sentences. By 1978, Corbett had become the longest-serving inmate at Cañon City's state prison. Since he'd been an exemplary prisoner credited with saving many prisoners' lives working in the infirmary as a lab technician (not quite hard labor), the parole board decided to release Corbett, but yielded to a public outcry led by the governor and the Coors family. A year later, the parole board again approved his release, this time unmoved by public opinion. Corbett flew to San Francisco to live with a cousin, only to violate his parole the next day by returning to Denver, where he was spotted by a reporter. An immediate manhunt ensued. Everyone believed Corbett was out for bloody revenge. The Coors plant beefed up security, and the Coors family received protection. A sheriff's deputy was posted at Hardesty's house.

It turned out Corbett was in Denver for only four hours to close a bank account, returning to San Francisco the same day. He was arrested five days later and returned to prison. He was paroled for the final time over a year later on December 12, 1980, at the age of fifty-two, having served only eighteen and a half years for murdering Ad Coors.

A lot had changed in almost two decades. He walked out of prison wearing a pastel blue leisure suit the same year the space shuttle *Enterprise* was towed through Denver on its way to California. He would live the rest of his life in Denver, only ten miles from where he murdered Ad Coors. He said he was going to get his degree and find a job as a lab technician, but as had been the case before, his plan was all talk, and the only steady work he could find outside prison was as a driver for the Salvation Army. When that stint was over, he lived off his meager Social Security checks. As an elderly man, Corbett said he was haunted by whispers, "There goes the guy who killed Adolph Coors." Perhaps what haunted him was his conscience.

Corbett shot and killed for a third and final time on August 24, 2009. Suffering from terminal cancer, he took his own life by a self-inflicted gunshot to the head while lying in bed in room 307 at the Royal Chateau Apartments in Denver, where he'd lived for twenty-nine years. He was eighty-two. He didn't leave a note and never admitted his guilt. The once intelligent college student with a bright future perhaps had become the last victim of the murderous side of Joe Corbett.

"I just take it in stride," Corbett had said in a brief final interview by *Denver Post* reporters though a cracked apartment door in 1996. "It's one of those bizarre things that happened. . . . I've put it behind me. It's a gruesome memory."

As for Mary Coors, it was impossible to put it behind her. She never recovered from the crippling blow. Mary's short life had been filled with deaths. Besides Ad dying at forty-four, Mary's mother died at the age of fifty, her father at fifty-nine, and most tragically of all, her daughter, Brooke, at the age of twenty-six from lymphoma, leaving behind a husband and a young son; and then Mary, who died at the age of sixty on July 26, 1975, from injuries suffered falling down stairs at a friend's home in Aspen. She is buried in a solitary setting under a large Douglas fir at Fairmount Cemetery in Denver beside her daughter, Brooke. She never remarried.

AUTHOR'S NOTE

The kidnapping and murder of Ad Coors was much more than simply the death of an heir; it was a horrible tragedy that struck a good man and his family. We and our loved ones have but a single lifetime on this earth and all of us wish to spend it happily and fruitfully free of grief and injustice. Yet misfortune shows no partiality. This story is a poignant illustration of that unpleasant truth.

Joe Corbett Jr. never admitted his guilt. No person in prison or any friend or family member ever came forward to say that Joe Corbett admitted he murdered Adolph Coors III. He refused interviews after his prison term, once saying, "It's not like I won the Nobel Peace Prize." In my mind, the circumstantial evidence collected by the Jefferson County Sheriff's Office and the Federal Bureau of Investigation leaves no doubt Corbett committed the crime.

I do not believe Corbett intended to kill Ad Coors when he planned the kidnapping. He was only after easy money. If Ad Coors had not resisted, he likely would have rejoined his family and presumably lived a long life like his brothers. That being said, Corbett's reflexive action was to shoot Ad Coors, killing him as he'd done another man a decade earlier in California, making Corbett a very dangerous man.

There was one lingering question of significance: Did Corbett act alone? Facts that indicated a potential accomplice centered on simple references in the ransom note to "kidnapers" and "we," a dark-colored Dodge sedan that was never traced to Corbett or located after the crime, and another man sometimes spotted riding with Corbett. The FBI concluded he did act alone, and though Corbett seems the type who would not snitch on his confederate even if it meant a lighter sentence, I agree with the FBI that he likely acted alone, though he might have had an associate who knew about the crime.

There is one obvious question that I have about this crime. How could someone supposedly as intelligent as Joe Corbett Jr. make so many mistakes after planning the kidnapping for so long? Besides killing Ad Coors and not collecting the ransom, he made the critical mistake of spending too much time near Ad's house and Turkey Creek Bridge in a yellow automobile bearing the actual license plate. James Cable's sighting of the partial plate number was Corbett's downfall. The plate connected the automobile to Walter Osborne and then to his apartment and the arson in Atlantic City and finally to Joe Corbett, escaped convict. Why would he buy a yellow car, keep it in a private garage so no one at his apartment could connect him with it, but then leave the actual license plate on the car when staking out the kidnapping site? And even more reckless was his stopping to speak with Hilton Pace at a mine. Inexplicable. Perhaps he thought he'd be in South America long before law enforcement put the pieces together. Whatever the case, it was not very clever.

Then there were the acts of burning his car in Atlantic City, which drew attention to his whereabouts on the East Coast; not changing his alias or appearance in Toronto, and though he changed his alias in Winnipeg, he didn't alter his appearance, resulting in a coworker and landlords contacting the authorities; writing bad checks in Winnipeg on his Toronto bank account and leasing a new red Pontiac convertible, for which he wrote another bad check, which kept the FBI on his trail and provided the FBI and Canadian authorities with the make and model of his vehicle that ultimately resulted in his capture.

Perhaps his overweening confidence was greater than his IQ.

Now a word about this book. This is a work of nonfiction. I have not created any characters or changed any names. Because the event occurred in 1960, firsthand knowledge of the abduction was difficult to obtain, yet I did locate and interview some individuals who were directly involved. I also visited many of the sites depicted, such as Ad Coors's Morrison and Denver houses, the kidnap and dump sites, Corbett's apartments, the Coors plant, and Fairmount Cemetery. Most of my extensive research, however, centered on contemporaneous accounts in newspapers and magazines, transcripts and records from courts, national and state archives, the Federal Bureau of Investigation, sheriff's departments, archival photos, and many other sources that I list in the Acknowledgments and Bibliography sections at the end of the book. I am very appreciative of the individuals and agencies that responded to my relentless requests. The story would not have been as accurate if not for them.

I have attempted to stay true to the facts uncovered during my exhaustive research while using literary techniques that I believe make the story more interesting and enjoyable. While the quoted material is accurate, I have deduced some scenes, remarks, and dialogue from the materials I gathered to convey information to the reader where details are unavailable. Despite some liberties, I believe the story reflects the factual truth.

To conclude, what follows is a summary of significant events following the 1961 trial:

- Sheriff Wermuth received criticism because many believed his hunger for media attention compromised the Coors investigation. Worse, he was indicted by a grand jury for misappropriation of $3,673 in county funds and resigned as sheriff on May 1, 1962, in lieu of prosecution. It has been suggested that he also allowed two prisoners to escape from jail in 1956 to receive notoriety upon their capture.

- On November 18, 1963, the Colorado Supreme Court denied all 103 counts of trial error asserted by Corbett's attorneys on appeal. In deciding that Corbett's conviction for murder would stand, Chief Justice Albert Frantz wrote: "It is deemed sufficient to convince even the most doubting Thomas that Joe Corbett Jr. is not the innocent victim of circumstances."

- Mr. and Mrs. Coors died in 1970 at the ages of eighty-six and eighty-five, respectively. According to one resource, Mary and her children were completely cut out of Mr. and Mrs. Coors's estates. I reviewed Mr. Coors's will that left his estate to his three living children and did exclude Ad's widow, Mary. Unfortunately, after repeated requests, the Jefferson County probate court was unable to locate the will or trust belonging to Mrs. Coors.

- Bill and Geraldine Coors divorced in 1962. Bill married his secretary, Phyllis Mahaffey, in 1963, and they had one son. Geraldine married again in 1965 to Joseph Jonas and divorced in 1971. Her struggles with alcohol continued for much of her life, and that, coupled with a heavy smoking habit, is believed to have contributed to her death in 1982. Tragically, one of Bill and Geraldine's three daughters, Geraldine "Missy" Coors Straus, committed suicide at the age of forty by leaping naked from her eleventh-floor Manhattan apartment on East Twenty-third Street, leaving behind two children. Bill and Phyllis Coors divorced in 1994. Bill married his third wife, Rita Bass, a year later, and though she died in 2015, at the time of print, Bill Coors is still living at the age of 100.

- Joe Coors became a considerable financial backer of the conservative political movement, assisting to create the Heritage Foundation, an influential conservative think tank, and being named to President Reagan's "kitchen cabinet." After forty-eight years of marriage, he and Holly divorced in 1988, and he married Anne Drotning months later. He moved away from his lifelong home of Golden to California, where he lived until his death in 2003 at the age of eighty-five. Holly died in 2009 at the age of eighty-eight.

- Turkey Creek Bridge is no longer standing as such, but its prior location can still be discerned by a clump of cottonwood trees in a tiny area between US-285 and the exit ramp connecting US-285 and C-470 near Morrison, Colorado. Not much of a memorial to what many consider the most notorious crime in Colorado history.

ACKNOWLEDGMENTS

I am exceedingly grateful to my agent, Richard Curtis, who believed in me and my manuscript, and without whose experience, guidance, and support, this book would not have been published. I also wish to thank Charlie Spicer, April Osborn, and everyone else at St. Martin's Press who've been so great. And thanks to freelance editor, John Paine, who knows how to skillfully cut a long manuscript without alienating his client.

During my research, I interviewed several people. I appreciate their time and generosity. However, there were two couples who were not only informative, but a pleasure and a privilege to meet:

First, Judge Ron Hardesty and his wife, Myrtsie. They welcomed me into their home in Grand Junction and were as cheerful and accommodating as anyone could be. Judge Hardesty communicated with me several times and he was always the same: interested, supportive, and considerate. I am saddened by their deaths.

Second, Bruce and Joan Buell. They were gracious and more than willing to help me with my research over dinner in Colorado Springs. Ms. Buell was very sweet and wore a lovely brooch given to her by Mary Coors. Mr. Buell has always kindly answered my questions.

I learned during my research that some documents, audio, and video of historical value to this story were unavailable because they were lost, destroyed, or legal, ethical, or proprietary barriers stood in the way of their disclosure; history is the loser. However, there is a legion of folks who did assist me, and many of them went above and beyond to respond to my pestering inquiries. I obtained a mountain of information. Though I thanked most of them at the time, and though they may have changed positions or locations from the time we last spoke, I would like to extend my gratitude once again—thank you:

Catherine Adkison, deputy solicitor general, Appellate Division, Office of the Attorney General, Criminal Justice Section, Denver, Colorado

Ardell Arfsten, former Douglas County, Colorado, deputy sheriff, Franktown, Colorado; deceased

Russ Banham and Dan Baum, whose books, *Coors: A Rocky Mountain Legend* and *Citizen Coors: A Grand Family Saga of Business, Politics, and Beer,* respectively, though very different, provided me with insight into the Coors family and their business, political, and theological views

Shaun Boyd, archivist, Douglas County History Research Center, Douglas County Libraries, Phillip S. Miller Library, Castle Rock, Colorado

Charles F. Brega, attorney, Fairfield & Woods, PC, Denver, Colorado; former legal associate of William Erickson

The Brentwood Library, Brentwood, Tennessee

Diane Burkhardt, interim library director, University of Denver, Sturm College of Law, Westminster Law Library, Denver, Colorado

Andrea Burns, community relations manager, Jefferson County Sheriff's Office, Golden, Colorado

California Department of Corrections and Rehabilitation, Sacramento, California

California State Archives, Sacramento, California

James Chipman, staff archivist, Colorado State Archives, Denver, Colorado

Dean Christopherson, technician, Community Resource Officer, District Four, Denver Police Department, Denver, Colorado

Jonathan A. Cline, coroner investigator, Jefferson County Coroner's Office, Golden, Colorado

Colorado Department of Corrections, Colorado Springs, Colorado

Jessica Corter, advancement assistant, Wells College, Office of Alumnae and Alumni Relations, Aurora, New York

J. Wendel Cox, Ph.D., senior special collection librarian, Western History and Genealogy, Denver Public Library, Denver, Colorado

Kathy Davis, past president 2010, Colorado Court Reporters Association, Denver, Colorado

Rebecca Daleske, Real Property GIS specialist, Jefferson County Assessor's Office, Golden, Colorado

Wonda Damron, Brentwood Library, Brentwood, Tennessee

Denver Public Library, Denver, Colorado

Eric Dew, judicial assistant, Denver Probate Court, Denver, Colorado

Barbara Dey, reference librarian, History Colorado, Denver, Colorado

Michael T. Dougherty, assistant district attorney, First Judicial District Attorney's Office, Golden, Colorado

Douglas County Libraries, Philip S. Miller Library, Castle Rock, Colorado

Coi E. Drummond-Gehrig, digital image collection administrator, Denver Public Library, Denver, Colorado

Keith Erffmeyer, deputy assessor / chief appraiser, Denver Assessor's Office, Denver, Colorado

David L. Erickson, attorney, Evergreen, Colorado

Doris Erickson, widow of William Erickson, Englewood, Colorado

Federal Bureau of Prisons Library, Washington, D.C.

Susan J. Festag, clerk of court, Colorado Supreme Court, Denver, Colorado

First Judicial District Attorney's Office, Golden, Colorado

Patrick J. Fraker, Stephen H. Hart Library & Research Center, Denver, Colorado

Megan K. Friedel, curator of Photography and Moving Images, History Colorado, Denver, Colorado

Johanna Harden, archivist, Douglas County Libraries, Douglas County History Research Center, Philip S. Miller Library, Castle Rock, Colorado

David Hardy, section chief, Record / Information Dissemination Section, Records Management Division, Federal Bureau of Investigation, Washington, D.C.

Mark Hargrove, correctional lieutenant, administrative assistant / public information officer, California Institution for Men, Chino, California

Ralph Hargrow, former chief global people officer, Molson Coors, Golden, Colorado

Thomas Haughton, archivist, National Archives and Records Administration, College Park, Maryland

Deena Havens, daughter of Alice M. Logan-Leuty, deceased juror, Elbert, Colorado

Ronda Hott, Fairmont Cemetery Office, Denver, Colorado

Thomas J. Infantino, CPA, Lakewood, Colorado (who arranged my interview with Edward Juhan)

Kathryn Isenberger, former assistant to Leo Bradley, former general counsel to Adolph Coors Company, Golden, Colorado

Jefferson County Public Library, Golden, Colorado

Linda Johnson, archivist, Reference Coordinator, California State Archives, Sacramento, California

Christina V. Jones, archivist, Archives II Reference Room, Textual Services Division, National Archives and Records Administration, College Park, Maryland

Edward N. Juhan, former assistant district attorney, First Judicial District, Golden, Colorado; deceased

Noel Kalenian, reference librarian, Western History and Genealogy Department, Denver Public Library, Denver, Colorado

Charles F. Luce Jr., attorney, Moye White LLP, Denver, Colorado

Kevin Luy, archivist, Colorado State Archives, Denver, Colorado

Vickie Makings, *The Denver Post* Research Library, Denver, Colorado

David Miller, archivist, National Archives and Records Administration, Rocky Mountain Region, Denver, Colorado

Nashville Public Library, Nashville, Tennessee

William "Ted" Nunes, Tedtoons, Nashville, Tennessee

Brenna Nurmi, court processing specialist II, Marin County Superior Court, San Rafael, California

Hannah Q. Parris, reference librarian, Western History/Genealogy, Denver Public Library, Denver Colorado

Beulah Pinson, widow of Edward Pinson, former Jefferson County Deputy Sheriff, Golden, Colorado

Dana Powell, document imaging / records manager, First Judicial District Attorney's Office, Golden, Colorado

Janice Prater, special collection librarian, Western History and Genealogy Department, Denver Public Library, Denver, Colorado

Tim Ryan, assistant news director, 9News & Channel 20/KUSA & KTVD, Denver, Colorado

Brandon Shaffer, Colorado State Board of Parole, Pueblo, Colorado

Bonnie M. J. Shriner, attorney / mediator, Denver, Colorado

David P. Sobonya, public information officer / legal administrative specialist, Service Request Unit, Record / Information Dissemination Section, FBI-Records Division, Winchester, Virginia

Sue Szostak, Poplar Bluff Municipal Library, Poplar Bluff, Missouri

Merrick and Janice Thomas, Morrison, Colorado (who own the ranch house built by Ad Coors, and who graciously showed me their beautiful home just prior to its renovation)

Charles "Chuck" Turner, executive director, Colorado Bar Association, Denver, Colorado

University of Denver, Sturm College of Law, Westminster Law Library, Denver, Colorado

RaeAn Waldheim, assessment information manager, Denver Assessor's Office, Denver, Colorado

Nancy R. Weber, legal assistant to Charles F. Brega, Fairfield & Woods, PC, Denver, Colorado

Elmer Werth, former Adolph Coors Company employee; deceased

BIBLIOGRAPHY

Abbott, Earl J. "Ransom: $500,000—Or Your Husband Dies!" *True Police Cases*, February 1961, 20–23, 70–73.

Adolph Coors III Estate files No. 6971 County Court. County of Jefferson, Golden, Colorado.

Adolph Coors III murder investigation collection, 1960–1961. Douglas County Historic Research Center, Douglas County Libraries, Castle Rock, Colorado.

Adolph Coors IV speech. Eighteenth Annual High Tech Prayer Breakfast 2009; Atlanta, Georgia; October 8, 2009.

Baltimore Sun. 28 photographs of Arthur Wermuth (as WWII hero) 1945 and 1946 and Coors family.

Banham, Russ. *Coors: A Rocky Mountain Legend*. Lyme, CT: Greenwich Publishing Group, 1998.

Baum, Dan. *Citizen Coors: A Grand Family Saga of Business, Politics, and Beer*. New York: William Morrow, 2000.

Bray, G. A., *Twenty-Six Years in Jail*. Payson, AZ: Leaves of Autumn Books, 2004.

Chino Champion. Chino, California. Archival clippings.

Church, F. L. "Man of the Year: William K. Coors," *Modern Metals*, January 1960, 88–98.

Clark, Blake. "How the Digest Helped Catch this Man," *Reader's Digest*, January 1961, 160–162.

Colorado State Archives. Colorado State Penitentiary, Joseph Corbett Jr. #33322. 1961 photographic file (36), CD.

Coors, Adolph IV, and John Fuller. "My Journey to Salvation I–II." *Focus on the Family Radio Broadcast*, July 12, 2012.

Corbett v. People, 153 Colo. 457, 387 P.2d 409 (1963).

Corbett v. Patterson, 272 F. Supp 602 (D.C. Colo. 1967).

Cornerstone Ministry. "What Happened to Adolph Coors?" Accessed April 30, 2010.

The Denver Post. Denver, CO. Archival clippings.

Dinar, Joshua. *Denver Then and Now*. San Diego: Thunder Bay Press, 2002.

Federal Bureau of Investigation. Records of COORNAP investigation, 163 pages, received pursuant to FOIA request.

Golden Pioneer Museum. *Images of America: Golden, Colorado*. Chicago: Arcadia Publishing 2002.

Golden Transcript. Golden, CO. Archival clippings.

Grossman, Evan O. "Is Coors the One?" *The Harvard Crimson*. March 5, 1987.

Jefferson County Sheriff's Office. *History of the Jefferson County Sheriff's Office: The Turbulent Sixties: 1960–1969*, 46–50. Accessed 2010. http:/www.jeffco.us/sheriff/documents/history-documents/1960-1969-the-turbutent-sixties.

Last will and testament, Adolph Coors Jr., dated November 18, 1969.

Life. 180 photographs of Sheriff Wermuth; Ad Coors' residence and ranch; Turkey Creek Bridge; miscellaneous, 1960.

Life. 68 photographs of California Institution for Men at Chino, 1950s.

Mary Grant Coors Estate files No. P-71073C. Probate Court Denver County, Denver, Colorado.

McPhee, John. Annals of Crime. "The Gravel Page." *New Yorker*, January 29, 1996, 44–52.

Murray, Raymond C. *Evidence from the Earth: Forensic Geology and Criminal Investigation*. Missoula, MT: Mountain Press Publishing, 2004, 95–96.

New York Times. Archival clippings.

People v. Corbett. District Court, Jefferson County, Colorado, No. 2815 case files.

Photographs (16) of sheriff's office, jail, and officers, Golden History Museums, Golden, Colorado.

Photographs (47) of Colorado State Penitentiary at Cañon City, Western History/Genealogy Department, Denver Public Library, 1937.

Photographs (168). Miscellaneous.

Pollack, Jack Harrison. "Florence Sternfels: The Amazing Mind Reader Who Solves Crimes." *Parade Magazine*, April 26, 1964, 4.

Potter, Dennis L. "Coornap: The Investigation into the 1960 Murder of Adolph Coors III." *Denver Westerners Roundup*, September/October 2010.

Prosecutive Summary Investigation Report of the Federal Bureau of Investigation regarding the Kidnapping of Adolph Coors III; U.S. National Archives & Records Administration; RG-65, Entry UD-UP 1B, Sections 49-51 (Serial 1166), boxes 263-264 (514 pages), location 230/900/02/07-03/01; dated November 14, 1960; received pursuant to FOIA request.

Queen, Ellery. "The Case of Colorado's Millionaire Brewer Coors," *Official Detective Stories*, February 1961, 10–48.

Rocky Mountain News. Archival clippings.

Sanchez, Robert. "Anatomy of a Murder." *5280*, February 2009. Accessed April 22, 2010. http://www.5280.com/2012/02/from-the-archives-anatomy-of-a-murder.

The Seattle Times. Archival clippings.

Stumbo, Bella. "Brewing Controversy: Coors Clan: Doing It Their Way (Part 1)." *Los Angeles Times*, September 18, 1988, 1, 30–33.

Thomas, Brian. "The FBI Wants this Man." *Reader's Digest*, November 1960, 115–119.

Reporter's Transcript of Proceedings, In the District Court in and for the County of Jefferson and State of Colorado, Criminal Action No. 2815: The People of the State of Colorado, Plaintiff, v. Joseph Corbett, Jr., alias Walter Osborne . . . Defendant; 1,683 pages (March 13–26, 1961).

Tully, Andrew. "An Affair at Turkey Creek." *Pictorial Living Colorado Magazine*, January 1966.

Vallier, Myron. *Historic Photos of Denver.* Nashville: Turner, 2007.

Whitacre, Christine. *The Denver Club, 1880–1995.* Denver, CO: Historic Denver Guides, 1998.

Williams, Brook. "Bungled Death of the Denver Millionaire." *True Detective*, February 1961, 26–31, 87–91.

Yetzbacher, Bill, ed. *Caps & Taps: Adolph Coors: 1873–1973.* Golden, CO: Adolph Coors Company, 1973.